The Great Virginia Triumvirate

THE GREAT
VIRGINIA
TRIUMVIRATE

George Washington,
Thomas Jefferson,
& James Madison

IN THE EYES OF THEIR CONTEMPORARIES

John P. Kaminski

University of Virginia Press   Charlottesville and London

University of Virginia Press
© 2010 by the Rector and Visitors of the University of Virginia
All rights reserved
Printed in the United States of America on acid-free paper

First published 2010
First paperback edition published 2014
ISBN 978-0-8139-3587-4 (paper)

1 3 5 7 9 8 6 4 2

The Library of Congress has cataloged the hardcover edition as follows:

LIBRARY OF CONGRESS CATALOGING-IN-PUBLICATION DATA
Kaminski, John P.
The great Virginia triumvirate : George Washington, Thomas Jefferson, and James
Madison in the eyes of their contemporaries / John P. Kaminski
    p.   cm.
Includes bibliographical references and index.
ISBN 978-0-8139-2876-0 (cloth : alk. paper)—ISBN 978-0-8139-2896-8 (e-book)
    1. Washington, George, 1732–1799. 2. Jefferson, Thomas, 1743–1826. 3. Madison,
James, 1751–1836. 4. Presidents—United States—Biography. 5. Statesmen—United
States—Biography. 6. Statesmen—Virginia—Biography. 7. United States—
Politics and government—1775–1783. 8. United States—Politics and government—
1783–1809. I. Title.
E176.1.K29 2010
973.3—dc22

                                                                    2009022153

Illustration credits: George Washington, by Charles Willson Peale, 1787, oil on canvas,
24 × 19⅛ in. [61.0 × 48.6 cm.], acc. no. 1912.14.3 (Courtesy of the Pennsylvania Academy
of Fine Arts, Philadelphia; bequest of Mrs. Sarah Harrison [The Joseph Harrison, Jr.,
Collection]). Thomas Jefferson, by Rembrandt Peale, 1805 (Snark/Art Resource, NY).
James Madison, by Gilbert Stuart, Washington, D.C., 1804, oil on twill weave canvas,
acc. no. 1945–23, image no. TC92–93 (The Colonial Williamsburg Foundation; gift of
Mrs. George S. Robbins).

For Alexander and Nicholas
Two little boys who have filled our lives with love and happiness

Contents

Preface

This trilogy utilizes a very different approach to writing biography. Each biography is largely composed of the words of the subject and his contemporaries to provide an otherwise unattainable immediacy. Vignettes and excerpts from letters, speeches, newspaper essays, diaries, journals, and memoirs have been interwoven with the narrative to create a fresh, intimate portrait of three familiar figures. Many of the quotations and vignettes found in these biographies are taken from obscure sources and have never been used by modern biographers. These biographies are written for students and teachers and for the general audience who would like to read brief but compelling accounts of the lives of the American founding generation. Nevertheless, because the sources are contemporaneous and have not been used recently, scholars will find many things of interest and of value, and some of the ideas developed will be new and challenging to prevailing interpretations.

For the last forty years, I have been editing *The Documentary History of the Ratification of the Constitution and the Bill of Rights*. During these many years I have immersed myself in the correspondence and political writings of the late eighteenth century. Less than half of my daily life is spent in the twenty-first century; the other time I live in the eighteenth.

For the last fifteen years, I have devoted much of my spare time to a new study. As a historical documentary editor, I knew that there were treasures buried in the thousands of documentary volumes published over the last two centuries. Especially important to me are the modern editions of so many of America's founders sponsored by the National Historical Publications and Records Commission and the National Endowment for the Humanities. The great Yale historian Edmund S. Morgan once wrote that the publication of these documentary editions was the single most important contribution to historical scholarship in the twentieth century. But in addition to these superb modern editions, there are countless older sources that are extremely valuable in re-creating the events and the times of the Revolutionary generation and capturing the public and private lives of America's founders. We, individually and as a nation, are enriched by the documentary heritage bequeathed to us by the founding generation. It is from this rich resource that the following biographies have been written.

Hundreds of volumes have been painstakingly examined page by page. Tentatively called "The Founders on the Founders," my database has grown to over 7,000 pages of descriptions of 430 individuals. Women as well as men are described, and women provided some of the best descriptions of their contemporaries. Some people have but one or two descriptions, while George Washington and John Adams each have over 300 entries. When an individual has many entries, a mosaic develops in which friends, enemies, family, acquaintances, and sometimes even the individuals themselves reveal the complexities and subtleties that are usually obscured by the fog of time and veneration.

In writing any kind of history, Thomas Jefferson believed that it was essential to get as many opinions as possible before making a final judgment. "Multiplied testimony, multiplied views will be necessary to give solid establishment to truth. Much is known to one which is not known to another, and no one knows everything. It is the sum of individual knowledge which is to make up the whole truth, and to give its correct current through future time."[1]

Jefferson rationalized to John Adams why he had not written a history of his times. His history was to be found in his correspondence, which was often "less guarded" because it was "not meant for the public eye, not restrained by the respect due to that; but poured forth from the overflowings of the heart into the bosom of a friend, as a momentary easement of our feelings."[2] "Written too in the moment, and in the warmth and freshness of fact and feeling," letters carry "internal evidence that what they breathe is genuine."[3]

Senator William Plumer of New Hampshire realized that he had drawn incorrect conclusions about President Jefferson. "The more critically & impartially I examine the character & conduct of Mr. Jefferson the more favorably I think of his integrity. I am really inclined to think I have done him injustice in not allowing him more credit for the integrity of heart that he possesses." It was important to gather perceptions from different people and at different times. "A city appears very different when viewed from different positions—& so it is with man. Viewed in different situations—different times—places—circumstances—relations & with different dispositions, the man thus examined appears unlike himself." Plumer's object, he said, "is truth—I write for myself—I wish not—I am determined not—to set down ought in malice, or to diminish anything from the fact."[4]

In selecting quotations and vignettes for these biographies, I included descriptions of character, mannerisms, physical and intellectual prowess, and common everyday activities. Some of the founders were very cautious in their assessments; others were brutally frank. Some, like Washington, rarely gossiped; others, like John Adams, couldn't resist the tittle-tattle of the day. Some founders used their private correspondence to vent off steam. Some avoided introspection, while others seemed almost obsessed with examining their own personalities. A few even subconsciously projected their own traits while describing others. Things often were written in letters, diaries, and memoirs that never would have been said in person. Abigail Adams wrote her husband that "my pen is always freer than my tongue. I have wrote many things to you that I suppose I never could have talk'd."[5] Friends, enemies, colleagues, family members, and occasionally their own introspective feelings provide over a period of time the individual tiles from which these biographical mosaics are constructed. In essence, the founders have become their own collective biographers, the painters of these word portraits.

The Great Virginia Triumvirate

Introduction

Virginia was the oldest, largest, wealthiest, and most populous of the thirteen North American English colonies to declare their independence in 1776. It consisted of present-day Virginia, West Virginia, Kentucky, Ohio, Indiana, Illinois, Michigan, Wisconsin, and part of Minnesota. As such, the other colonies looked to the Old Dominion for leadership. Even after it ceded to Congress all of its territory north and west of the Ohio River, the other states still deferred to Virginia, and Virginians continued to fill key national leadership positions. Three remarkable Virginians stand out in their service to the new nation: George Washington as commander in chief during the Revolution, Thomas Jefferson as the philosophic voice of the country, and James Madison as the chief architect of the nation's new constitutional system. Each man also served eight years as president of the United States. The three biographical essays that follow illustrate how each Virginian helped to mold the new American republic.

George Washington

THE GREATEST MAN ON EARTH

Early Life

George Washington was born into a middle-gentry family in tidewater Virginia in 1732. When George was only eleven years old, his father died, and George then looked up to his half brother Lawrence, fourteen years his senior, as a father figure. As an adolescent George lived with Lawrence at the family estate recently renamed Mount Vernon. Lawrence's marriage into the wealthy Fairfax family opened opportunities for young George Washington. He regularly visited neighboring Belvoir, the brick mansion on the Potomac River occupied by William Fairfax, Lawrence's father-in-law. It was at Mount Vernon and Belvoir that Washington learned how to carry himself: how to walk, how to eat, how to converse, how to dance. In essence, it was during these formative years that Washington learned to be a Virginia gentleman.

Sometime before he turned sixteen, Washington decided to strive for greatness. His ambition was to become a wealthy tidewater planter with all the accoutrements, power, and privileges of elite Virginia society. Deprived of the "gentleman's education" that his two half brothers received in England, Washington made the most of his limited education, first supplied by his father and then by hired tutors. Reading, writing, and basic mathematics came first and were then applied in learning the skill of surveying land. He became obsessed with self-improvement; he copied, learned, and practiced 110 "Rules of Civility and Decent Behaviour in Company and Conversation" taken from an English translation of the maxims of a fifteenth-century French Jesuit. The first six rules were:

> (1) Every action done in company ought to be done with some sign of respect to those that are present, (2) When in company, put not your hands to any part of the body not usually discovered, (3) Show nothing to your friend that may affright him, (4) In the presence of others, sing not to yourself with a humming noise or drum with your fingers or feet, (5) If you cough, sneeze, sigh, or yawn, do it not loud but privately; and speak not in your yawning, but put your handkerchief or hand before your face and turn

aside, (6) Sleep not when others speak, sit not when others stand, speak not when you should hold your peace, walk not on when others stop.

Fifty years later, at the age of sixty-four, Washington advised his step-grandson, perhaps in a way reminiscent of his own father's advice. "You are now extending into that age of life when good or bad habits are formed. When the mind will be turned to things useful and praise-worthy, or to dissipation and vice. Fix on whichever it may, it will stick by you; for you know it has been said, and truly, 'that as the twig is bent, so it will grow.'"[1]

Washington grew into an impressive young man. While other Virginia boys stopped growing at about five feet six inches, Washington towered over them at six foot three. He had strong shoulders, powerful arms, a slender waist, and an easy grace. Others readily perceived in him an extraordinary sense of self-assuredness.

Washington's character and bearing impressed Lord Fairfax, who used his influence to have the seventeen-year-old appointed surveyor of Culpeper County on the Virginia frontier. Although at first glance this appointment might not seem too important, it proved fortuitous, because in colonial Virginia surveyors were recognized as gentlemen and "were numbered among the colony's practical-minded elite."[2] With wealth measured by the acres of good land owned, surveyors were uniquely positioned to assist the wealthy in locating and purchasing choice lands. Surveyors also assisted the many settlers laying claim to more modest tracts of land. An ambitious, hardworking surveyor became locally prominent, made important connections with wealthy investors, and earned sizable fees. Surveyors often acquired large landholdings themselves and in partnership with others. Within a year Washington saved enough money to purchase 1,500 acres on Bullskin Creek in the Shenandoah Valley, the beginning of his vast property holdings.

❦ The First War

In 1753, as tension with the French became critical, Virginia lieutenant governor Robert Dinwiddie appointed Washington as an emissary to warn the encroaching French to leave Virginia territory and return to Canada. Washington, who the year before had been commissioned a major in the militia by Dinwiddie, was well qualified for the dangerous assignment. His experience as a surveyor fashioned Washington into a skilled frontiersman with an intimate knowledge of Indians. Traveling for a month during November and December in Indian territory until he reached the French Fort Le Boeuf, not far from Lake Erie, Washington delivered his governor's ultimatum. The French responded defiantly. Surviving an Indian ambush and nearly drowning in the icy waters of the Monongahela River, Washington returned to Virginia and became a hero after the publication of his journal. Promoting him to lieutenant colonel and second in command of the Virginia militia, Dinwiddie ordered Washington to build a fort at the Forks of the Ohio River (later Pittsburgh). As Washington marched through the frontier, he learned that the French had already constructed Fort Duquesne at the Forks and that a small French force was marching southward. Washington ambushed the French troops, killed ten men, including the commander, and took twenty-two prisoners. The French denounced the attack on what they called a peaceful diplomatic mission. Soon the conflict escalated into a world war, the fourth colonial war of the eighteenth century between Britain and its colonies on one side and France and Spain and their colonies on the other. Washington stayed on the frontier, and although forced to surrender in July 1754 to a superior force at the ill-designed Fort Necessity, he returned to Virginia a hero and retired from active military duty.

In 1755 Washington joined British general Edward Braddock's army as an unpaid volunteer. Washington hoped that his services might be rewarded with a commission in the British army. He learned a great deal from Braddock about how to command an army, but unfortunately Braddock did not heed Washington's advice on wilderness warfare. Shortly after Braddock's army crossed the Monongahela River, the French and Indians ambushed them and, in a battle lasting almost five hours, wounded more than 400 redcoats and killed another 500, including Braddock. Washington was one of only a handful of officers who escaped unscathed. Two of his horses were killed beneath him, and bullets pierced his coat four times and shot off his hat. He rallied the survivors and led them on a forced retreat. Washington again returned to Virginia a hero. Throughout his engagements in battle, he found something exhilarating. He wrote his younger brother that he heard the bullets whistle and found "something charming in the sound."[3]

Named commander in chief of the Virginia militia, Washington served another three years until the British regular army relieved the militia on the frontier. Although saddened by the deaths he saw in war, Washington felt that when the cause is just, "who is there that does not rather Envy, than regret a Death that gives birth to Honour & Glorious memory." Recognized throughout the colonies as a hero, he was disappointed when the British denied him a commission in the regular army. Washington retired from active duty, and his fellow militia officers bid farewell to their twenty-six-year-old commander: "In our earliest infancy, you took us under your tuition, trained us in the practice of that discipline which alone can constitute good troops. . . . Your steady adherence to impartial justice, your quick discernment and invariable regard to merit—wisely intended to inculcate those genuine sentiments of true honor and passion for glory, from which the greatest military achievements have been derived—first heightened our natural emulation, and our desire to excel." The officers lamented for their country (i.e., their colony) because of the loss of Washington. No one else could provide "the military character of Virginia."[4]

When he retired from the militia, Washington was described by George Mercer, a fellow officer.

Straight as an Indian, measuring 6 feet 2 inches in his stockings and weighing 175 pounds. . . . His frame is padded with well-developed muscles, indicating great strength. His bones and joints are large, as are his hands and feet. He is wide shouldered but has not a deep or round chest; is neat waisted, but is broad across the hips and has rather long legs and arms. His head is wellshaped, though not large, but is gracefully poised on a superb neck. A large and straight rather than a prominent nose; blue grey penetrating eyes which are widely separated and overhung by a heavy brow. His face is long rather than broad, with high round cheek bones, and terminates in a good firm chin. He has a clear though rather colorless pale skin which burns with the sun. A pleasing and benevolent though a commanding countenance, dark brown hair [actually it was more reddish] which he wears in a cue. His mouth is large and generally firmly closed, but which from time to time discloses some defective teeth. His features are regular and placid with all the muscles of his face under perfect control, though flexible and expressive of deep feeling when moved by emotions. In conversation, he looks you full in the face, is deliberate, deferential, and engaging. His demeanor at all times composed and dignified. His movements and gestures are graceful, his walk majestic, and he is a splendid horseman.[5]

First Retirement

Washington's exploits in the French and Indian War won him fame throughout the colonies. Other than Benjamin Franklin, Washington was the single most known American. Mount Vernon had started to attract many visitors. In 1773 Charles Willson Peale, already a well-respected artist, traveled to Virginia to paint Colonel Washington's portrait. Peale described the leisure activities of some of the young visitors to Mount Vernon as they pitched the bar to see who was the strongest among them. Suddenly the colonel appeared and asked to be shown the pegs that marked the farthest throws. "Smiling, and without putting off his coat," Washington held out his hand. As soon as the heavy lead weight felt the grasp of his hand, according to Peale, "it lost the power of gravitation, and whizzed through the air, striking the ground far, very far, beyond our utmost limits." The young men stood astonished as Washington walked away, saying, "When you beat my pitch, young gentlemen, I'll try again."[6]

In 1770 when Washington toured his lands in the Ohio country, a party of Indians led by an old chief rode to see him. An interpreter told Washington that the chief had been at Braddock's defeat in 1755. He and other Indians had fired repeatedly at Washington without success. After two hours the Indians sensed that the Great Spirit would not allow the young officer to be killed in battle, so they fired at other men. When the chief heard that Washington was nearby, he wanted to pay homage to "the Great Knife," the name Indians had given Washington, the brave warrior who had been so divinely protected.[7]

In January 1759 Washington married Martha Dandridge Custis, the widow of Daniel Parke Custis, a wealthy planter. It was a pivotal event in Washington's life. Although born into a similar social class as Washington, Martha Dandridge had married into wealth and high society. She brought to Washington thousands of acres of land, a couple hundred slaves, and access to elite Virginia society. She also brought two small children, John Parke Custis (Jackie) and Martha Parke Custis (Patsy). The Washingtons never had children themselves, but their forty-one-year marriage seems to have been happy. After they had been together twenty-five years, Washington wrote that he "always considered Marriage as the most interesting event of one's life. The foundation of happiness or misery." He felt that "more permanent and genuine happiness is to be found in the sequestered walks of connubial life than in the giddy rounds of promiscuous pleasure." Washington described Martha as "a quiet wife, a quiet soul." Martha, who regularly was plagued with nagging illnesses (called by Washington the "billious cholick"), said that she enjoyed "the pleasant duties of an old fashioned Virginia house-keeper, steady as a clock, busy as a bee, and as cheerful as a cricket." Throughout their life together, Martha served as the hostess to the innumerable guests that visited Mount Vernon. In all the accounts of these visits, no person ever spoke ill of her, and everyone commented on her graciousness. A young Polish nobleman visiting described Mrs. Washington as "one of the most estimable persons that one could know, good, sweet, and extremely polite. She loves to talk and talks very well about times past. . . . I was not as a stranger but a member of the family in this estimable house. They took care of me, of my linen, of my clothes, etc."[8]

After retiring from the militia, Washington threw himself into the role of a Virginia planter. He inherited Mount Vernon when his brother's widow died and added to the estate when he married Martha. Repeated purchases of land increased Washington's holdings, and he twice enlarged the mansion house. Of his 8,000 acres, less than half were under cultivation. Washington by 1765 had abandoned the cultivation of tobacco when it became obvious that it not only was extremely labor-intensive and hard on the land but also placed planters at the economic mercy of the Scottish factors who dominated the British tobacco trade. He would raise only enough tobacco for local consumption. Instead, Washington concentrated on grains and vegetables that were consumable at home and marketable regionally as well as in the Caribbean.

Indian corn, wheat, and peas were the primary crops. For the rest of his life, Washington was an experimental farmer, always searching for a better crop or a more productive method of farming. Over the years he planted sixty different crops. He was happiest when he was farming. After the Revolution he wrote that "agriculture has ever been amongst the most favorite amusements of my life." "The life of a Husbandman of all others," he wrote, "is the most delectable. It is honorable—It is amusing—and, with Judicious management, it is profitable. To see plants rise from the earth and flourish by the superior skill, and bounty of the labourer fills a contemplative mind with ideas which are more easy to be conceived than expressed." Even more than that, farming was also patriotic. "I know of no pursuit in which more real and important service can be rendered to any country than by improving its agriculture." After several days' conversing with Washington, Robert Hunter, a young London merchant, wrote in 1785 that "his greatest pride now is to be thought the first farmer in America. He is quite a Cincinnatus, and often works with his men himself: strips off his coat and labors like a common man."[9]

In addition to cultivating the land, Mount Vernon sustained an enormous fishery along the shore of the estate's entire length of the Potomac River. A wide variety of fish (shad, herring, bass, carp, perch, sturgeon, crawfish, and catfish) and river turtles provided an important supplemental cash crop, a valuable source of protein for Washington's slaves, and diversity to the table for family and visitors, while the fish heads and entrails provided a cheap, effective fertilizer for the fields. While attending the Constitutional Convention in Philadelphia in August 1787, Washington explored the market potential for barrels of herring.[10] Mount Vernon also had a thriving whiskey distillery that produced at least fifty gallons daily, while the mash was used to feed the hogs. Cider was also distilled in large quantities. Large quantities of mint and rose water were produced and manufactured into soap under Martha Washington's direction. A water mill refined the wheat into flour. Washington also bred livestock: horses, mules, cattle, sheep, hogs, and chickens. The manure from these animals served to replenish the soil.

Washington strove to make Mount Vernon self-sufficient. The estate was divided into five farms, each with its own overseer (often a slave himself), who managed the plantation's 300 slaves, indentured servants,

and hired laborers. In addition to working in the fields and digging irriga-
tion ditches, slaves practiced a variety of trades; they were blacksmiths,
carpenters, coopers, shoemakers, brewers, brick makers, masons, weav-
ers, bakers, dairymen, seamstresses, cooks, or gardeners, in addition to
farmhands and house servants. When not busy with plantation work,
Washington's slaves did work for neighbors both on and off the estate.
Carpenters, for example, were used to frame buildings in Alexandria
and in the new federal capital that was being built during the last ten
years of Washington's life. When Washington attended the Constitutional Convention in Philadelphia in 1787, he first saw Venetian blinds.
He obtained the dimensions of one window in the mansion house and
purchased one pair of custom-made blinds; the estate's carpenters then
used that set of blinds as the prototype for the others that they made. In
the management of the estate, Washington kept elaborate books that his
secretary told a friend "were as regular as any merchant whatever."[11]

Washington regularly contributed to charitable causes. His ledgers
are filled with one-time donations as well as annual donations made to
specific organizations such as the Alexandria Academy, which received
$100. When he went north to command the army in 1775, he instructed
his cousin left in charge of Mount Vernon that "the Hospitality of the
House, with respect to the Poor, be kept up. Let no one go hungry away.
If any of this kind of people should be in want of corn, supply their ne-
cessities, provided it does not encourage them in Idleness; and I have
no objection to your giving my money in charity, to the amount of forty
or fifty pounds a year, when you think it well bestowed. What I mean
by having no objection is, that it is my desire that it should be done."
He advised his nephew to "let your heart feel for the afflictions and dis-
tresses of everyone, and let your hand give in proportion to your purse,
remembering . . . that it is not everyone who asketh that deserveth
charity." He admonished his grandson to "never let an indigent person
ask, without receiving *something*, if you have the means." When Washington returned to Philadelphia after the terrible yellow fever epidemic
of 1793 had subsided, he wrote to a city clergyman asking where charitable relief was most needed. "To obtain information, and to render the
little I can afford, without ostentation or mention of my name, are the
sole objects of these inqueries."[12]

With full days either on the plantation or in the army, Washington had little time for amusements. Early in life he became an expert horseman, and horseback riding was always both pleasurable and a necessary part of life for him. He greatly enjoyed foxhunting, either by himself when a fox would appear while he was making the everyday rounds of the property or on planned occasions when a large group would ride to the hounds. Washington also enjoyed horse racing, attending both as a spectator placing a bet and as a breeder who raised horses for racing. Outdoors, Washington also enjoyed fishing and duck hunting. He actively bred dogs to be skilled in both fox and duck hunting.

Indoors, Washington enjoyed playing cards and billiards. He acquired a substantial library and read extensively in agriculture, English history, and military matters. Often he received complimentary books and pamphlets from authors on a host of subjects—particularly on politics and economics—that he read with interest. He subscribed to almost a dozen newspapers and several magazines, including the monthly *Pennsylvania Museum* begun in January 1787. He enjoyed dancing, which helped to alleviate the monotony of winter encampments and provided a social gathering where townsmen and women could meet him. When in large towns he frequently attended plays, concerts, and museums. He was fascinated by natural wonders and visited factories, waterworks, and internal improvements.

After the Revolution, Washington ardently supported the development of canals as a means to tie the new western settlements with the East both economically and politically. With Washington's prestige and James Madison's legislative skill, they obtained state charters for the Potomac River Company and the James River Company. Both companies sought to extend the western and northern navigation of their rivers by building canals around nonnavigable falls. Only about twenty miles of highways would be needed to connect each river with tributaries of the Ohio River. The 700-mile distance between Detroit and Alexandria was considerably shorter than the distance between the West and New Orleans, New York, Quebec, or Montreal. With the Spanish in control of New Orleans and the southernmost 150 miles of the Mississippi River and with the British in control of the Great Lakes and the St. Lawrence River, Washington's canal system was the safest way to transport goods and the best way to keep western settlers in the American Union. "The Western settlers," Washington feared, "stand as it were upon a pivot—the touch of a feather, would turn them any way." "The consequences to the Union [of opening Virginia's rivers] . . . are immense—& more so in a political, than a Commercial point. . . . For unless we can connect the New [western] States, which are rising to our view . . . with those on the Atlantic by interest . . . they will be quite a distinct People; and ultimately may be very troublesome neighbours to us." Washington became the president of the Potomac River Company, and both companies worked hard to accomplish his dream. After almost forty years, however, both companies lost their charters to the Chesapeake and Ohio Canal Company, which abandoned river improvements in favor of one still-water canal paralleling the Potomac River. This effort also failed as railroads became the prime carrier of goods east and west.[13]

❧ The Revolutionary Movement

When the imperial crisis first developed between Britain and its American colonies, Washington could best be described as a reluctant rebel. For his whole life he had aspired to become a country gentleman. Now with that goal realized, Parliament's policies and the violent American reaction placed him in an awkward position. Despite his reluctance to oppose British law, Washington never hesitated to support the constitutional rights of his country. In 1769 he condemned the policies of "our lordly Masters in Great Britain," who would "be satisfied with nothing less than the deprivation of American freedom." He knew that something had to be done to protect that freedom and "maintain the liberty which we have derived from our Ancestors; but the manner of doing it to answer the purpose effectually is the point in question." However reluctant he was to use violence, Washington believed "that no man shou'd scruple, or hesitate a moment to use arms in defence of so valuable a blessing, on which all the good and evil of life depends." But arms, he felt, "should be the last resource." Petitioning the king and Parliament had already failed. Economic boycotts should be the next tactic.[14]

When in 1774 the British overreacted to the dumping of privately owned tea into Boston harbor, Washington vowed in the House of Burgesses to raise and lead 1,000 men at his own expense to relieve Massachusetts from the oppression of British power. He saw "as clear as the sun in its meridian brightness" that Parliament was attempting to enslave Americans by wresting the taxing power from colonial assemblies. The ministry was "pursuing a regular Plan at the expence of Law & justice, to overthrow our Constitutional Rights & liberties." "As Englishmen, we could not be deprived of this essential, & valuable part of our Constitution." By opposing British policy, Americans were merely "claiming a Right which by the Law of Nature & our Constitution we are ... indubitably entitled to." For his part, Washington did "not undertake to say where the Line between Great Britain and the Colonies should be drawn, but I am clearly of opinion that one ought to be drawn; & our Rights clearly ascertained." He wished "that the dispute had been left to Posterity to determine, but the Crisis is arrived when we must assert our Rights, or Submit to every Imposition that can be heap'd upon us; till custom and use, will make us as tame, & abject Slaves, as the Blacks we Rule over with such arbitrary Sway." According to Washington, it was not the wish of Americans to become independent of Great Britain, but he was sure "that none of them will ever submit to the loss of those valuable rights & priviledges which are essential to the happiness of every free State, and without which, Life, Liberty & property are rendered totally insecure." It was "the ardent wish of the warmest advocates for liberty, that peace & tranquility, upon Constitutional grounds, may be restored, & the horrors of civil discord prevented." But if the British failed to alter their policies, "more blood will be spilt on this occasion ... than history has ever yet furnished instances of in the annals of North America."[15]

Commander in Chief

In 1774 Washington served in the First Continental Congress and supported the Continental Association that provided for an economic boycott of Britain in the hopes of getting British merchants and manufacturers to exert pressure on Parliament to change its policies. Elected to the Second Continental Congress, he arrived in Philadelphia in May 1775 wearing the uniform of a Virginia militia colonel, the only delegate attired in a military uniform. He impressed the delegates with his modesty and with his manner of speaking in a "cool but determined Style & Accent."[16] Washington seemed to be the natural choice to command a Continental military force. He had but one challenger, President of Congress John Hancock of Massachusetts. To assure his own selection, Hancock arranged for fellow Massachusetts delegates John and Samuel Adams to nominate the commander. In his nominating speech John Adams called for a man of independent wealth, who could not be bribed by the British and who would willingly go home after the hostilities ended rather than usurp power as was done by Oliver Cromwell after the English civil war in the 1640s. Hancock, the heir of a huge estate, was one of the wealthiest men in the colonies. Adams suggested that the commander in chief should be a man of excellent accomplishments. Hancock felt that his position as president of Congress proved his worth. And finally, Adams called for the commander in chief to be a man of impeccable character. Fixing his eyes upon Washington, Adams then said, we need a man from Virginia. We need George Washington. Stunned, Hancock nearly fell off his chair. Samuel Adams took the floor and seconded Washington's nomination. Washington immediately left the hall, and the delegates unanimously elected him commander in chief. Knowing the difficulties ahead, Washington accepted the appointment with humility and refused to accept a salary. He would accept only payment for his expenses. Shortly after his appointment, Washington met with Virginia congressman Patrick Henry and with tears in his eyes told him that "from the day I enter upon the command of the American armies, I date my fall, and the ruin of my reputation."[17] To his brother Jack, Washington wrote:

> I am Imbarked on a wide Ocean, boundless in its prospect & from whence, perhaps, no safe harbour is to be found. I have been called upon by the unanimous Voice of the Colonies to take the Command of the Continental Army—an honour I neither sought after, nor desired, as I am thoroughly convinced; that it requires greater Abilities, and much more experience, than I am Master of, to conduct a business so extensive in its nature, and arduous in the execution, but the partiallity of the Congress, joined to a political motive, really left me without a Choice. . . . That I may discharge the Trust to the Satisfaction of my Imployers, is my first wish—that I shall aim to do it, there remains as little doubt of— how far I may succeed is another point.[18]

Washington wrote to his wife telling her of his appointment, which "destiny . . . has thrown upon me." He explained that "it was utterly out of my power to refuse this appointment without exposing my Character to such censures as would have reflected dishonour upon myself, and given pain to my friends." Surely, he wrote, she would not have wanted him to decline the appointment; if he had, it would "have lessen'd me considerably in my own esteem." Uncertain of the future, "common prudence" dictated that he have his will drafted, and he sent it to her.[19]

Wherever Washington went he inspired confidence. John Adams wrote his wife Abigail that "Congress have made Choice of the modest and virtuous, the amiable, generous and brave George Washington Esqr. to be the General of the American Army. . . . This Appointment will have a great Effect, in cementing and securing the Union of these Colonies. . . . The Liberties of America depend upon him, in a great Degree." Connecticut delegate Eliphalet Dyer saw that Washington's appointment put southern delegates to Congress at ease by removing their fear that a successful "Enterprising eastern New England General . . . might with his Victorious Army give law to the Southern & Western Gentry. . . . He is Clever, & if anything too modest. He seems discrete & Virtuous, no harum Starum ranting Swearing fellow, but Sober, steady, & Calm." Even John Hancock had to admit that Washington "is a fine man." A young officer delivered a letter to Washington "and was deeply impressed with an awe I cannot describe in contemplating that great man, his august person, his majestic mien, his dignified and commanding deportment." Abigail Adams wrote her husband about her impressions of the general. "You had prepared me to entertain a favorable opinion of him, but I thought the one half was not told me. Dignity with ease, and complacency, the Gentleman and Soldier look agreeably blended in him. Modesty marks every line and feature of his face." Philadelphian Benjamin Rush suggested that Washington "seems to be one of those illustrious heroes whom providence raises up once in three or four hundred years to save a nation from ruin. . . . he has so much martial dignity in his deportment that you would distinguish him to be a general and a soldier from among ten thousand people. There is not a king in Europe that would not look like a valet de chambre by his side."[20]

On his way to take command of the New England army then laying siege to the British army in Boston, Washington stopped in New York

City where he was feted at a dinner by the provincial congress. The New Yorkers asked Washington if he and his fellow officers would promise to surrender their commissions at the end of the hostilities. Somewhat taken aback, Washington thoughtfully responded that when he and his fellow officers put on their uniforms, they never ceased to be citizens. They were citizens first and soldiers second. They assuredly would surrender their commissions at the end of the hostilities and "sincerely rejoice with you in that happy hour when the establishment of American Liberty, upon the most firm and solid foundations, shall enable us to return to our Private Stations in the bosom of a free, peaceful and happy Country."[21]

Washington's initial actions as commander in chief were quite successful. He appeared outside Boston and looked every part the general. Virginia congressman Richard Henry Lee praised Washington for "the discipline you have introduced into the Camp," while John Hancock told the general "that under your Directions, an undisciplined Band of Husbandmen, in the Course of a few Months became Soldiers."[22] The emplacement of captured cannon from Fort Ticonderoga on Dorchester Heights forced the British army to evacuate Boston, never to return.

In April 1776 Washington moved his army south to New York to defend against an expected British attack. With too many strategic locations to defend, Washington unwisely spread thin his 19,000-man army composed of inexperienced Continentals and untrained militia. He had no artillery, no cavalry, and no naval support. In late June the British started arriving with an army of 30,000, thirty major naval vessels armed with 1,200 cannon, and 10,000 sailors. The British easily defeated the American forces in every engagement, forcing Washington to abandon New York City and retreat across the Hudson River into New Jersey and then across the Delaware into Pennsylvania. Miraculously Washington always managed to escape keeping an army intact and the struggle alive. But by December 1776 he had only 2,300 men left, many of whom were militiamen whose time of service was up at the end of the year. On December 20 he wrote President Hancock that "ten days more will put an end to the existence of our Army." At the same time the enemy was "gathering strength from the disaffected. This strength, like a Snowball by rolling, will increase, unless some means can be devised to check effectually, the progress of the Enemy's Arms." It was one of the lowest points of the Revolution, especially for the commander in chief. Second in command General Charles Lee and his supporters indiscreetly conspired to replace Washington. Disgruntled congressmen refused to supply the army adequately with men, food and clothing, and matériel, yet they complained about Washington's ignominious retreat across New Jersey. Congressman John Adams suggested that had he been a commander, even if outnumbered, he would attack and run, attack and run, provoking and winning these ongoing skirmishes. "Defeat," in his opinion, "appears to be preferable to total Inaction." Discouraged, Washington wrote that it appeared as if "the game is pretty near up."[23]

But then, in perhaps the most important two-week period of the entire war, American fortunes reversed. The commander in chief, faced with the prospect of losing his entire army during a long winter encampment, hatched a bold and extremely dangerous plan to attack several isolated New Jersey settlements occupied by both British redcoats and German mercenaries. In November, Washington had ordered Thomas Paine to leave the army and write something that would inspire the army and the American people. Pennsylvania general Thomas Mifflin was ordered to go on a whirlwind recruitment tour which raised Washington's forces up to 6,000. Paine responded with the first number of his *American Crisis* series, which was read to Washington's troops on the banks of the Delaware on December 23, 1776. "These are the times that try men's souls," wrote Paine in some of the greatest rhetoric of the Revolution. "The summer soldier and the sunshine patriot will, in this crisis, shrink from the service of his country; but he that stands it now, deserves the love and thanks of man and woman."[24]

On December 24 Pennsylvania congressman Dr. Benjamin Rush spent over an hour in private with the general. "Washington appeared much depressed, and lamented the ragged and dissolving state of his army in affecting terms." Rush assured Washington that Congress supported him. While they were talking, Rush noticed that Washington was doodling on several small pieces of paper. "One of them by accident fell upon the floor near my feet. I was struck with the inscription upon it. It was 'Victory or Death.'"[25]

On December 25, beginning at 11:00 p.m., Washington with 2,400 men crossed the ice-choked Delaware River and then marched nine long miles to Trenton through a storm of wind, rain, hail, and snow.

Surprising the 1,200 Hessians at about 8:00 a.m., the Americans won a decisive victory. Only a handful of Americans were wounded and but two died from freezing. The Hessians lost 106 killed and wounded and over 900 captured. The American troops used the phrase "Victory or Death" as their countersign. Washington retreated back across the Delaware but a few days later again crossed the river and won another victory at Princeton. Other American victories occurred at Borden-town and Burlington before Washington's rejuvenated army went into winter encampment at Morristown. These victories were really quite inconsequential militarily; for morale, they were monumental. They allowed the American cause to continue. They brought in new recruits and a new confidence in the commander in chief. Abigail Adams wrote that she believed "that our late misfortunes have called out the hidden Excellencies of our Commander in chief—'affliction is the good man's shining time.' The critical state of our affairs has shown him to great advantage." Thomas Paine wrote of Washington that "there is a natural firmness in some minds which cannot be unlocked by trifles, but which, when unlocked, discovers a cabinet of fortitude." Congressman William Hooper of North Carolina marveled at "how often America has been rescued from ruin by the mere strength of [Washington's] genius, conduct & courage encountering every obstacle that want of money, men, arms, Ammunition could throw in his way; an impartial World will say with you that he is the Greatest Man on Earth. Misfortunes are the Element in which he shines."[26]

But there were pessimists. John Adams told Congress that he was "distressed to see some members disposed to idolise an image which their own hands have molten. I speak here of the superstitious venera-tion that is sometimes paid to General Washington. Altho' I honour him for his good qualities, yet in this house I feel myself his Superior. In private life I shall always acknowledge that he is mine. It becomes us to attend early to the restraining our army." Benjamin Rush predicted that Washington would not "close the present war with G. Britain," because revolutions usually do not end with those they begin with, because his talents were better suited to unite the people against Britain "than to give them Afterwards a national complexion," because "his talents are unequal" to the task, and because "he is idolized by the people of Amer-ica." These fears seemed justified when Congress conferred dictatorial powers on Washington. Congressman Charles Carroll of Maryland hoped that Washington would use these new powers wisely because "unless he does, our affairs will never go well." Carroll's greater concern was that Washington would not use these new powers because "he is so humane & delicate."[27]

When General Horatio Gates accepted the surrender of British general John Burgoyne at Saratoga in October 1777 and Washington failed to defeat the British at Brandywine and Germantown, the conspiracies and cabals revived. Jonathan Dickinson Sergeant savaged the commander. "We are so attached to this Man that I fear we shall rather sink with than throw him off our Shoulders. And sink we must under his Management." None of these cabals amounted to much, however, because Washington's supporters in Congress were always dominant and because he always maintained the loyalty of his soldiers. President of Congress Henry Laurens, a South Carolina planter, wrote the marquis de Lafayette not to worry. The commander "is out of the reach of his Enemies." The cabals against him amounted "to little more than tittle tattle." To others Laurens acknowledged that there was unjustified criticism of Washington but that the general understood how important it was to the country for him to continue in command. "This great & virtuous Man has not acted the *half patriot*, by a hasty resignation . . . he will not take a Step which may greatly injure thirteen United States. . . . No internal Enemy can hurt him without his own consent."[28]

Washington was not a brilliant military strategist, nor did he generally take risks when the likelihood of success was uncertain. He told President of Congress Hancock, "We should on all occasions avoid a general action or put anything to the risk unless compelled by a necessity, into which we ought never to be drawn."[29] He, unlike his subordinate generals, could not afford the luxury of being captured. His capture could have been catastrophic for the Revolution.

Washington continually had to be diplomatic with both Congress and his own generals as well as with the enemy. In 1776 Washington refused to accept letters from British naval commander Admiral Sir Richard Howe or his brother, British commander in chief General Sir William Howe. The letters were addressed to "George Washington, Esq." and were sent to his camp where the commander in chief's pennant was flying, clearly indicating that the general was in residence. When

General Howe's aide arrived and personally presented another letter to Washington again without his military rank indicated, Washington once again refused to accept the letter and told the aide that he would never accept a "letter directed to him as a private Person when it related to his publick Station."[30] Finally, General Howe understood and addressed his next letter to "General George Washington, Esq.," and it was accepted. Until this time British forces had considered the Americans as rebels, and captured American soldiers were treated accordingly. Washington wanted to make it clear that the war was no longer a colonial rebellion. The former colonies were an independent nation. Captured American soldiers should be treated as captured British soldiers were treated: as prisoners of war.

Washington's understanding of psychology again was displayed on the eve of the battle of Germantown. General Howe recently had captured Philadelphia, and the two armies prepared to fight what was expected to be the climactic battle of the war. Reinforcements flooded in to both armies. At this critical juncture, on the morning of October 6, 1777, Washington wrote a card to General Howe informing him that the Americans had in their possession a dog with a collar inscribed "General William Howe." The card and the dog were delivered to Howe. Later that day Washington wrote a letter to Howe asking the British commander to control his troops in the ensuing battle. In previous engagements British and Hessian soldiers had raped, killed, pillaged, and burned. Washington asked that the civilian population of Philadelphia be spared. By showing Howe humanity in returning the general's dog, Washington was now asking Howe in return to show humanity toward Philadelphia's civilians.[31]

On occasion Washington upset his officers and men by endangering himself. Samuel Shaw wrote that "our army love our General very much, but yet they have *one thing against him,* which is the little care he takes of himself in any action. His personal bravery, and the desire he has of animating his troops by example, make him fearless of any danger. This, while it makes him appear great, occasions us much uneasiness. But Heaven, who has hitherto been his shield, I hope will still continue to guard so valuable a life."[32]

Probably the most dramatic case of Washington's disregard for his own personal safety occurred during the battle of Monmouth in central

New Jersey in July 1778. General Charles Lee was assigned command of American forces sent to attack General Howe's troops as they evacuated Philadelphia and marched toward New York City. Soon the engagement became a rout as the Americans, including Lee, ran from the counterattacking British. Washington rode down amid the confusion, ordered the insubordinate Lee to the rear, and restored order among the troops. The day ended with a standoff as the British slipped away at night. Alexander Hamilton, Washington's aide-de-camp, described the scene to New Jersey congressman Elias Boudinot.

> As we approached the supposed place of action we heard some flying rumors of what had happened in consequence of which the General rode forward and found the troops retiring in the greatest disorder and the enemy pressing upon their rear. I never saw the general to so much advantage. His coolness and firmness were admirable. He instantly took measures for checking the enemy's form and make a proper disposition. He then rode back and had the troops formed on a very advantageous piece of ground. . . . The sequel is, we beat the enemy and killed and wounded at least a thousand of their best troops. America owes a great deal to General Washington for this day's work; a general rout, dismay and disgrace would have attended the whole army in any other hands but his. By his own good sense and fortitude he turned the fate of the day. Other officers have great merit in performing their parts well; but he directed the whole with the skill of a Master workman. He did not hug himself at a distance and leave an Arnold to win laurels for him [an indirect, although not too subtle, reference to Horatio Gates, who stood back while Benedict Arnold led the American attack at Saratoga]; but by his own presence, he brought order out of confusion, animated his troops and led them to success.[33]

Boudinot responded that "the General I always revered & loved ever since I knew him, but in this Instance he has rose superior to himself. Every Lip dwells on his Praise." A year later Lafayette, back briefly in France, asked Washington's forgiveness for what he was about to say. "I can't help reminding you that a commander in chief should never too much expose himself, that in case General Washington was killed, Nay was seriously wounded, there is no officer in the army who might fill that place." If such a calamity occurred, not only would a battle be lost, but the entire army and "the American cause itself would perhaps be entirely Ruined."[34]

Often Washington had to make hard, heart-wrenching decisions as commander in chief. Such was the case in April 1778 when Colonel Matthias Ogden of the First New Jersey Regiment asked Washington for permission to rescue between twenty and thirty American officers held captive by the British on Long Island. Ogden had gotten information that the officers were being held one or two each in private homes. Only Loyalist militia were left to guard against an escape. Ogden's plan seemed certain of success in freeing at least some of the prisoners. After painstaking consideration Washington rejected Ogden's proposal. A gentleman's agreement among the British commanding officer, Washington, and the captured American officers allowed the prisoners lenient treatment and mild accommodations on Long Island. Freeing these twenty or thirty would put six times as many other captured officers (and all future prisoners as well) under "a stricter & much more limited confinement than they now experience." Even if the rescue attempt was successful, too much would be lost that would endanger the lives of many more prisoners. Washington reluctantly ordered Ogden not to proceed.[35]

Only once was it rumored that large portions of the army had become disaffected from Washington. At the beginning of 1783, with the war all but over as the peace negotiators in Paris were finishing the peace treaty, the officers and the army encamped at Newburgh, New York, were upset with Congress's failure to pay them and to deliver on pension promises to the officers made in the depths of the war in 1780. The soldiers and officers knew that Washington would not support any "unlawful proceeding" against Congress.[36] Mutiny was in the air. Washington might have to be replaced with a commanding officer willing to stand against Congress.

Washington sensed the danger. "The predicament in which I stand as Citizen & Soldier, is as critical and delicate as can well be conceived. It has been the subject of many contemplative hours. The sufferings of a complaining army on one hand, and the inability of Congress and tardiness of the States on the other, are the forebodings of evil; & may be productive of events which are more to be deprecated than prevented."

To forestall "the blackest designs" of those who wanted to blackmail Congress, Washington took extraordinary action. He ordered the officers to assemble and then, contrary to custom, he personally attended and formally addressed the 500 officers. Washington asked them to be patient, to use "cool, deliberative thinking, and that composure of Mind which is so necessary to give dignity and stability to measures." He asked them to trust him to intervene for them with Congress. The nation, he said, owed them a debt, not an ordinary debt but a debt of honor that the officers had paid with their blood. He would go to Congress and plead their case. He was confident that Congress, which "entertain[ed] exalted sentiments of the Services of the Army ... will do it compleat justice." He hoped the officers would not "cast a shade over that glory which has been so justly acquired; and tarnish the reputation of an Army which is celebrated thro' all Europe, for its fortitude and Patriotism." He begged the officers to oppose those who "wickedly" made "attempts to open the flood Gates of Civil discord, and deluge our rising Empire in Blood." He ended his formal address by saying that by preserving "the dignity of your Conduct, [it would] afford occasion for Posterity to say, when speaking of the glorious example you have exhibited to Mankind, 'had this day been wanting, the World had never seen the last stage of perfection to which human nature is capable of attaining.'"[37]

After his formal address, which had not yet convinced the hostile officers to put their trust in him, Washington asked their permission to read a letter he had just received from a reassuring member of Congress. As he started to read the letter, he stumbled. Washington was not a good public speaker. He paused, and then pulled from his coat pocket a pair of spectacles. No one had previously seen him wear glasses in public. He asked the officers' forbearance: "Gentlemen, you will permit me to put on my spectacles, for I have not only grown gray but almost blind in the service of my country." According to one observer, "There was something so natural, so unaffected, in this appeal, as rendered it superior to the most studied oratory; it forced its way to the heart, and you might see sensibility moisten every eye." The reporter of these events, Samuel Shaw, praised the patriotism of both the army and its leader.

> I rejoice, in the opportunities I have had of seeing this great man in a variety of situations — calm and intrepid where the battle

raged, patient and persevering under the pressure of misfortune, moderate and possessing himself in the full career of victory. Great as these qualifications deservedly render him, he never appeared to me more truly so, than at the assembly we have been speaking of. On other occasions he has been supported by the exertions of an army and the countenance of his friends; but in this he stood single and alone. There was no saying where the passions of an army, which were not a little inflamed, might lead; but it was generally allowed that longer forbearance was dangerous, and moderation had ceased to be a virtue. Under these circumstances he appeared, not at the head of his troops, but as it were in opposition to them; and for a dreadful moment the interests of the army and its General seemed to be in competition! He spoke — every doubt was dispelled, and the tide of patriotism rolled again in its wonted course. Illustrious man! what he says of the army may with equal justice be applied to his own character. "Had this day been wanting, the world had never seen the last stage of perfection to which human nature is capable of attaining."

Shortly after the conspiracy at Newburgh was stifled, Washington received word of the peace. He shed tears and said that "it was the happiest hour of his life."[38]

Washington became immortal in the eyes of his countrymen in June 1783 when in a circular letter to the states he announced his resignation. As soon as the peace treaty was accepted, he planned to retire to Mount Vernon, never again to serve in public office. But before retiring, he offered his countrymen one last piece of advice. Washington suggested that America was at a crossroads. The winning of independence alone would not guarantee greatness.

There is an opinion still left to the United States of America, whether they will be respectable and prosperous, or contemptible and miserable as a nation. This is the time of their political probation; this is the moment, when the eyes of the whole world are turned upon them, this is the moment to establish or ruin their national character forever; this is the favorable moment to give such a tone to the federal government, as will enable it to answer the ends of its institution; or this may be the ill-fated moment for relaxing the powers of the union, annihilating the cement of the confederation, and exposing us to become the sport of European politics, which may play one State against another, to prevent their growing importance, and to serve their own interested purposes. For, according to the system of policy the States shall adopt at this moment, they will stand or fall; and, by their conformation or lapse, it is yet to be decided, whether the revolution must ultimately be considered as a blessing or a curse; not to the present age alone, for with our fate will the destiny of unborn millions be involved.[39]

Four things, Washington said, must be done to make America great. First, the Union must be maintained and the powers of Congress strengthened. Second, public justice had to be preserved, by which he meant that Congress must properly compensate public creditors, domestic and foreign; the army and its officers; and the widows and orphans of those who died in the war. Third, a proper peacetime military establishment must be created. The war had shown the ineffectiveness of the militia system, and a standing army of sorts had to be established. Finally, Washington stressed that after twenty years of fighting against British despotism, Americans should "cultivate a spirit of subordination and obedience to government." They should also reject the spirit of sectionalism that had developed and "entertain a brotherly affection and love for one another." This advice should "be considered as the legacy of one who has ardently wished, on all occasions, to be useful to his country." Only by pursuing these policies could Americans "hope to be a happy Nation."[40]

The war continued for another five months. The treaty of peace was ratified in September 1783, and a month later Congress discharged those soldiers who had enlisted for the duration of the war and allowed officers on furlough to retire. On November 2, 1783, Washington sent his farewell address to the armies of the United States. In his address Washington wanted to recall the past, explore the soldiers' future prospects, advise them on their future pursuits, and conclude with the obligations he felt to them for the "spirited and able assistance" he had received from them.

Washington felt that all Americans had to be astonished, grateful, and inspired at what had been accomplished. Faced with tremendous "disadvantageous circumstances," the army with "the singular interposition of Providence" had wrought what "was little short of a standing miracle." He remembered how "raw" recruits with no military experience taken from separate regions of the continent that had traditionally "despise[d] and quarrel[ed] with each other" "instantly became but one patriotic band of Brothers."

The future prospect for America with its independence and sovereignty obtained "exceeds the power of description." Brave and indomitable soldiers would now become farmers, merchants, and fishermen and, above all else, would never be excluded "from the rights of Citizens and the fruits of their labour." Washington also predicted that no state would refuse to pay its federal requisitions (i.e., taxes) thereby threatening "a national bankruptcy and a dissolution of the union." Congress would receive the state payments with which it could pay the nation's debt to its army. The commander in chief knew that his soldiers would be patient in awaiting their just compensation; that they would be "not less virtuous and useful as Citizens, than they have been persevering and victorious as Soldiers." America's soldiers would possess "the private virtues of œconomy, prudence, and industry" as civilians just as while soldiers they possessed "the more splendid qualities of valour, perseverance, and enterprise . . . in the Field." Washington had confidence that his soldiers would be able "to change the military character into that of the Citizen" because of "their good sense and prudence." As "the Curtain of separation" was about to be drawn between him and his men, Washington could only pray that "their grateful country" would provide "ample justice" here on earth while "the God of Armies" would reward them with "the choicest of heaven's favours."[41]

The British finally evacuated New York City on November 25, 1783. General Washington and New York governor George Clinton rode into the city after nearly seven years of British occupation. Residents, returning refugees, and the army celebrated. When it came time for Washington to depart, he called his officers together at Fraunces Tavern to say farewell. He raised a glass of wine to toast them. With a heart filled with love and gratitude, he hoped that their latter years would be as happy and prosperous as their former ones were honorable and glorious. He could not go to each officer individually, but he asked them to come and take him by the hand. With that comment, General Henry Knox, Washington's commander of artillery, who was standing next to him, turned to Washington, embraced him and kissed him on the cheek. The other officers followed the example and they all wept knowing, in all likelihood, that they would never see their "father general" again.[42]

Washington left New York with but one last official act to perform. He stopped on the way home to surrender his commission to Congress then meeting in Annapolis, Maryland. On Monday, December 22, Congress honored Washington with a dinner. Between 200 and 300 attended. After the obligatory thirteen toasts, Washington made a final additional toast. "Competent powers to Congress for general purposes." That evening the governor of Maryland hosted a ball at the statehouse. "The General danced every set, that all the ladies might have the pleasure of dancing with him, or as it has since been handsomely expressed, *get a touch of him.*"[43]

The formal ceremony surrendering Washington's commission was held on Tuesday morning, December 23. Congressman James McHenry, a former aide-de-camp to Washington, described the scene to his fiancée.

> Today my love the General at a public audience made a deposit of his commission and in a very pathetic [that is, emotional] manner took leave of Congress. It was a Solemn and affecting spectacle; such an one as history does not present. The spectators all wept, and there was hardly a member of Congress who did not drop tears. The General's hand which held the address shook as he read it. When he spoke of the officers who had composed his family, and recommended those who had continued in it to the present moment to the favorable notice of Congress he was obliged to support the paper with both hands. But when he commended the interests of his dearest country to almighty God, and those who had the superintendence of them to his holy keeping, his voice faultered and sunk, and the whole house felt his agitations. After the pause which was necessary for him to recover himself, he proceeded to say in the most penetrating manner, "Having now finished the work assigned me I retire from the great theater of action, and bidding an affectionate farewell to this august

body under whose orders I have so long acted I here offer my commission and take my leave of all the employments of public life." So saying he drew out from his bosom his commission and delivered it up to the president of Congress. . . . This, [McHenry continued,] is only a sketch of the scene. But, were I to write you a long letter I could not convey to you the whole. So many circumstances crowded into view and gave rise to so many affecting emotions. The events of the revolution just accomplished—the new situation into which it had thrown the affairs of the world—the great man who had borne so conspicuous a figure in it, in the act of relinquishing all public employments to return to private life—the past—the present—the future—the manner—the occasion—all conspired to render it a spectacle inexpressibly solemn and affecting.[44]

The next day, Washington was home to spend the first Christmas at Mount Vernon in eight years. A month later, Washington asked Congress to return the commission "to have it deposited amongst my own Papers. It may serve *my Grand Children* some fifty or a hundred years hence for a theme to ruminate upon" On January 29, 1784, North Carolina delegate Hugh Williamson moved "that his late Commission be returned to General Washington in a neat gold box to be preserved among the archives of his family."[45]

❦ Private Citizen

Washington was delighted to be back home as "a private citizen on the banks of the Potomac . . . free from the bustle of a camp & the busy scenes of public life." He was now free to pursue the "tranquil enjoyments" unattainable by the soldier pursuing his own fame or the statesman advancing the welfare of his country. Not only was he retired from all public employment, but he was retiring within himself. He was "envious of none." His aim was but to repair the damage suffered by his plantation during his long absence.[46]

Despite Washington's withdrawal from public life, the public did not withdraw from him. He remained the most popular person in the country, and a stream of visitors daily paraded to Mount Vernon. During the more than five years he spent at home between his retirement from the army and his inauguration as president, there were only a few days when Martha and her husband did not entertain guests. Washington compared Mount Vernon "to a well resorted tavern, as scarcely any strangers who are going from north to south, or from south to north do not spend a day or two at it." Sometimes guests stopped for only a few hours or a day, but more typically they stayed for several days at a time. Not only guests had to be accommodated, but their servants (often slaves) and their horses needed to be housed and fed. David Humphreys, a former aide-de-camp, stayed for a year and a half! Washington enjoyed the company of his friends; "their visits," he wrote, "can never be unseasonable." Hospitality was ever present. In writing a friend who had recently returned to England, Washington told him that "should your Son who is lately arrived from England be prompted by business or inclination to travel into this State it would give me much pleasure to shew him every civility in my power—the same to any branch of your family—or any of your friends."[47] One condition, however, that Washington always insisted upon was that his guests allow him to do his work on the plantation.

Washington's daily schedule remained fairly constant while he was at home, as he devoted mornings to business and afternoons to guests. He rose at sunrise. Late in life he advised his stepgrandson to "rise early, that by habit it may become familiar, agreeable, healthy, and profitable. It may for a while be irksome to do this, but that will wear off and the practice will produce a rich harvest forever thereafter." He dressed and went out briefly to check on various "hirelings," whom he expected also to rise with the sun. After two hours he was back home at around seven for breakfast. Late in life his breakfast consisted of "tea and *caks* made from maize; because of his teeth he makes slices spread with butter and honey." Then he would answer some of his voluminous correspondence and read some of the dozen newspapers and magazines he subscribed to. Next he would "mount my horse and ride round my farms."[48] Between two and three in the afternoon, he would return to the house and briefly chat with his visitors and family, which included his two young stepgrandchildren. He then excused himself, changed for dinner, powdered his hair, which he tied neatly in a long queue, and returned to his company. After dinner they enjoyed Madeira and talked about the events of the Revolution; the latest state, national, or international news; or new developments in canal building or farming techniques. Again the general would go off to his study to read newspapers and answer correspondence. At 7:00 p.m. he would rejoin his guests for tea and conversation until 9:00 when he would retire to his bedroom where again he would read and write until the candle burned low.

In the summer of 1784, Washington greatly enjoyed a visit from the marquis de Lafayette, who during the war had become almost an adopted son. The Frenchman described the sublime simplicity of Washington: "he is as completely involved with all the details of his lands and house as if he had always lived here." Washington was saddened when his dear friend left, expecting that they would never see each other again. He remembered his own youthful days that "had long since fled to return no more." He realized that he "was now descending the hill, I had been 52 years climbing." Knowing that his family was not blessed with long life, he soon expected "to be entombed in the dreary mansions of my father's." These brief somber periods always vanished, pushed aside by his busy schedule. He vowed not to repine. But he thought, "I have had my day."[49]

Visitors to Mount Vernon often came not knowing what to expect. They always left sensing that they had been in the presence of greatness but at the same time found that this great man was a kind, thoughtful person. Their experience would never be forgotten; they would record it in their diaries and tell their grandchildren.

Elkanah Watson of New York was typical. Armed with several letters of recommendation from friends of Washington, Watson described his feelings as he neared Mount Vernon: "No pilgrim ever approached Mecca with deeper enthusiasm. . . . I trembled with awe as I came into the presence of this great man. . . . He soon put me at ease, by unbending, in a free and affable conversation. . . . I observed a peculiarity in his smile, which seemed to illuminate his eye; his whole countenance beamed with intelligence, while it commanded confidence and respect. . . . I remained alone in the enjoyment of the society of Washington, for two of the richest days of my life." Watson remembered that he and Washington sat alone at the table uninterrupted for an hour. Unfortunately, Watson was sick with a cold and coughed excessively. Washington offered various remedies, but Watson declined them. When he retired for the night, Watson's cough worsened. After a while a knock on the door caused Watson to pull back his bed curtains. To his "utter astonishment, I beheld Washington himself, standing at my bedside, with a bowl of hot tea in his hand." Watson was stunned. Such an act of kindness might be expected "with an ordinary man, . . . but as a trait of the benevolence and private virtue of Washington, deserves to be recorded."[50]

Robert Hunter, a young Scotsman, visited Mount Vernon in November 1785. He described the retired general as "about six foot high, perfectly straight and well made, rather inclined to be lusty. His eyes are full and blue and seem to express an air of gravity. His nose inclines to the aquiline; his mouth small; his teeth are yet good; and his cheeks indicate perfect health. His forehead is a noble one, and he wears his hair turned back, without curls (quite in the officer's style) and tied in a long queue behind. Altogether, he makes a most noble, respectable appearance, and I really think him the first man in the world." A Rhode Islander described meeting the Washington family "without any ceremonious parade. The general converses with great deliberation, & with ease, except in pronouncing some few words, in which he has a hesitancy of speech."[51]

Painters often visited Mount Vernon hoping to capture Washington on canvas. Frequently the artist would have one life sitting with Washington and then copy that original painting in numerous others. In introducing Robert Edge Pine, a famous English painter who had been sympathetic to the American cause during the Revolution, Francis Hopkinson wrote Washington that Pine wanted to paint scenes from the war "wherein you bore so conspicuous a Part, [that they] cannot be *faithfully* represented if you are omitted. I know you have already suffer'd much Persecution under the Painter's Pencil—& verily believe that you would rather fight a Battle, on a just Occasion, than sit for a Picture, because there is Life and Vigour in *Fortitude*, & *Patience* is but a dull Virtue. I would not insinuate that you have not much Patience, but am very sure that you have a great deal of Good Nature." Washington wrote: "I am so hackneyed to the touches of the Painters pencil, that I am *now* altogether at their beck, and sit like patience on a Monument whilst they are delineating the lines of my face. It is a proof among many others, of what habit & custom can effect. At first I was as impatient at the request, and as restive under the operation, as a Colt is of the Saddle—The next time, I submitted very reluctantly, but with less flouncing. Now, no dray moves more readily to the Thill [the two shafts between which a horse is hitched to a wagon], than I do to the Painters Chair."⁵² Washington was less at ease with sculptors who made life masks. American artist Joseph Wright, commissioned by Congress to sculpt an equestrian statue of Washington, and the great French sculptor Jean Antoine Houdon, hired by the Virginia legislature to prepare a full-length statue of Washington, came to Mount Vernon in the summer of 1783 and in October 1785, respectively. For the face mask, Houdon had Washington lie on his back and then covered his head and shoulders with plaster. Straws placed in each nostril allowed Washington to breath. A combination of pain and claustrophobia accompanied the difficult removal of the set plaster.

After the Revolution, Washington increased his real estate holdings by purchasing western lands far from Mount Vernon. In the summer of 1783, he and New York governor George Clinton purchased 6,071 acres near present-day Utica, New York. Clinton put up the cash for the transaction and managed the holdings. He explained to his partner what kind of investment worked best. The land should be well watered, sprinkled with timber and orchards, near a good road, and not far from towns that could provide necessary goods and markets for farm produce. Half the land should be sold quickly at a modest profit. Settlers would improve that land, causing an escalation of surrounding land values. By 1796, when Washington was thinking about retiring from the presidency, Clinton reported that they still retained 1,446 acres valued at over five dollars per acre. Clinton recommended holding onto the land because "the soil is good and in proportion to the rapid settlement of that Part of the Country the value of those Lands continue to increase." The two old surveyors had done well as a team. With a quarter of their land still available, the investment had already turned a handsome profit.⁵³

Washington developed his own marketing strategy for renting or selling his western lands that aimed at long-term profits rather than quick financial returns. First he identified an agent who would be given the power of attorney over the land. The agent would then place as many tenants on the land as seemed practical. Landholdings would not be initially surveyed but would be determined by natural boundaries such as rivers and rock formations. As an incentive to settle the land, tenants would be exempt from rent for three years provided they made "certain reasonable improvements," such as building "comfortable houses," putting a certain portion of the land under cultivation and establishing another portion as meadowland, and planting a minimum number of fruit trees. With the fourth year of occupancy, tenants would pay one-third of what they raised to the agent, who would sell the produce, keep a commission, and pay the balance to the landlord. The landlord reserved all mineral rights. The agent then would set a term limit on the rented property, preferably not to exceed ten years. The lease could be extended at the agent's discretion, but not for life.[54]

The Master and His Slaves

Throughout his life Washington owned slaves; they were an integral part of his well-ordered life. Usually he referred to his slaves by some euphemistic term: his family, his servants, or "my people." One of the 110 rules of civility that Washington lived by provided that "artificers & persons of low degree ought" to be treated by "those of high degree . . . with affability and courtesy, without arrogancy." Consequently Washington treated his slaves with a degree of humanity not always found among owners of large numbers of slaves. He encouraged marriages and family life among slaves, he made some slaves overseers, and he prepared young slaves for their eventual freedom. In an undated memorandum probably written late in his life, Washington stated his goal: "To make the Adults among them as easy & as comfortable in their circumstances as their actual state of ignorance & improvidence would admit; & to lay a foundation to prepare the rising generation for a destiny different from that in which they were born; afforded some satisfaction to my mind, & could not I hoped be displeasing to the justice of the Creator." In 1793, while serving as president, Washington responded to a question about his slaves, declaring "that I do not like to even think, much less talk of it." His idea was that if he was not "principled agst selling negroes, as you would do cattle in the market, I would not, in twelve months from this date, be possessed of one, as a slave. I shall be happily mistaken, if they are not found to be a very troublesome species of property."[55] While resident in Philadelphia, Washington regularly rotated his slaves home to Mount Vernon so as not to be subject to a Pennsylvania law that allowed slaves resident for longer than six months to sue for their freedom.

Washington inherited ten slaves from his father. When, at the age of twenty-two, Washington acquired Mount Vernon, he obtained another eighteen slaves with the estate. In 1754 he bought two males and a female. Two years later he bought from the governor a slave woman and her child. In 1758 he purchased another male, and the following year (the year of his wedding), he purchased eleven more males and a woman and her child. In 1762 he purchased nine males, and in 1764 he purchased three men, two women, and a child. Four years later he purchased two mulatto men and two boys. In 1772 he made what he hoped would be his last slave purchase, of five more males. When George and Martha Washington married in 1759, she brought with her and her two children the full estate of her late husband. Washington would control almost 200 additional slaves that were part of Martha's dower and her children's inheritance.[56]

By 1791 Washington controlled nearly 300 slaves, twice as many as he thought he needed. Although the surplus slaves strained the plantation's resources, he could not bring himself to sell them "because I am principled against this kind of traffic in the human species." To hire them out was also unacceptable because families would be split, to which Washington had "an aversion." He felt that "it would be for my interest to set them free, rather than give them victuals and cloaths."[57]

Occasionally throughout the years Washington, perhaps less often than other large slave owners, confronted the problem of runaways. In 1760 he advertised for his first runaway. In 1786 he wrote that he "abominate[d]" runaways. A decade later he asked a friend about a runaway girl in New England, justifying his actions by saying that "however well disposed I might be to a gradual abolition, or even to an entire emancipation of that description of People (if the latter was in itself practicable at this moment) it would neither be politic or just to reward *unfaithfulness* with a premature preference, and thereby discontent before hand the minds of all her fellow-servants who by their steady attachments, are far more deserving than herself of favor." He thought it likely that slaves would continue to run away and that if returned to their rightful masters, runaways should not "be retained . . . as they are sure to contaminate and discontent others."[58]

When Washington discovered that a runaway from a former guest, William Drayton of Charleston, South Carolina, was staying at Mount

Vernon, he arranged to have the runaway returned, sending him "under the care of a trusty Overseer" to Baltimore "under the impression of assisting in bringing" some mules back to Mount Vernon. "The real design," however, was to place the runaway on a ship to Charleston. While awaiting the departure of the vessel, the overseer attempted to put the runaway in jail, but when the jailer hesitated because of the lack of an order from a judge, the runaway escaped and took off for Philadelphia. Washington wrote Drayton of the events and complained that it was difficult to capture and return runaways "where there are numbers that had rather facilitate the escape of slaves, than apprehend them." The runaway eventually was returned to Charleston from Philadelphia.[59]

In 1786 Washington was told about a new divisiveness between the North and the South. When a personal slave or two accompanied southerners visiting Philadelphia, Quakers attempted to liberate them. The slaves would be encouraged to run away, and the wealthy Quakers would bring one "vexatious lawsuit" after another against the slave owner. Asked to intervene, Washington wrote his friend Robert Morris, the wealthy Philadelphia merchant who had been superintendent of finance during the war, seeking his assistance in getting the Quakers to desist, or else "none of those whose *misfortune* it is to have slaves as attendants, will visit the City if they can possibly avoid it." Washington hoped that his intervention in this matter would not imply

that it is my wish to hold the unhappy people, who are the subject of this letter, in slavery. I can only say that there is not a man living who wishes more sincerely than I do, to see a plan adopted for the abolition of it; but there is only one proper and effectual mode by which it can be accomplished, and that is by Legislative authority; and this, as far as my suffrage will go, shall never be wanting. But when slaves who are happy and contented with their present masters, are tampered with and seduced to leave them; when masters are taken unawares by these practices; when a conduct of this sort begets discontent on one side and resentment on the other, and when it happens to fall on a man, whose purse will not measure with that of the Society [of Friends], and he loses his property for want of means to defend it; it is oppression in the latter case, and not humanity in any; because it introduces more evils than it can cure.[60]

Washington always instructed his overseers to treat his slaves humanely and to care for them when sick. A clause was inserted in the contract of each overseer binding him "to take all necessary and proper care of the Negroes committed to his management using them with proper humanity and descretion." When sick, slaves should be provided "timely applications and remedies." If they were sufficiently ill, a doctor was to be called from Alexandria. But Washington was always aware that some slaves took advantage of this concern. "I never wish my people to work when they are really sick, or unfit for it; on the contrary, that all necessary care should be taken of them when they are so; but if you do not examine into their complaints, they will lay by when no more ails them, than all those who stick to their business, and are not complaining from the fatigue and drowsiness which they feel as the effect of night walking and other practices which unfit them for the duties of the day."[61]

By the time of the American Revolution, Washington realized the inconsistency of the American struggle for liberty against British oppression and the institution of slavery. He decided, "unless some particular circumstances should compel me to it," never "to possess another slave by purchase; it being among my first wishes to see some plan adopted, by the legislature by which slavery in this Country may be abolished by slow, sure, & imperceptable degrees."[62]

On occasion Washington pressed some of his debtors to pay him so that he could avoid selling land or slaves to make payments to his own creditors and workers. When John Francis Mercer was unable to pay cash for the debt that his father's estate owed Washington, Washington reluctantly agreed to take payment in slaves, but only a certain kind of slave. "The Negroes I want are males. Three or four young fellows for Ditchers; and the like number of well grown lads for artificers." All of the slaves should be healthy, none should be "addicted to running away," and none should be women or children, who "would not suit my purposes on *any terms.*"[63] When the slaves Mercer identified objected to be separated from their wives and families, Washington rejected the arrangement and agreed "to await the money in any manner you shall please to offer it."[64]

After the Revolution advocates of emancipation regularly sought Washington's endorsement for their proposals. Washington, however, realized his important position in the country and that any public statement he might make against slavery could severely divide the Union. In February 1783 Lafayette asked Washington to join him in purchasing a plantation in the west of Virginia and freeing slaves to settle thereupon as tenants to show that freedmen could succeed. Such an act would also make a public statement that Washington endorsed the abolition of slavery, thereby encouraging other southern slave owners to follow his example. Washington responded to Lafayette, "I shall be happy to join you in so laudable a work; but will defer going into a detail of the business, till I have the pleasure of seeing you" next year.[65]

A year later, historian William Gordon took the occasion of Lafayette's visit to Mount Vernon to write Washington that "you wished to get rid of all your Negroes, & the Marquis wisht that an end might be put to the slavery of all of them. I should rejoice beyond measure could your joint counsels & influence produce it, & thereby give the finishing stroke & the last polish to your political characters." Nothing seems to have been settled on the matter during Lafayette's two visits to Mount Vernon in 1784. In late 1785, however, Lafayette proceeded on his own by purchasing a plantation on Cayenne, an island in the French West Indies, and freeing the slaves "in order to make that experiment which you know is my hobby horse."[66]

In 1785 Methodist ministers asked Washington to sign their petition to the Virginia legislature seeking emancipation. Washington told the ministers that he held similar sentiments and that he had told the state leaders how he felt about slavery. The general, however, awkwardly refused to sign the petition but promised to send his sentiments to the legislature if it considered the petitions. The next year Washington wrote Lafayette congratulating him on his West Indian experiment. "Would to God a like spirit would diffuse itself generally into the minds of the people of this country, but I despair of seeing it." He informed Lafayette that the Methodist petitions had failed in the legislature; "they could scarcely obtain a reading." Perhaps, Washington lamented, it would be wrong to emancipate all of the slaves immediately because it would "be productive of much inconvenience and mischief." A gradual emancipation offered by legislative authority seemed more likely to succeed.[67]

Washington once told a visiting Englishman "that nothing but the rooting out of slavery can perpetuate the existence of our union by consolidating it in a common bond of principle." If, however, slavery divided America, Washington revealed to Edmund Randolph, "he had made up his mind to move and be of the northern."[68]

In December 1793 Washington wrote Arthur Young, an English agricultural reformer, that he wanted to bring "*good* farmers" to Mount Vernon as tenants. Washington would retain only the mansion house farm itself; the other four Mount Vernon farms would be leased to the English farmers. "Many of the Negroes, male and female, might be hired by the year as labourers" to work the land. In this way Washington could "liberate a certain species of property which I possess, very repugnantly to my own feelings."[69] In essence, rather than freeing his slaves and hiring them directly himself, Washington searched for a buffer that would insulate him from the criticism of his fellow Virginians.

As president of the United States, Washington occasionally felt that freeing his slaves might serve as an example for other southerners to free their slaves, but he also felt that such a public act by him might drive the North and the South farther apart. With Washington as an example, the North might redouble its abolition efforts, while a beleaguered South might become increasingly more defensive. Rather than risk such divisiveness, Washington again avoided any public stance on slavery. Only in his will would he take action.

Believing that Martha would outlive him and knowing that his slaves and her dower slaves had intermarried and had had children together, Washington realized the heartbreak that would occur if he freed only his slaves in his will. Therefore, Washington freed only one slave in his will, William Lee, who had faithfully served as Washington's valet throughout the war and after. In 1785 while assisting Washington in surveying his lands, Lee had broken a kneecap in an accident that made it difficult for him to walk, especially when coupled with a severe case of rheumatism. Washington specified that Lee could stay on the plantation as long as he wished and was to be given an annual pension of $30 in addition to his regular clothing and food allowance. All of the other slaves were to be freed upon Martha's death. Those who were old and suffered infirmities were to be provided for by Washington's heirs. The young without parents were to be made wards of the court until they were twenty-five, during which time they should be taught to read and write and "some useful occupation."

After Washington's death it did not take long before the slaves realized that their freedom was dependent upon Martha's death. Martha soon realized that the slaves were aware of this. She therefore, freed all of the slaves in 1801, a year before her death.

Religion

George Washington was like many of his Virginia contemporaries when it came to religion. Outwardly he was a member in good standing of the Anglican Church, which after the Revolution became known as the Episcopalian Church. He was baptized and married in the church and served as godfather to several children. For over twenty years, from 1763 to 1784, he was on the Truro Parish vestry, playing an active role until 1774. Even so, Washington usually attended Sunday services only once a month, choosing instead on the other Sundays to ride, hunt, read, write correspondence, update his plantation records, and entertain guests. While attending the Constitutional Convention in Philadelphia for four months in 1787, Washington attended church only twice, once for the ordination of a Catholic priest. As president, however, Washington more regularly attended Sunday services at St. Paul's Chapel or Trinity Church in New York City and St. Peter's in Philadelphia. During this time he did not participate in the sacrament of Communion. Years later the Reverend James Abercrombie remembered that Washington and others of the congregation left the chapel after the sermon on Communion Sunday, leaving Mrs. Washington, who always took Communion. One Sunday, Abercrombie's sermon criticized those (especially public figures) who set a bad example by eschewing Communion. Sympathetic to Abercrombie's position yet unwilling to give the impression that he was now taking Communion because of his elevated status as president, Washington thereafter made it a point not to attend church on Communion Sunday. Washington probably did not take Communion because his head and heart were not in tune with the doctrine of that sacrament and he did not wish to be hypocritical.

Washington, like many others at the time, felt that *"Religion and morality* are the essential pillars of Civil society." He believed that there are certain "eternal rules of order and right which Heaven itself has ordained." Any people who deviate from these rules can never expect "the propitious smiles of Heaven." In his Farewell Address announcing his retirement from the presidency, Washington wrote:

> Of all the dispositions and habits which lead to political prosperity, Religion and morality are indispensable supports. In vain would that man claim the tribute of Patriotism, who should labour to subvert these great Pillars of human happiness, these firmest props of the duties of Men & citizens. The mere Politician, equally with the pious man ought to respect & to cherish them. A volume could not trace all their connections with private & public felicity. Let it simply be asked where is the security for property, for reputation, for life, if the sense of religious obligation desert the Oaths, which are the instruments of investigation in Courts of Justice? And let us with caution indulge the supposition, that morality can be maintained without religion. Whatever may be conceded to the influence of refined education on minds of peculiar structure—reason & experience both forbid us to expect that National morality can prevail in exclusion of religious principle.[70]

Washington believed that God smiled upon America and played a crucial role in its development. Heaven had blessed America with a bountiful land, with varied climates, and advantageously located navigable rivers. Never before was a people given "a fairer opportunity for political happiness." It would be left for the people of America to determine whether or not they should "be completely free and happy."[71] When Americans faced uncertainties during the mid-1780s, Washington continued to have faith in God.

> It is indeed a pleasure from the walks of private life to view in retrospect, all the meanderings of our past labors—the difficulties through which we have waded—and the fortunate Haven to which the ship has been brought! Is it possible after this that it should founder? Will not the all wise, & all powerfull director of human events, preserve it? I think he will, he may however for wise purposes not discoverable by finite minds, suffer our indiscretions & folly to place our national character low in the political

Scale—and this, unless more wisdom & less prejudice take the lead in our governments, will most assuredly be the case.[72]

Later events would justify Washington's faith. With God's help Americans had won their independence and drafted and ratified a new federal Constitution. "No People," Washington said in his first inaugural address,

> can be bound to acknowledge and adore the invisible hand which conducts the Affairs of men more than the People of the United States. Every step, by which they have advanced to the character of an independent nation, seems to have been distinguished by some token of providential agency. And in the important revolution just accomplished in the system of their United Government, the tranquil deliberations, and voluntary consent of so many distinct communities, from which the event has resulted, cannot be compared with the means by which most Governments have been established.[73]

Washington staunchly advocated religious freedom. He wrote his neighbor George Mason that "no man's sentiments are more opposed to *any kind* of restraint upon religious principles than mine are." Because "religious controversies are always productive of more acrimony and irreconcilable hatreds than those which spring from any other cause," Washington was grateful that Americans were "with slight shades of difference . . . the same Religion."[74] He believed that "every man, conducting himself as a good citizen and being accountable to God alone for his religious opinions, ought to be protected in worshipping the Deity according to the dictates of his own conscience." To the Society of New York Quakers, Washington professed that "the liberty enjoyed by the People of these States, of worshipping Almighty God agreable to their Consciences, is not only among the choicest of their *Blessings,* but also of their *Rights.*" To the members of the New Jerusalem Church of Baltimore, Washington wrote that "in this land of equal liberty, it is our boast, that a man's religious tenets will not forfeit the protection of the laws, nor deprive him of the right of attaining and holding the highest offices that are known in the United States."[75]

To Washington, religious freedom and toleration did not mean a total separation of church and state. He encouraged his troops both in the French and Indian War and during the Revolution to attend worship services, and he supported the appointment of chaplains. He recognized congressional days of thanksgiving and even proclaimed them himself. And unlike James Madison and Thomas Jefferson, Washington favored the use of a special tax to support the ministers of each person's faith. "I am not amongst the number of those who are so much alarmed at the thoughts of making people pay towards the support of that which they profess, if of the denominations of Christians; or declare themselves Jews, Mahomitants or otherwise, & thereby obtain proper relief." Religion and morality were so important that the state should make certain that ministers earned livable salaries. But the tremendous public debate generated by the general assessment bill to levy a tax for the support of ministers in 1785 made Washington wish that the bill had never been introduced and "that the Bill could die an easy death; because I think it will be productive of more quiet to the State, than by enacting it into a Law; which, in my opinion, wou'd be impolitic, admitting there is a decided majority for it, to the disgust of a respectable minority." If the bill died, the controversy "will soon subside." If the assessment bill passed, "it will rankle, & perhaps convulse the State."[76]

Washington, like many of the other founders, shared some beliefs in deism but with some semblance of stoicism. Eighteenth-century deists believed in the classical virtues and in one great initiator who designed and started the universe, which was subject to a panoply of unimpeachable "natural laws" propagated by the Supreme Architect of the Universe. Deists also believe in a life after death but are uncertain what that afterlife entails. Thomas Jefferson, who along with Benjamin Franklin and Thomas Paine might well be classified as deists, wrote that "when I was young I was fond of the speculations which seemed to promise some insight into that hidden country, but observing at length that they left me in the same ignorance in which they had found me, I have for very many years ceased to read or to think concerning them, and have reposed my head on that pillow of ignorance which a benevolent creator has made so soft for us, knowing how much we should be forced to use it." On a few occasions Washington alluded not merely to "the impervious shades of death" but to an afterlife in a world of spirits. Consoling his sister upon his mother's death, Washington had "a hope that she is translated to a happier place." Similarly, he expressed "no doubt" that the recently deceased former Connecticut governor Jonathan Trumbull would find "immeasurable happiness hereafter."[77]

Washington accepted these tenets but also, contrary to deists, believed that God intervenes in the ongoing development of his universe, but only in conjunction with human beings. In essence, God takes sides, supporting the just and moral against the perverse and ignoble. Consequently, God interposed in favor of Americans in their righteous struggle for independence and their just pursuit of good government. Washington explained to Lafayette, "I rely much on the good sense of my Countrymen & trust that a superintending Providence will disappoint the hopes of our enemies." This divine intervention applied to individuals as well as nations. Washington firmly believed that it was his destiny—his fate—to lead the American people and that on several occasions God had intervened to spare his life. After the disastrous defeat at the battle of the Monongahela in 1755, in which Washington escaped unscathed while almost every other officer was killed, Washington wrote that he had been left in the land "of the livg by the miraculous care of Providence, that protected me beyond all human expectation." After the Revolution, Washington wrote to Henry Knox that he felt like "a wearied Traveller must do, who, after treading many a painful step, with a heavy burden on his Shoulders, is eased of the latter, having reached the Goal to which all the former were directed—& from his House top is looking back, & tracing with a grateful eye the Meanders by which he escaped the quicksands and Mires which lay in his way, and into which none but the All-powerful guide, & great disposer of human Events could have prevented his falling."[78]

Washington rarely used the word *God*, choosing instead to use the terms *Heaven* or *Providence*, along with the non-gender-specific pronoun *it*. Frequently he reverted to Masonic or deist terminology, such as the Great Ruler of Events, the Governor of the Universe, the Supreme Architect of the Universe, the Sovereign Dispenser of life and health, the Grand Architect, or the Director of Human Affairs. He virtually never used the name Jesus Christ in writing but in his June 1783 circular to the states (his farewell address on leaving the army) did call upon Americans "to do justice, to love mercy, and to demean ourselves with that

charity, humility, and pacific temper of mind, which were the characteristics of the Divine Author of our blessed religion; without an humble
imitation . . . we can never hope to be a happy nation."[79]

Washington pictured God as omnipotent and benign. Through
his "Infinite Wisdom," God dispensed justice to all, the good and the
wicked and everyone in between. Astonishment, adoration, and gratitude were due this divine Being, whose actions were often inscrutable.
At the end of the harsh winter encampment at Valley Forge, Washington
wrote that "the determinations of Providence are always wise—often
inscrutable—and, tho' its decrees appear to bear hard upon us at times,
is, nevertheless meant for gracious purposes."[80]

God's inscrutability was particularly apparent when it came to illness and death. Human beings should hope for the best as long as
there was hope, but once death either was imminent or occurred, the
good Christian would gracefully acquiesce. Washington wrote that the
death of his favorite nephew was "a loss I sincerely regret; but as it
is the will of Heaven, whose decrees are always just & wise, I submit
to it without a murmur." To Henry Knox, his former artillery commander and secretary of war, Washington wrote that it "is not for man
to scan the wisdom of Providence. The best he can do, is to submit to
its decrees. Reason, religion and Philosophy, teaches us to do this, but
'tis time alone that can ameliorate the pangs of humanity, and soften
its woes." In mourning his aged mother, he wrote his sister that "awful, and affecting as the death of a Parent is, there is consolation in
knowing that Heaven has spared ours to an age, beyond which few
attain, and favored her with the full enjoyment of her mental faculties,
and as much bodily strength as usually falls to the lot of four score.
Under these considerations . . . it is the duty of her relatives to yield
due submission to the decrees of the Creator." In pondering his own
inevitable but unforeseeable death, Washington wrote to the marquis
de Lafayette that "I will move gently down the stream of life until I
sleep with my fathers." The trees that he had planted grew rapidly and
reminded him of his own "declination, & their disposition to spread
their mantles over me, before I go hence to return no more." He hoped
that "when the summons comes, I shall endeavor to obey it with a
good grace."[81]

❧ Library

As the "Father of His Country," George Washington is remembered for many things. Unlike Thomas Jefferson, however, he is not remembered for his library. In fact, because of the descriptions of him by a handful of his contemporaries, Washington is not associated with books and reading. Alexander Hamilton said that Washington read virtually nothing at all and that his aides did all of his writing. Fifteen years after Washington's death, Jefferson described his literary skills more temperately, stating that Washington "wrote readily, rather diffusely, in an easy and correct style. This he had acquired by conversation with the world, for his education was merely reading, writing and common arithmetic, to which he added surveying at a later day. His time was employed in action chiefly, reading little, and that only in agriculture and English history. His correspondence became necessarily extensive, and with journalizing his agricultural proceedings, occupied most of his leisure hours within doors."[82]

Washington himself occasionally wrote to friends that his time was almost totally consumed in "rural amusements" and in correspondence, "the drudgery of the pen." He was far more likely to order and receive a case of wine from European merchants than a box of books. Later in life he advised his stepgrandson that "light reading (by this, I mean books of little importance) may amuse for the moment but leaves nothing solid behind."[83]

In reality, Washington was more bookish than most of his contemporaries would have us believe. Not a bibliophile like Jefferson or James Madison, not an avid reader like John Adams, Washington had an extensive personal library that could be divided into five segments: (1) an archive of personal and public papers, (2) public records, (3) atlases and maps, (4) newspapers and magazines, and (5) books and pamphlets.

Like many of his contemporaries, Washington believed that he and his generation had a special destiny. They studiously saved their correspondence and public papers as a testament to their effort to obtain independence and preserve liberty. Six wagonloads of Washington's papers arrived overland at Mount Vernon at the end of the Revolution, too valuable a cargo to be shipped by sea. Secretary of Congress

Charles Thomson told Washington that these papers were "invaluable documents from which future historians will derive light & knowledge. I consider it as a most fortunate circumstance that through all your dangers and difficulties you have happily preserved them entire."[84]

Washington dictated many of his letters to his secretaries, who recorded them in letter books that remained in Washington's library. Washington then personally copied the letters (sometimes changing a word here and there) and sent the result to the addressees. When Washington's papers arrived at Mount Vernon in 1784, some had been recently sorted and copied in letter books, but others were still in disarray. In May 1786 Washington hired Tobias Lear, a twenty-four-year-old New Hampshire native and recent Harvard graduate, to tutor Washington's two stepgrandchildren living at Mount Vernon, assist with correspondence, arrange the general's papers, and care for the library. The warm relationship between Washington and Lear lasted throughout Washington's life.

Several friends and acquaintances encouraged Washington to write either a history of the Revolution or his memoirs. He never gave a thought to doing either and, in fact, did not want anyone to have access to his public papers before his death unless Congress would first open its papers for historical research. He told a friend "that any memoirs of my life, distinct & unconnected with the general history of the war, would rather hurt my feelings than tickle my pride whilst I lived. I had rather glide gently down the stream of life, leaving it to posterity to think & say what they please of me, than by an act of mine to have vanity or ostentation imputed to me. . . . I do not think vanity is a trait of my character."[85]

Washington had a mind that could not easily grasp what he read. To fully comprehend and remember information, he had to write things down or copy them. Consequently, he kept minutely detailed plantation records that helped him (and subsequently us) understand the economies of an eighteenth-century planter who experimented with over sixty different crops to maintain the viability of Mount Vernon.

As a surveyor and military commander, Washington had a keen interest in maps. At the time of his death, his library contained at least six atlases, 150 individual maps, and a book on navigational charts. Most interesting was a portfolio of thirty-five maps he had used in various

Revolutionary War campaigns, as well as the most modern atlas, published by Mathew Carey in Philadelphia in 1796.

Washington's library also contained a large collection of printed public documents. Included among these were parliamentary records, debates, and laws; the laws of Virginia and other colonies and states; the journals of Virginia's colonial House of Burgesses and postwar House of Delegates; the journals and debates of the state conventions that adopted the Constitution of 1787; Indian treaties; Washington's and Adams's presidential addresses to Congress; the cabinet secretaries' reports; the laws of the United States under the new Constitution; the journals of the U.S. House of Representatives and Senate; and numerous miscellaneous pieces. He also for a time retained the records of the Constitutional Convention that drafted the new Constitution of 1787. The delegates to that convention nearly voted to destroy its records but decided better to entrust them with Washington, instructing him to turn them over to proper authorities if the Constitution was adopted. As president in March 1796, Washington turned over these records to the State Department, which had cognizance over not only foreign affairs but also interior matters.

Washington irregularly subscribed to or received complimentary copies of more than a dozen newspapers and magazines. Most of the newspapers were American weeklies with a few dailies sprinkled in, while the magazines were all monthly publications. The magazines— including the Philadelphia *American Museum* and *Columbian Magazine,* the *New York Magazine,* and London's *Gentleman's Magazine* and *The Remembrancer*—were all compilations of literature, poetry, political and philosophical writings, history, historical documents, news from around the world, medical advice, commercial information, religious writings, items on food and drink, geography, grammar, accounts of humorous events, and so on. He usually had the issues of each title bound together every six months, making them easy to store and reference. Washington tried to set aside a certain portion of the day to read this periodical literature which kept him abreast with the affairs of the world, but he told his commercial agent in Philadelphia in the mid-1780s that "my other avocations, will not afford me time to Read them oftentimes; & when I do attempt it, find them more troublesome, than Profitable."[86] Consequently, Washington canceled most of his newspaper subscriptions.

Washington's library contained about 900 books and over 100 pamphlets, which he kept at Mount Vernon in the upstairs study, in the south room on the first floor, and on tables and in bookcases throughout the house. Washington usually signed his name on the upper right-hand corner of the title page and often placed his bookplate in the back of the book. The specially designed bookplate has a dove alighting atop a shield with two horizontal stripes and three stars (Washington was a three-star general). Below the shield is a Latin phrase: "exitus acta probat [all's well that ends well]." A cursive "George Washington" appears at the bottom. Relatively few of these items were purchased by Washington for either his own use or for the use of Martha or her children and grandchildren.

Most of the books and pamphlets were received as complimentary copies from the authors. A goodly number of these works were even dedicated to Washington, as was Thomas Paine's first volume of *Rights of Man* (1790), even though Washington discouraged this practice. In one case, Nicholas Pike, the author of *A New and Complete System of Arithmetic,* asked Washington for permission to dedicate the work to him. Washington declined the honor, but in the interim the book was published with the dedication. Embarrassed, Pike apologetically wrote to Washington explaining how the book went to press before Washington's disclaimer had arrived. Washington graciously responded, praising the author for such a valuable work and hoping that it would be financially profitable for Pike.

Washington read some of the volumes in his library avidly, particularly the pamphlets written during the public debate over the ratification of the U.S. Constitution from 1787 to 1789, while others were of little or no interest to him. Occasionally he loaned volumes to friends or sent them to political associates, sometimes asking them to pass the book or pamphlet along to others. Often Washington's guests, such as Lafayette in 1784, spent time reading from the library while Washington attended to his daily plantation duties. When Washington returned home, the guests and he would discuss what they had been reading as well as the events of the Revolution, agricultural matters, and the affairs of the day. Washington could not read any foreign language, but Lafayette sent him Jacques Necker's popular work on the finances of France anyway, suggesting that Washington could "find translators enough."[87]

Authors who sent Washington complimentary copies had a variety of motivations. All wanted to pay tribute to the great man. Most wanted Washington to be aware of their authorship, especially those who wrote under a pseudonym. These authors usually accompanied their publication with a short cover letter subtly indicating their authorship. Some hoped that Washington might assist in the sales of their volumes. William Gordon, for instance, persuaded a reluctant Washington to circulate subscription papers for his history of the Revolution. Uncertain whether to send Washington a complimentary copy of his history of New Hampshire, the Reverend Jeremy Belknap asked his friend and literary agent Ebenezer Hazard for advice. Hazard, postmaster general of the United States since 1782 and a compiler and editor of a two-volume collection of American state papers published in 1792 for which President Washington subscribed, wrote that "I think it will be quite polite to present General Washington with a copy of your History, and it will produce a letter from him in *his own handwriting,* which will be worth preserving. I have several, which I intend to hand down carefully to posterity as highly valuable." Belknap sent Washington a copy of his book accompanied by a letter praising Washington "with a degree of respect approaching to veneration." As usual, Washington responded with brevity. Belknap told Hazard that though Washington's response was "short and expresses but little, [it] means something very pertinent and interesting. I shall, as you guess, rank it among my valuables."[88]

The books that most interested Washington dealt with practical matters about how to run the plantation. He had many works on agriculture, horticulture, gardening, and animal husbandry, including a series of about 100 tracts from the British Board of Agriculture. He needed the rudimentary medical and veterinary works that were available to care for the family, guests, slaves, and animals. Slave owners and overseers provided the first medical attention for those who were sick; only severe illnesses or accidents required calling physicians to the plantation from Alexandria. He also had gathered a wide variety of military studies dealing with artillery, bayonet exercises, cavalry, the code of military standing, discipline, duties, engineering, fortifications, maneuvers, the militia, ordnance, projectiles, tactics, uniforms, and lists of British and Canadian officers who had served during the Revolution.

Washington's library also contained literary works, such as plays by

Shakespeare, Laurence Sterne's *Tristram Shandy,* Cervantes's *Don Quixote,* Jonathan Swift's *Gulliver's Travels,* and Daniel Defoe's *Robinson Crusoe;* poetry by Joseph Addison, Joel Barlow, Robert Burns, Samuel Butler, Philip Freneau, David Humphreys, Ossian, Alexander Pope, William Preston, James Thomson, and Mercy Otis Warren; the classical writings of Horace and Seneca ; seventeenth-century works including the *Travels of Cyrus* by Andrew Michael Ramsay, the memoirs of his patron, the duc de Sully, Henry IV's chief minister, and the works of John Locke; histories of England, France, Greece, Ireland, Prussia, Rome, Scotland, Spain, Sweden, Kentucky, Maine, New Hampshire, Virginia, the church in New England, and Shays's and the Whiskey rebellions and William Bligh's account of the mutiny on the *Bounty;* histories of the Revolution by Jonathan Boucher, William Heath, Richard Price, David Ramsay, and William Gordon; diplomatic works on Frederick the Great, the Barbary States, and Citizen Genêt and descriptions of and treaties with various Indian tribes; legal works on the law of nature, the law of nations, reports of judicial cases including *Chisholm v. Georgia,* James Wilson's lectures for his law course, and the landlord's law; dictionaries and reference works, among them Samuel Johnson's dictionary and books on grammar; religious works, including several Bibles, a concordance, and many sermons printed as pamphlets; geographies such as Jedidiah Morse's *American Geography* and *American Gazetteer* and a European gazetteer; travel accounts by William Bartram, Brissot de Warville, Andrew Barnaby, Jonathan Carver, the marquis de Chastellux, and John Drayton; works on politics—including the *Letters of Junius* and the two-volume edition of *The Federalist* written by Alexander Hamilton, James Madison, and John Jay under the pseudonym Publius—and political economy, encompassing works on paper currency, banks, and Adam Smith's *Wealth of Nations;* science and natural history, with works on population, Thomas Jefferson's *Notes on the State of Virginia,* and Walter Minto's books on mathematics and the planets; and a variety of works on social reform, including the movement for penitentiaries and antislavery pamphlets, particularly those by Quaker Anthony Benezet and Englishman Granville Sharp.

Washington left his public papers to his nephew Bushrod Washington, who had recently been appointed to the U.S. Supreme Court by President John Adams. The private papers, books, and pamphlets were also to go to Bushrod but only after Martha Washington's death. Martha could save those that "are worth preserving." Wanting to preserve a degree of privacy after her husband's death, Martha destroyed all the letters in her possession between her and her husband.

Bushrod Washington occupied Mount Vernon after Martha's death in 1802 and died in 1829. Over these three decades, he added to the library. He gave much of the original library (658 volumes) to his nephew George C. Washington and a large part of his additions (486 volumes and most of the pamphlets) to another nephew, John A. Washington. All of the law books and state documents were to go to his grandnephew Bushrod Washington Herbert if he became trained in the law. By acts of Congress in 1834 and 1849, the federal government purchased Washington's public and private papers, which were placed under the control of the State Department. In 1908 the papers were transferred to the Library of Congress where they remain today. George C. Washington sold his portion of Washington's library to Henry Stevens, a book dealer, who announced in 1847 that he was going to send the books to the British Museum. Outraged, a group of men from Boston and Cambridge took up a subscription of $5,000 and bought the volumes from Stevens for $3,800. The subscribers gave the books to the Boston Athenæum where they reside today.[89]

Coming Out of Retirement

After his retirement the country did not heed Washington's advice in his 1783 circular to the states. Congress seemed impotent, state politics became increasingly partisan and virulent, the wartime debt largely went unpaid, calls for separate confederacies were openly and increasingly discussed, and a nascent desire for the restoration of monarchy surfaced. A deep economic depression gripped the country, and animosity between debtors and creditors escalated in every state. Violence flared in most states. Debtor farmers in western Massachusetts closed the civil courts to stop foreclosure proceedings, while in Virginia debtors burned courthouses, thereby destroying tax records and obliterating their obligations. Every attempt to strengthen Congress and to amend the Articles of Confederation had failed. Washington wrote that there were combustibles in every state ready to be ignited by a single spark.[90]

Although he advocated radical change in the Articles of Confederation, Washington cautioned against monarchy, "admitting the utility—nay necessity of the form—yet that the period is not arrived for adopting the change without shaking the Peace of this Country to its foundation." In this explosive situation, with the very principles of the Revolution at stake, Washington wholeheartedly supported calling a general convention to address the crisis. He wrote to James Madison that the proposed convention should "adopt no temporising expedient, but probe the defects of the Constitution [i.e., the Articles of Confederation] to the bottom, and provide radical cures, whether they are agreed to or not. A conduct like this, will stamp wisdom and dignity on the proceedings, and be looked to as a luminary, which sooner or later will shed its influence."[91]

In December 1786 the Virginia legislature elected Washington a delegate to the general convention, which was to meet in Philadelphia in May 1787. He declined the appointment, alluding to his 1783 public promise never to serve in public office again. He had other concerns also. Suffering from rheumatism, he was not feeling well. His mother and sister were both seriously ill. Another major concern was the Society of the Cincinnati. This fraternal order of former military officers established in 1784 had elected Washington as its president. The society scheduled its triennial convention for Philadelphia in the spring of 1787. Washington, who did not wish to be president of the society, declined an invitation to attend its convention. Now to accept an appointment to the Federal Convention in the same city at the same time would seem to be an insult to his fellow former officers.

Many of Washington's friends, whose advice he sought and respected, pleaded with him to attend the Philadelphia convention. Virginia governor Edmund Randolph told him that the country's gloomy prospects admitted "one ray of hope, that those, who began, carried on & consummated the revolution, can yet rescue America from the impending ruin." James Madison wrote Washington, "It was the opinion of every judicious friend whom I consulted that your name could not be spared from the Deputation to the Meeting." Two weeks later Madison again pleaded that the "dark and menacing" clouds threatening "our national existence or safety" superseded all of Washington's reasons for not returning to public life. Writing more bluntly than anyone else would dare, Secretary for Foreign Affairs John Jay told Washington well before a convention was ever called that he must "favor your country with your counsels on such an important & single occasion." Jay had told Washington that "altho' you have wisely retired from public Employment, and calmly view from the Temple of Fame, the various Exertions of the Sovereignty and Independence which Providence has enabled You to be so greatly & gloriously instrumental in securing to your country; yet I am persuaded you cannot view them with the Eye of an unconcerned Spectator."[92]

Unsure of what to do, Washington sought the advice of two of his most trusted friends: David Humphreys of Connecticut and Henry Knox of Massachusetts, then serving in New York City as the Confederation's secretary at war. Washington was especially worried that if he refused to attend the convention, it would be "considered as a dereliction to republicanism," or worse, he might be accused of wanting the convention to fail so that he could become king. Humphreys, "disclosing the very sentiments of my soul without reservation," advised Washington not to attend the convention. It was doomed to fail, and if it did, Washington's "character would be materially affected." When the convention failed, Humphreys wrote, Washington's "personal influence & character" would be "justly considered, the last stake which America has to play." Rhetorically, Humphreys asked Washington, "Should you not reserve yourself for the united call of a Continent entire?" The army, Humphreys implied, with Washington at its head, would use "compulsion" to make necessary changes.[93]

Knox agreed that Washington should not attend the convention if "only amendments and patch work" revision of the Articles of Confederation were expected. Washington's "reputation would in a degree suffer" from such halfway measures. But if Washington attended the convention, he would certainly be elected its president. And if the convention proposed "an energetic, and judicious system to be proposed under Your signature," he would have doubly earned "the glorious republican epithet—THE FATHER OF YOUR COUNTRY."[94] Washington could not refuse; he would attend the convention.

Washington was indeed elected president of the convention. But most of the time during the first six weeks of the convention he did not preside, because the delegates sat as a committee of the whole. Even so, he did not participate in the debates. His mere presence, however, cast an aura over the proceedings within the convention, in Philadelphia, and throughout the country.

Early in the convention's proceedings, as Washington was about to convene the session, a delegate came forward and handed him a sheet of paper with notes on the convention's debate that had been found on the floor. Washington said nothing about this breach of the convention's rule of secrecy until the day's session ended. Before adjourning the meeting, Washington stood and said: "Gentlemen, I am sorry to find that some one member of this Body, has been so neglectful of the secrets of the Convention as to drop in the State House a copy of their proceedings, which by accident was picked up and delivered to me this Morning. I must entreat Gentlemen to be more careful, lest our transactions get into the News Papers, and disturb the public repose by premature speculations. I know not whose Paper it is, but there it is (throwing it down on the table), let him who owns it take it." According to William Pierce, a delegate from Georgia, Washington bowed, picked up his hat, and left the room "with a dignity so severe that every Person seemed alarmed."

Several delegates, among them Pierce (who recorded and preserved this anecdote), anxiously fumbled through their papers to see if their notes were missing. Unable to find his notes, Pierce timidly approached the table to claim the lost paper. He was relieved, however, to find that the handwriting was not his. Greatly relieved, Pierce left the convention and found his missing notes in the pocket of another coat left in his boardinghouse. All of the delegates felt the power and intensity of Washington's earnestness, and no one ever claimed the paper.[95]

Washington's presence in the convention instilled confidence. The popular feeling was that this convention, with General Washington and Benjamin Franklin as members, would succeed in recommending desperately needed changes to the Articles of Confederation when all previous attempts had failed. The *Massachusetts Centinel,* April 14, 1787, in an article that was reprinted thirteen times from Vermont to New York, reported that it was reasonable to expect that the convention led by Washington and Franklin "cannot but produce the most salutary measures." The names of these two patriots affixed to the convention's recommendations "will stamp a confidence in them, which the narrow-soul'd, antifederal politicians in the several States, who, by their influence, have hitherto damn'd us a nation, will not dare to attack, or endeavour to nullify." The Petersburg *Virginia Gazette*, July 26, 1787, wrote, in an article that was reprinted seven times from Massachusetts to South Carolina, that "the Grand Fœderal Convention it is hoped will act wisely, for on their determination alone, and our acquiescence, depends our future happiness and prosperity; and if there lives a man equal to so arduous a task, it is a WASHINGTON!"

Some people, however, saw that Washington's role in the convention had resulted in a dangerous situation. Thomas Jefferson, serving as America's minister to France, and the "Federal Farmer," perhaps the most articulate writer opposed to the Constitution, suggested that the Constitution gave great powers to the president only because the convention expected that Washington would be the first to fill that office. Washington would never violate the public trust, but what would happen after Washington stepped down? What would happen under "President Slushington"?[96]

Washington kept busy during his four months in Philadelphia. When the convention did not sit, he visited factories, inspected militia units, and attended concerts, museums, and plays. Evenings were spent with fellow delegates and other friends except for two nights a week. On these evenings Washington sequestered himself and wrote letters that would go out the following day in the stagecoach mail. When the convention recessed for ten days to allow the Committee of Detail to arrange the agreed-upon resolutions in the form of a draft constitution, Washington abandoned his usual schedule and accepted an invitation from Pennsylvania delegate Gouverneur Morris to go fishing. Though an avid fisherman, Washington at first rejected Morris's invitation because of previous commitments. Although Morris enticed Washington with descriptions of a well-stocked trout stream on his brother-in-law's farm, Washington still declined. But when Morris told Washington that the farm and stream were near Valley Forge, he could not refuse. On the first day of their trip, Washington recorded that he and Morris fished with little success. The next day Morris went fishing alone, while Washington spent the entire day at the camp ruins recalling the awful hardships endured during that bitter winter a decade earlier.[97]

On his way back to the farmhouse, Washington saw several farmers in a field. Dismounting his white stallion, he jumped over a fence and introduced himself, asking what they were doing. The astonished farmers told Washington they were planting buckwheat. He asked for details about sowing, tending, and harvesting the crop. That night, Washington wrote to his nephew George Augustus Washington, who was overseeing Mount Vernon in the general's absence, relating all he had learned about buckwheat and instructing him to plant this new crop. That same evening, the farmers must have excitedly told their incredulous wives and friends of their encounter with the great man.

Ratifying the New Constitution

The convention approved the Constitution on September 17, 1787. Washington signed as president of the convention and as a Virginia delegate. He also signed a letter prepared by the convention to explain the convention's actions:

> In all our deliberations we kept steadily in our view, that which appears to us the greatest interest of every true American, the consolidation of our Union, in which is involved our prosperity, felicity, safety, perhaps our national existence. This important consideration, seriously and deeply impressed on our minds, led each State in the Convention to be less rigid on points of inferior magnitude, than might have been otherwise expected; and thus the Constitution, which we now present, is the result of a spirit of amity, and of that mutual deference and concession which the peculiarity of our political situation rendered indispensable.

The Constitution would not satisfy every state completely. But the delegates believed that it would "promote the lasting welfare of that country so dear to us all, and secure her freedom and happiness."[98] Although Washington, as much as possible, refrained from public participation in the debate over ratifying the Constitution, this letter with his signature was printed repeatedly along with the new Constitution throughout the country in newspapers, broadsides, pamphlets, magazines, and almanacs. It also was quoted frequently in Federalist essays defending the Constitution. The letter strongly supported a powerful argument made by those who supported the Constitution: "If Washington supports the Constitution, who are you to oppose it?" It was a difficult question to answer.

The Presidency

ACCEPTING THE OFFICE

Everyone presumed Washington would be elected the first president under the Constitution. But would he accept the position? He preferred retirement. All could readily agree with a young Frenchman visiting America: "This is a very happy man and one who deserves to be. Everyone mentions him for president . . . if he is not it, there is no new Constitution." His friends and advisers told him he must accept his country's call. Alexander Hamilton said that by attending the Constitutional Convention he had made a commitment to the new plan of government and that he was, in essence, *"pledged"* to assume the presidency. General Anthony Wayne wrote to Lafayette on July 4, 1788, that the Constitution had been ratified and that "our Illustrious friend *Genl. Washington*" would be elected president. Wayne ended his letter, "I wish he had a *son.*" (Perhaps Wayne was hinting to Lafayette that he should come to America and become Washington's adopted son and be next in line to become president or elective king; as a citizen of Virginia, Maryland, and Connecticut, Lafayette would have been eligible to be president.) In April 1789, with Washington still uncommitted, Wayne wrote the general that he must accept the presidency. The task would be arduous, but he was capable. "The unbounded confidence placed in you, by every class of Citizens (which no other man cou'd expect or hope for) will contribute to render it less difficult—in fact—it is a Crisis that requires a Washington!"[99]

Perhaps the most convincing argument came from Gouverneur Morris early in the debate over ratifying the Constitution. Morris was certain that Washington's attendance at the Philadelphia convention had "been of infinite Service" in gaining supporters. But,

> should the Idea prevail that you would not accept of the Presidency it would prove fatal in many Parts. Truth is, that your great and decided Superiority leads Men willingly to put you in a Place which will not add to your personal Dignity, nor raise you higher

than you already stand: but they would not willingly put any other Person in the same Situation because they feel the Elevation of others as operating (by Comparison) the Degradation of themselves. And however absurd this Idea, you will agree with me that Men must be treated as Men and not as Machines, much less as Philosophers, & least of all Things as reasonable Creatures. . . .

Thus much for the public Opinion on these Subjects, which must not be neglected in a Country where Opinion is every Thing. . . . You are best fitted to fill that Office. Your cool steady Temper is indispensibly necessary to give a firm and manly Tone to the new Government. To constitute a well poised political Machine is the Task of no common Workman; but to set it in Motion requires still greater Qualities. When once a-going, it will proceed a long Time from the original Impulse. Time gives to primary Institutions the mighty Power of Habit, and Custom, the Law both of Wise Men and Fools serves as the great Commentator of human Establishments, and like other Commentators as frequently obscures as it explains the Text. No Constitution is the same on Paper and in Life. The Exercise of Authority depends on personal Character; and the Whip and Reins by which an able Charioteer governs unruly Steeds will only hurl the unskillful Presumer with more speedy & headlong Violence to the Earth. The Horses once trained may be managed by a Woman or a Child; not so when they first feel the Bit. And indeed among these thirteen Horses now about to be coupled together there are some of every Race and Character. They will listen to your Voice, and submit to your Control; you therefore must, I say must, mount the Seat.

Morris understood Washington's reluctance to serve. He knew that Washington's service would be more important to the country than pleasant for himself. But Morris assured Washington that his continued public service would provide "that interior Satisfaction & Self Approbation which the World cannot give, and you will have in every possible Event the Applause of those who know you enough to respect you properly."[100]

Washington knew that becoming president would be the popular thing for him to do. But he did not seek popularity. "Though I prize, as

I ought, the good opinion of my fellow Citizens; yet if I know myself, I would not seek or retain popularity at the expence of one social duty or moral virtue." He would follow his conscience "as it respected my God, my Country and myself. . . . And certain I am, whensoever I shall be convinced the good of my Country requires my reputation to be put in risque, regard for my own fame will not come in competition with an object of so much magnitude." Although Martha Washington objected to her husband becoming president—"it was much too late for him to go into publick life again"—she realized that "it was not to be avoided."[101] When the time came, Washington decided that duty required him to accept the presidency.

INAUGURAL ADDRESS

Washington asked his old friend David Humphreys, on a protracted visit to Mount Vernon, to draft his inaugural address. Several friends advised Washington not to deliver Humphreys's two-and-a-half-hour speech. Washington painstakingly copied the draft in order to digest it fully and agreed that it was too magisterial as well as far too long for the occasion. He asked James Madison to write another draft, outlining to him the things that should be included.

Washington, clad in a dark brown suit of Connecticut broadcloth with metal wing-spread eagle buttons, white silk stockings, and a magnificent ceremonial sword, took the oath of office about 1:00 p.m. on April 30, 1789, on the balcony of Federal Hall (the Old City Hall) located where Wall Street meets Broad and Nassau in New York City. New York's Chancellor Robert R. Livingston, the highest ranking judicial officer in the state, administered the oath, after which Livingston proclaimed, "Long Live George Washington, President of the United States." As the crowd shouted, "God bless our Washington! Long live our beloved president," Washington, Vice President John Adams, and the other attending dignitaries reentered the building and proceeded to the Senate chamber where Washington delivered his four-page address in about twelve minutes to a joint session of Congress.[102]

Massachusetts congressman Fisher Ames sat close to Washington at the ceremony. "Time," Ames wrote, "has made havoc upon his face." The speech itself was dramatic. "His aspect grave, almost to sadness; his modesty, actually shaking; his voice deep, a little tremulous, and so low as to call for close attention . . . produced emotions of the most affecting kind upon the members. I . . . sat entranced. It seemed to me an allegory in which virtue was personified."[103]

Washington performed his "first official Act" as president with great anxiety. Although he preferred to spend "the asylum of my declining years" in retirement at Mount Vernon, he could not reject this latest call to duty. He understood "the magnitude and difficulty of the trust in which the voice of my Country called me." He was uncertain whether he had the ability to succeed in leading the country's "civil administration" under the new Constitution. "It would be peculiarly improper [at this time] to omit . . . my fervent supplications to that Almighty Being who rules over the Universe, who presides in the Councils of Nations, and whose providential aids can supply every human defect." Only through the benediction of "the Great Author of every public and private good" would Americans retain their "liberties and happiness."

Washington acknowledged that Americans had just passed through their second revolution, a peaceful one, changing "the system of their United Government, [through] the tranquil deliberation, and voluntary consent of so many distinct communities." This revolution "cannot be compared with the means by which most Governments have been established."

One duty of the executive department of the new government was to make proposals for Congress to consider. Instead, however, Washington acknowledged "the talents, the rectitude, and the patriotism" of the members of the First Congress. He was confident that "no local prejudices, or attachments; no separate views, nor party animosities, will misdirect the comprehensive and equal eye which ought to watch over this great Assemblage." America's "national policy, will be laid in the pure and immutable principles of private morality. . . . the propitious smiles of Heaven, can never be expected on a nation that disregards the eternal rules of order and right." "The sacred fire of liberty, and the destiny of the Republican model of Government, are justly considered as *deeply,* perhaps as *finally* staked, on the experiment entrusted to the hands of the American people."

Washington advocated that Congress propose amendments to the new Constitution not to change the structure of the government but in the form of a bill of rights to ameliorate the fear expressed by Antifederalists during the ratification struggle. "A reverence for the characteristic rights of freemen, and a regard for the public harmony, will sufficiently influence" Congress's deliberations on this matter.

Following the address, the company walked about 700 yards to St. Paul's Episcopal Chapel for services conducted by the Reverend Dr. Samuel Provost, the newly elected chaplain of the Senate. After the services the president was escorted to his residence where he dined with a small group of friends and advisers. The inaugural events ended that evening with a brilliant display of fireworks.

Committees of each house of Congress responded favorably to the speech. The House committee, chaired by James Madison, said that the House would pay particular attention to Washington's request for a bill of rights. The Senate rejoiced with all Americans "that, in Obedience to the Call of our common Country, you have returned once more to public life." It told Washington that "in you all Interests unite; and we have no doubt that your past Services, great as they have been, will be equalled by your future Exertions; and that your Prudence and Sagacity as a statesman will tend to avert the Dangers to which we were exposed, to give stability to the present Government, and Dignity and Splendor to that country, which your Skill and Valor as a Soldier, so eminently contributed to raise to independence and Empire." The Senate promised to work with the president "in every Measure, which may strengthen the Union, conduce to the Happiness, or secure and perpetuate the Liberties of this great confederated Republic." Washington thanked each house for the warm remarks and wrote that he would "readily engage" with them "in the arduous, but pleasing, task, of attempting to make a Nation happy."[104]

Presiding over the Experiment

Washington hoped to serve only two years as president, but his advisers pleaded with him to finish his four-year term. With war raging in Europe, no one else, they told him, could lead the country through such perilous times. He agreed to finish the term and asked James Madison to draft a farewell address. As the term neared completion, his advisers again argued that the country could not afford to lose him; no successor could unite the different sections of the country. He must stay on for another term. He alone, "as the Atlas of the New Government," could preserve the Union.[105] Archibald Stuart of Virginia captured the sense of the country. "I never knew the Minds of men so much disposed to acquiesce in public Measures as at present. Their Language is all is well. While G. Washington lives he will crush both men & Measures that would abridge either our happiness or Liberty. In short we are all in the same State of Security with Passengers on board a Vessel navigated by an Able captain & skillful Mariners." Abigail Adams, the vice president's wife, felt that no one else "could rule over this great peopl[e] & consolidate them into one mighty Empire." She described Washington as having "so happy a faculty of appearing to accommodate & yet carrying his point, that if he was not really one of the best intentioned men in the world he might be a very dangerous one. He is polite with dignity, affable without familiarity, distant without Haughtyness, Grave without Austerity, Modest, wise & Good. These are traits in his Character which peculiarly fit him for the exalted station he holds, and God Grant that he may Hold it with the same applause & universal satisfaction for many many years."[106]

On several occasions during his presidency, Washington was gravely ill. Fear of his death gripped everyone. Early in the administration Madison told Edmund Randolph that Washington's "death at the present moment would have brought on another crisis in our affairs." A year later the president again was ill. Georgia congressman Abraham Baldwin said that he had never seen Washington "more emaciated. . . . It is so important to us to keep him alive as long as he can live, that we must let him cruise as he pleases, if he will only live and let us know it." Postmaster General Samuel Osgood told Secretary of War Henry Knox that everyone was upset over the president's illness. "He must not, he shall not die, at least not for 10 years. God knows where our troubles would end. . . . He alone has the confidence of the People. In Him they believe and through him they remain United." Abigail Adams astutely understood the importance of Washington's life. "It appears to me that the union of the states, and consequently the permanency of the Government depend under Providence upon his Life. At this early day when neither our Finances are arranged nor our Government sufficiently cemented to promise duration, His death would I fear have had most disastrous consequences. I feared a thousand things which I pray I never may be called to experience." Vice President John Adams agreed that Washington's "life is of vast importance to us." The marquis de Lafayette wrote Washington that "Your preservation is the life of Your friends, the Sall-vation of Your Country—it is for You a Relligious duty, Not to Neglect Any thing that May Concern Your Health."[107]

Washington survived his illnesses, and he even agreed to serve a second term, but he required a promise from his closest advisers. If he should die in office, these friends were to inform posterity that he did not seek this continuation. He was not a Cromwell. He had wanted to retire to the peace and serenity of his beloved Mount Vernon. But, even more, he wanted to give the young republic a chance to survive in a hostile world. Only with this purpose in mind did Washington agree to a second term as president.

DINNERS AND LEVEES

President Washington attempted to run the presidential mansion as efficiently as he ran Mount Vernon. Expenses, however far outdistanced his annual salary of $25,000. He paid his steward and fourteen servants their wages, supplied all food and drink, and maintained his own stable. The servants and steward alone cost $600 per month. He held weekly dinners, a levee once weekly, and special events like an annual Fourth of July party open to the public. Martha Washington held a weekly levee as well, which Washington regularly attended.

Washington held his dinners for "as many as my table will hold" on Thursdays at 4:00 p.m. Guests gathered in the drawing room about twenty minutes earlier, and the president spoke with each person. He allowed a five-minute grace period before dinner was served. Those arriving late were told, "We are too punctual for you. I have a cook who never asks whether the company has come, but whether the hour has come."[108]

The president's table was handsomely spread with a variety of roast beef, veal, turkey, duck, and other fowl, and ham; puddings, jellies, oranges, apples, almonds and other nuts, figs, and raisins; and a variety of wines and punch. Four or five liveried servants waited on the guests. Often Mrs. Washington attended, sitting across from her husband at the middle of the table. The president's two secretaries, Tobias Lear and David Humphreys, sat at the ends of the table.

Some guests reported much hilarity; others, like the somewhat neurotic William Maclay of Pennsylvania, had mixed reactions. During his two-year term as a U.S. senator, Maclay sometimes thoroughly enjoyed the dinner but at other times "considered it as a part of my duty as a Senator to submit to it, and am glad it is over" even though he felt that the dinner "was the best of the kind I ever was at." After some dinners Maclay described Washington as "a cold formal Man." At other times he found the president "Melancholy" without a "chearing ray of Convivial Sunshine brook[ing] thro' the cloudy Gloom of settled seriousness. At every interval of eating or drinking he played on the Table with a fork or knife like a drumstick," even though one of the 110 rules of civility Washington studied in his youth prohibited a drumming "with your fingers or feet." At his last presidential dinner, Maclay wrote that his host "seemed more in good humor than ever I saw him. Tho he was so deaf that I believe he heard little of the Conversation."[109]

Knowing of Maclay's hostility to Treasury Secretary Hamilton's economic plan, the president paid Maclay a great deal of personal attention. Maclay was proud that the president's attention could not change his stance on Hamilton's plan. When seemingly skipped over for another dinner, the neurotic senator criticized Washington: "How Unworthy of a great Character, is such littleness? He is not aware however that he is paying me a Compliment that none of his Guests can claim. He places me above the influence of a dinner, even in his own Opinion. Perhaps he means it as a punishment, for my opposition of Court Measures. Either way I care not a fig for it. I certainly feel a pride arising, from a consciousness, that the greatest Man in the World, has not Credit enough with me to influence my conduct in the least."[110] Somewhat shattering his own sense of importance, however, Maclay received another dinner invitation the very next week.

Maclay felt that the dining room "was disagreeably warm." He described the menu: "First was soup. Fish roasted & boiled meats Gammon Fowls &ca. This was the dinner. The middle of the Table was garnished in the usual tasty way, with small Images flowers (artificial), &ca. The dessert was, first Apple pies, pudding, &ca.; then iced creams, Jellies, &ca.; then Water Melons, Musk Melons, apples, peaches, nuts." No toasts were offered until "the President filling a Glass of Wine, with great formality drank the health of every individual by name round the Table." After a while, Mrs. Washington withdrew, taking the other ladies with her. The men remained seated, involved in small chitchat, during which time the president "played with his Fork striking on the Edge of the Table with it." Soon Washington rose and went upstairs to drink coffee; "the Company followed." Maclay described Washington's appearance. "In Stature about Six feet, with An Unexceptionable Make, but lax Appearance, his frame Would seem to Want filling Up. His Motions rather slow than lively, tho he showed no Signs of having Suffered either by Gout or Rheumatism. His complexion pale Nay Almost Cadaverous. His Voice hollow and indistinct Owing As I believe to Artificial teeth before in his Upper Jaw."[111]

Washington's biweekly levees were held on Tuesday and Friday afternoons at three o'clock. Soon, the Friday levee became a three-hour evening affair hosted by Martha Washington. During the week Abigail Adams had a levee on Monday evenings; Lady Temple, wife of the British consul general, on Tuesday evenings; Lucy Knox, wife of the secretary of war, on Wednesdays; and Sarah Jay, wife of Chief Justice John Jay, on Thursdays.

The levees were more formal than the presidential dinners. William Sullivan described Washington's hour-long Tuesday afternoon ritual.

> At three o'clock or at any time within a quarter of an hour afterward, the visitor was conducted to his dining room, from which all seats had been removed for the time. On entering, he saw Washington, who stood always in front of the fire-place, with his face towards the door of entrance. The visitor was conducted to him, and he required to have the name so distinctly pronounced that he could hear it. He had the very uncommon faculty of associating a man's name, and personal appearance, so durably in his memory, as to be able to call one by name, who made him a second visit. He received his visitor with a dignified bow, while his hands were so disposed of as to indicate, that the salutation was not to be accompanied with shaking hands. This ceremony never occurred in these visits, even with his most near friends, that no distinction might be made. As visitors came in, they formed a circle round the room. At a quarter past three, the door was closed, and the circle was formed for that day. He then began on the right, and spoke to each visitor, calling him

by name, and exchanging a few words with him. When he completed his circuit, he resumed his first position, and the visitors
approached him in succession, bowed and retired. By four o'clock
the ceremony was over.[112]

The president dressed elegantly for his levees. One visitor described
him as wearing purple satin. Another recorded Washington as "clad in
black velvet; his hair in full dress, powdered and gathered behind in a
large silk bag; yellow gloves on his hands; holding a cocked hat with a
cockade in it, and the edges adorned with a black feather about an inch
deep. He wore knee and shoe buckles; and a long sword, with a finely
wrought and polished steel hilt, which appeared at the left hip; the coat
worn over the sword, so that the hilt, and the part below the coat behind, were in view. The scabbard was white polished leather."[113]

Washington was less formal at his wife's Friday evening levees, which
began at 8:00 p.m. Colonel David Humphreys or Tobias Lear, Washington's personal secretaries, welcomed the women entering the room,
brought them forward, and introduced them to "Lady Washington,"
who sat in a chair on a raised platform. After a curtsy and a brief conversation, the visitor would be escorted to a seat. The president, con-
sidering himself as a private gentleman, wearing neither hat nor sword,
approached each woman and conversed "with a grace, dignity & ease,
that leaves Royal George far behind him." One chair was placed to the
right of Martha's on the dais. Whenever Abigail Adams attended the
levee, which was usually every other week, the president would make
sure that the second chair was vacated. If another woman was occupy-
ing the chair when Mrs. Adams arrived, Washington would engage the
seated woman in conversation and then tactfully offer to introduce her
to another woman across the room so that Mrs. Adams could take her
rightful spot. Guests quickly understood that the chair must be given
up when Abigail Adams attended the levee. The guests were served tea,
coffee, lemonade, cake, and, in the summer, ice cream. After two to three
hours, all the guests would have left.[114]

President Washington also hosted an annual Fourth of July party.
The president's mansion overflowed, and long tables were placed in
the yard. Not only was Congress invited if still in session but "all the
Gentlemen of the city, the Governor and officers and companies." The

president provided the refreshments at his own expense, more than 200 pounds of cake, two quarter casks of wine, and other spirits, all costing more than $500.[115]

THE FIRST LADY

Martha Washington was described as combining "in an uncommon degree, great dignity of manner with most pleasing affability." Abigail Adams came to respect and admire her. At their first meeting in New York City after their husbands had been elected president and vice president under the new Constitution, Abigail described Martha as "plain in her dress, but that plainness is the best of every article. . . . Her Hair is white, her Teeth beautifull, her person rather short than otherways. . . . Her manners are modest and unassuming, dignified and femenine, not the Tincture of ha'ture about her." Two weeks later, after their second meeting, Abigail again praised Mrs. Washington as "one of those unassuming characters which create Love & Esteem. A most becoming pleasantness sits upon her countenance & an unaffected deportment which renders her the object of veneration and Respect. With all these feelings and Sensations I found myself much more deeply impressed than I ever did before their Majesties of Britain." According to Mrs. Adams, "We live upon terms of much Friendship & visit each other often. While the Gentlemen are absent we propose seeing one another on terms of much sociability. Mrs. Washington is a most friendly, good Lady, always pleasant and easy, doatingly fond of her Grandchildren, to whom she is quite the Grandmamma." "No Lady," Abigail wrote, "can be more deservedly beloved & esteemed than she is, and we have lived in habits of intimacy and Friendship."[116]

ACCOMPLISHMENTS

Despite all the dangers facing the country, Washington's two terms as president were highly successful. Through the force of his own personality, Washington maintained American neutrality while all of Europe flamed with war and destruction. The financial policies of his secretary of the treasury restored solvency to the formerly bankrupt confederation. Tax uprisings were easily suppressed, and the authority of the federal government over the states and the people was successfully asserted and maintained; yet during the same years a bill of rights, staunchly advocated by James Madison and seconded by Washington, assured former Antifederalists that the new Constitution would not be oppressive. Thoughtful appointments—especially to the federal judiciary—instilled confidence in the new government. Treaties with peaceful southern Indians and forceful measures against the powerful hostile tribes in the Northwest Territory opened new lands for settlement. A treaty with Great Britain kept the peace and obtained the evacuation of British troops from nearly a dozen Revolutionary War forts on American soil near the Canadian border. A treaty with Spain promoted friendly relations between the two countries with an expansion of commerce and the Spanish opening of the Mississippi River to the navigation by Americans. A treaty with Algiers reestablished peace for American merchantmen in and around the Mediterranean and obtained the release of two crews of American seamen who had been held in slavery by Algiers for over a decade. Washington's every act created precedent to be followed by his successors. His eight years in office saw the formation of two political parties that under any other person might have divided America into two or more competing countries. But, as Gouverneur Morris had predicted, the able charioteer guided and tamed the wild horses and made them manageable for his successors.

Tours of the States

One of Washington's hopes as president was to visit every state in the Union. Illness kept him from traveling until October 1789 when he set out on a six-week eastern tour. The president traveled with remarkable informality. Nine men made up the entire presidential entourage: two private secretaries, Tobias Lear and William Jackson; a valet; a postilion; and four horsemen. No military guard: the people, Washington said, would protect him. Inundated with invitations to be guests in private homes, the party stayed only in public inns and usually started traveling at 6:00 each morning. The president did not want to inconvenience anyone, and he certainly did not wish to play favorites. During the long stretches between towns, Washington traveled in a coach pulled by four horses. Just before entering a town, he would leave the carriage and mount his white stallion. The party was often met on the outskirts of town by the local militia or light-horse cavalry. Parades, processions of citizens, congratulatory addresses, odes, and music became customary.

He comes! He comes! the HERO comes!
Sound, sound your trumpets, beat, beat your drums;
From port, to port, let cannon roar
He's welcome to New-England's shore!
Welcome, welcome, welcome, welcome,
Welcome to New-England's shore.[117]

Formal dinners and evenings balls were held in the major towns. Washington enjoyed dancing every set with the local beauties attired in their finest dresses with sashes emblazoned with the initials "GW."

In addition to his public duties, Washington found time to do enjoyable things. He attended concerts, visited internal improvements and manufacturing facilities, inspected a French 24-gun man-of-war in Portsmouth, fished whenever possible, and talked to farmers about crops. Portrait sitting was an unpleasant concomitant.

After Rhode Island ratified the Constitution on May 29, 1790, the president made a special effort personally to welcome the prodigal state back into the Union. Sailing from New York City, Washington was accompanied by Secretary of State Thomas Jefferson, New York governor George Clinton, Supreme Court justice John Blair, Rhode Island senator Theodore Foster, South Carolina representative William Loughton Smith, David Humphreys, and secretaries William Jackson and Thomas Nelson. The group visited both Newport and Providence. Washington was particularly moved by an address from the Hebrew congregation of Newport. As Jews, who were traditionally deprived "of the invaluable rights of free citizens," they asked the president to extend religious freedom and the "immunities of citizenship" to them. Washington responded:

> The citizens of the United States of America, have a right to applaud themselves for having given to mankind examples of an enlarged and liberal policy—a policy worthy of imitation. All possess alike liberty of conscience, and immunities of citizenship. It is now no more that toleration is spoken of, as if it was by the indulgence of one class of people, that another enjoyed the exercise of their inherent natural rights. For happily the government of the United States, which gives to bigotry no sanction—to persecution no assistance, requires only that they who live under its

protection should demean themselves as good citizens, in giving it on all occasions their effectual support.[118]

Washington's three-and-a-half-month southern tour started from Philadelphia, the new federal capital, on March 21, 1791. To avoid the bad roads between Delaware and Maryland, the eight-man presidential party sailed aboard a ship to Annapolis. The inexperienced or incompetent captain grounded the ship during a storm at the mouth of the Severn River leading to Annapolis; after dislodging the ship, he ran it aground again. There, throughout the night, the crew and passengers feared the ship would founder, causing loss of life. When morning came, a rescue ship took the passengers off the marooned ship.

The southern tour proceeded much as its eastern counterpart had. The party usually traveled between thirty-five and forty-five miles each day. Starting at first at 6:00 a.m., soon, to avoid the heat of afternoon, the party began traveling each day by 5:00 a.m. and then during the last three weeks by 4:00. The public's adoration was universal.

> He comes! he comes! the Hero comes!
> Sound, sound your trumpets, beat your drums.
> From port to port let cannons roar,
> He's welcome to our friendly shore.
>
> Prepare! prepare! your songs prepare!
> Loud, loudly read the echoing air;
> From pole to pole, his praise resound,
> For virtue is with glory crown'd.[119]

At Charlotte Court House in Virginia, crowds waited to see the president. One observer scribbled in his diary: "Strange is the impulse which is felt by almost every breast to see the face of a great good man—sensation better felt than expressed." The next day, the same diarist recorded the feelings at Prince Edward County, Virginia, where crowds waited "anxious to see the saviour of their country and object of their love."[120] After a journey of almost 2,000 miles, the president returned to Philadelphia on July 6, 1791.

Washington was pleased with his presidential tours. In a letter to North Carolina governor Alexander Martin, he said that his purpose in visiting the states "was not to be received with parade and an ostentatious display of opulence. It was for a nobler purpose. To see with my own eyes the situation of the Country, and to learn on the spot the condition and disposition of our Citizens. In these respects I have been highly gratified, and to a sensible mind the effusions of affection and personal regard which were expressed on so many occasions is no less grateful, than the marks of respect shewn to my official Character were pleasing in a public view." To David Humphreys he confided that "each days experience of the government of the United States seems to confirm its establishment, and to render it more popular. A ready acquiescence in the laws made under it shews in a strong light the confidence which the people have in their representatives, and in the upright views of those who administer the government."

The presidential tours did much to unify the country behind President Washington and the new federal government. Opponents of the Constitution saw firsthand the tremendous support the people had for the new experiment. In a way, the tours marked the end of the Revolution. The *Gazette of the United States* reported that "the time to pull down, and destroy, is now past." It was now time "to build up, strengthen and support" the Constitution. The tours had demonstrated that these sentiments "pervade the minds of the people."[121]

FAREWELL ADDRESS

In his Farewell Address, revised for him by Alexander Hamilton, Washington announced to the American people that he would not seek a third term as president. He felt that he had done his duty and that it was time to retire to the shadow of private life. He was happy "that, while choice and prudence invite me to quit the political scene, patriotism does not forbid it." He had entered the presidency knowing his frailties and the "weight of years" had only increased his desire for "the shade of retirement." Washington thanked the American people for the opportunity to serve them and for the "steadfast confidence" with which they had supported him. He admitted that there had been difficult times, but "the constancy of their support" had always been his "essential prop." He hoped that God would continue to watch over the American

Union and stamp every department of the government "with wisdom and virtue."

Perhaps, Washington stated, he should stop at this point. But his concern for his country, "which cannot end but with my life," and the dangerous world at home and abroad forced him to recommend "some sentiments" that were "the result of much reflection" on "the permanency of your felicity as a people." These sentiments, Washington said, were offered as "the disinterested warnings of a parting friend, who can possibly have no personal motive to bias his counsel."

Washington's theme throughout the address was the importance of the "national Union to your collective and individual happiness." Union, he said, "is a main pillar in the edifice of your real independence, the support of your tranquillity at home; your peace abroad; of your safety; of your prosperity; of that very Liberty which you so highly prize." Many at home and abroad would attempt "covertly and insidiously" to weaken the importance of Union, but Americans must always "cherish a cordial, habitual and immovable attachment" to the Union. It must be thought of as "the Palladium of your political safety and prosperity."

Washington stressed the importance of American citizenship. "Citizens by birth or choice, of a common country, that country has a right to concentrate your affections.—The name of AMERICAN, which belongs to you, in your national capacity, must always exalt the just pride of patriotism, more than any appellation derived from local discriminations." He cautioned against being drawn into the treacherous affairs of European politics. "Observe good faith & justice towards all Nations. Cultivate peace & harmony with all," but "steer clear of permanent Alliances, with any portion of the foreign world."

He warned against the growing hostility of the contentious political parties at home that could start "a fire not to be quenched." He urged respect and allegiance to the new government under the Constitution as the culmination of the Revolutionary era.

This government, the offspring of our own choice uninfluenced and unawed, adopted upon full investigation & mature deliberation, completely free in its principles, in the distribution of its powers, uniting security with energy, and containing within itself a provision for its own amendment, has a just claim to your confidence and your support.—Respect for its authority, compliance with its Laws, acquiescence in its measures, are duties enjoined by the fundamental maxims of true Liberty.—The basis of our political systems is the right of the people to make and to alter their Constitutions of Government.—But the Constitution which at any time exists, 'till changed by an explicit and authentic act of the whole people, is sacredly obligatory upon all.—The very idea of power and the right of the People to establish Government presupposes the duty of every Individual to obey the established Government.

Washington hoped that "these counsels of an old and affectionate friend" would have a "strong and lasting impression" on his countrymen. He hoped that in his retirement he would feel "the benign influence of good laws under a free government, the ever favorite object of my heart, the happy reward, as I trust, of our mutual cares, labors, and dangers."

It had been Washington's aim to serve as president and help the new American republican experiment establish roots. "With me, a predominant motive has been to endeavour to gain time to our country to settle & mature its yet recent institutions, and to progress without interruption, to that degree of strength & consistency, which is necessary to give it, humanly speaking, the command of its own fortunes."[122] The American Revolution was over. The new institutions of government were solidly established. It was time for Washington to go home. He had done his duty. He compared himself "to the wearied traveller who sees a resting place, and is bending his body to lean thereon."[123]

Shortly before his retirement, Washington was visited by Benjamin Henry Latrobe, a young English-born engineer and architect. Latrobe saw that

> Washington has something uncommonly majestic and commanding in his walk, his address, his figure and his countenance. His face is characterized however more by intense and powerful thought, than by quick and fiery conception. There is a mildness about its expression; and an air of reserve in his manner lowers its

tone still more. He is 64, but appears some years younger, and has sufficient apparent vigor to last many years yet. He was frequently entirely silent for many minutes during which time an awkwardness seemed to prevail in every one present. His answers were often short and sometimes approached to moroseness. He did not at any time speak with very remarkable fluency:—perhaps the extreme correctness of his language which almost seemed studied prevented that effect. He seemed to enjoy a humourous observation, and made several himself. He laughed heartily several times and in a very good humoured manner. On the morning of my departure he treated me as if I had lived for years in his house; with ease and attention, but in general I thought there was a slight air of moroseness about him, as if something had vexed him.

Latrobe thought that if Horace had lived at the time, he would have described Washington as "the man [who is] just and firm in purpose."[124]

Last Retirement

The Washingtons happily returned to their private lives at Mount Vernon. They left dear friends behind in Philadelphia and found that many old Virginia friends had passed away. "Our circle of *friends* of course is contracted without any disposition on our part to enter into *new friendships,* though we have an abundance of acquaintances and a variety of visitors." Martha Washington wrote Lucy Knox that "I cannot tell you, My dear friend, how much I enjoy home after having been deprived of one so long, for our dwelling in New York and Philadelphia was not home, only a sojourning. The General and I feel like children just released from school or from a hard taskmaster." Nothing would now tempt them away from their "sacred roof-tree again."[125]

Although some visitors saw Washington as reserved and taciturn, others felt that "he does not avoid entering into conversation when one furnishes him with a subject. . . . At the table after the departure of the ladies, or else in the evening seated under the portico, he often talked with me for hours at a time. His favorite subject is agriculture, but he answered with kindness all questions that I put to him on the Revolution, the armies, etc. He has a prodigious memory."[126]

❧ The End

Rumors of Washington's illness and death amused the former president. Martha now endearingly referred to her husband as "the withered Proprietor." He jokingly said that he was "glad to hear before hand, what will be said of him" after his death. He, Robert Morris, and several other men had entered into an agreement "not to quit the theatre of this world before the year 1800." Washington was committed "that no breach of contract shall be laid to him on that account." But in the summer of 1799, he had a dream that he would soon die, leaving Martha a widow. Deeply affected by the dream, Washington put his will and other papers in final order. On December 14, 1799, after only two days of catching a severe cold that worsened into a throat swollen shut, Washington died.[127]

Innumerable eulogies praised the dead hero. Typically Timothy Dwight, president of Yale College, wrote that "to his conduct, both military and political, may, with exact propriety, be applied the observation, which has been often made concerning his courage; that in the most hazardous situations no man ever saw his countenance change." In describing the aura about Washington, Dwight said that "wherever he appeared, an instinctive awe and veneration attended him on the part of all men. Every man, however great in his own opinion, or in reality, shrunk in his presence, and became conscious of an inferiority, which he never felt before. Whilst he encouraged every man, particularly every stranger, and peculiarly every diffident man, and raised him to self-possession, no sober person, however secure he might think himself of his esteem, ever presumed to draw too near him."[128]

Many years later, James Madison remembered some of the things that made Washington great.

> The strength of his character lay in his integrity, his love of justice, his fortitude, the soundness of his judgment, and his remarkable prudence to which he joined an elevated sense of patriotic duty, and a reliance on the enlightened & impartial world as the tribunal by which a lasting sentence on his career would be pronounced. Nor was he without the advantage of a Stature & figure, which however insignificant when separated from greatness of character do not fail when combined with it to

aid the attraction. But what particularly distinguished him, was a modest dignity which at once commanded the highest respect, and inspired the purest attachment. Although not idolizing public opinion, no man could be more attentive to the means of ascertaining it. In comparing the candidates for office, he was particularly inquisitive as to their standing with the public and the opinion entertained of them by men of public weight. On important questions to be decided by him, he spared no pains to gain information from all quarters; freely asking from all whom he held in esteem, and who were intimate with him, a free communication of their sentiments, receiving with great attention the different arguments and opinions offered to him, and making up his own judgment with all the leisure that was permitted.[129]

No one, however, captured the uniqueness and the importance of Washington as well as Jefferson.

I think I knew General Washington intimately and thoroughly; and were I called on to delineate his character, it should be in terms like these.

His mind was great and powerful, without being of the very first order; his penetration strong, though not so acute as that of a Newton, Bacon, or Locke; and as far as he saw, no judgment was ever sounder. It was slow in operation, being little aided by invention or imagination, but sure in conclusion. . . . He was incapable of fear, meeting personal dangers with the calmest unconcern. Perhaps the strongest feature in his character was prudence, never acting until every circumstance, every consideration, was maturely weighed; refraining if he saw a doubt, but, when once decided, going through with his purpose, whatever obstacles opposed. His integrity was most pure, his justice the most inflexible I have ever known, no motives of interest or consanguinity, of friendship or hatred, being able to bias his decision. He was, indeed, in every sense of the words, a wise, a good, and a great man. His temper was naturally high toned; but reflection and resolution had obtained a firm and habitual ascendancy over it. If ever, however, it broke its bonds, he was most tremendous in his wrath. In his expenses he was honorable, but exact; liberal in contributions to whatever promised utility; but frowning and unyielding on all visionary projects and all unworthy calls on his charity. His heart was not warm in its affections; but he exactly calculated every man's value, and gave him a solid esteem proportioned to it. His person, you know, was fine, his stature exactly what one would wish, his deportment easy, erect and noble; the best horseman of his age, and the most graceful figure that could be seen on horseback. Although in the circle of his friends, where he might be unreserved with safety, he took a free share in conversation, his colloquial talents were not above mediocrity, possessing neither copiousness of ideas, nor fluency of words. In public, when called on for a sudden opinion, he was unready, short and embarrassed. . . . On the whole, his character was, in its mass, perfect, in nothing bad, in few points indifferent; and it may truly be said, that never did nature and fortune combine more perfectly to make a man great, and to place him in the same constellation with whatever worthies have merited from man an everlasting remembrance. For his was the singular destiny and merit, of leading the armies of his country successfully through an arduous war, for the establishment of its independence; of conducting its councils through the birth of a government, new in its forms and principles, until it had settled down into a quiet and orderly train; and of scrupulously obeying the laws through the whole of his career, civil and military, of which the history of the world furnishes no other example.

He was no monarchist from preference of his judgment. The soundness of that gave him correct views of the rights of man, and his severe justice devoted him to them. He had often declared to me that he considered our new constitution as an experiment on the practicability of republican government, and with what dose of liberty man could be trusted for his own good; that he was determined the experiment should have a fair trial, and would lose the last drop of his blood in support of it.[130]

The experiment succeeded to a great measure thanks to George Washington.

In addressing a joint session of Congress for his eighth State of the Union speech in December 1796, Washington said that he could not "omit the occasion, to congratulate you and my Country, on the success of the [American] experiment." He repeated from his first inaugural address his "fervent supplications to the Supreme Ruler of the Universe, and Sovereign Arbiter of Nations, that his Providential care may still be extended to the United States; that the virtue and happiness of the People, may be preserved; and that the Government, which they have instituted, for the protection of their liberties, may be perpetual."

Thomas Jefferson

PHILOSOPHER & POLITICIAN

Introduction

America has been blessed with few Renaissance men. Certainly Thomas Jefferson is among this group; some would argue that only he and Benjamin Franklin fall into this category. Among his many accomplishments, Jefferson was a statesman, parliamentarian, codifier of laws, antiquarian, historian, surveyor, philosopher, diplomat, scientist, architect, inventor, educator, lawyer, farmer, breeder, manufacturer, botanist, horticulturist, anthropologist, archaeologist, meteorologist, paleontologist, lexicologist, linguist, ethnologist, biblicist, mathematician, astronomer, geographer, librarian, bibliophile, bibliographer, classicist, scholar and historian of religions, cryptographer, translator, writer, editor, musician, and gastronome and connoisseur of wine.

Jefferson's skill as a writer has accentuated many of his accomplishments. Partly because of his preference for style and euphony over a rigid adherence to the rules of grammar, he was perhaps the most eloquent of all American writers. Congressman John Adams, in identifying the thirty-three-year-old Virginian as the person who should write the Declaration of Independence, said that Jefferson had "a masterly Pen" and "a remarkable felicity of expression."

More than most of the founders, Thomas Jefferson is hard to understand, even paradoxical, not only for us today but also for the people of his own time. Though he was far more the theoretical philosopher than his contemporaries, he incessantly left the safety and seclusion of his mountaintop retreat to brave the violence and turbulence of revolution and diplomacy, of partisan politics and public service. He served almost continuously, though sometimes reluctantly, in the colonial and state legislatures, the Continental and Confederation congresses, as governor of Virginia, minister to France, secretary of state, political party leader, and as the second vice president and third president of the United States. Jefferson not only wrote the words of the Declaration of Independence, but he thoroughly believed in the revolutionary principles they espoused and consistently attempted to implement those principles in the real world of practical politics.

As a political philosopher, Jefferson was greatly admired and savagely condemned by his contemporaries. Jefferson's political enemies (as well as some later historians) belittled him. Alexander Hamilton saw him "as a man of sublimated & paradoxical imagination—cherishing notions incompatible with regular and firm government." Hamilton saw Jefferson's politics as "tinctured with fanaticism" and believed that he was "too much in earnest in his democracy." He believed Jefferson's posture as the detached philosopher to be the ruse of "a man of profound ambition & violent passions." Even after Jefferson's first administration, perhaps the most successful term of any American president, skeptics remained. New Hampshire senator William Plumer described President Jefferson as "a man of science. . . . he knows little of the nature of man—very little indeed. . . . He has much knowledge of books—of insects—of shells & of all that charms a virtuoso—but he knows not the human heart. He is a closet politician—but not a practical statesman. He has much *fine sense* but little of that *plain common sense* so requisite to business—& which in fact governs the world." The gossipy John Nicholas, clerk of Jefferson's Albemarle County, told George Washington that Jefferson was "one of the most artful, intriguing, industrious and double-faced politicians in all America."[1]

Admirers, however, like James Madison could readily forgive Jefferson's sometimes impractical ideas because they so admired his commitment to republican principles and his remarkable ability to express those principles with an eloquence that approached poetry. It seemed to Margaret Bayard Smith, the matriarch of Washington society, "impossible, for any one personally to know him & remain his enemy."[2]

Jefferson believed that every man owed his country "a debt of service . . . proportioned to the bounties which nature & fortune have measured to him." Some men were "born for the public. Nature, by fitting them for the service of the human race on a broad scale, has stamped them with the evidences of her destination & their duty." The Revolutionary generation, Jefferson believed, had been "thrown into times of a peculiar character, and to work our way through them has required services & sacrifices from our countrymen generally, and, to their great honor, these have been generally exhibited, by every one in his sphere, & according to the opportunities afforded."[3]

Jefferson was convinced that he was "conscientiously called" to his "tour of duty" and was confident that he faithfully responded. His "affections were first for my own country, and then generally for all mankind." Jefferson was a revolutionary who welcomed change, with one exception: "the inherent and unalienable rights of man" were unchangeable and needed constant vigilance to protect. To safeguard these rights, Jefferson made difficult decisions that sometimes meant choosing "a great evil in order to ward off a greater." But throughout his life his guiding principle was "to do whatever is right, and leave consequences to him who has the disposal of them." He hoped that his contemporaries and posterity would understand. "The only exact testimony of a man is his actions, leaving the reader to pronounce on them his own judgment."[4]

Early Life

Born on April 13, 1743, on the fringe of the Virginia frontier, Thomas Jefferson was the eldest of seven children, five girls and two boys. Jefferson's father, Peter, was a prosperous, self-made Albemarle County planter and surveyor. His marriage to Jane Randolph, the daughter of a wealthy planter from a distinguished family, not only assisted Peter financially but contributed to his rise socially and politically. Peter, a vestryman in his local Anglican congregation, served Albemarle County as a colonel in the militia, sheriff, justice of the peace, and burgess in Virginia's colonial legislature.

Young Thomas Jefferson was truly shaped by his times. He was raised and imbued with the spirit of the Enlightenment, which recognized the perfectibility of both man and government through education and the discovery of well-designed natural laws using man's innate reason. Although always an optimist, Jefferson's immersion in the Whig political writings of seventeenth- and eighteenth-century England instilled in him a pervasive skepticism of government officials who often sought to expand their authority at the expense of the rights of their constituents. During his darkest political hour, Jefferson suggested that "it would be a dangerous delusion were a confidence in the men of our choice to silence our fears for the safety of our rights: that confidence is everywhere the parent of despotism—free government is founded in jealousy, and not in confidence; it is jealousy and not confidence which prescribes limited constitutions, to bind down those whom we are obliged to trust with power. . . . In questions of power, then, let no more be heard of confidence in man, but bind him down from mischief by the chains of the Constitution."[5]

Jefferson acknowledged the influence of several individuals in shaping his character and philosophy of life. His mother, he readily admitted, had little influence; but his father, who died when Jefferson was only fourteen, was a primary influence. At the age of five, Jefferson began to attend local schools conducted for the gentry's sons by impoverished but educated clergymen, where he continued until his father's death. For the next two years Jefferson studied at the school of a more capable teacher, the Anglican minister James Maury, concentrating on Latin and Greek, literature and mathematics, and the Bible. Although well trained in the Bible and, like his father, a parish vestryman, Jefferson never accepted the Bible as divine scripture. He read it more as history and readily embraced the philosophical teachings of Jesus.

At the age of seventeen, Jefferson left Shadwell, the family plantation, and attended the College of William and Mary in Williamsburg, Virginia's provincial capital. For the next three years, the lanky, ruddy, freckle-faced youth with tousled reddish hair, blue-gray eyes, and a sometimes disheveled appearance studied with Dr. William Small, the college's professor of mathematics, an immigrant from Scotland.

In 1762 Small introduced Jefferson to George Wythe, who at thirty-five was a member of the House of Burgesses and on his way to becoming the most prominent lawyer in the colony. Wythe not only instructed Jefferson in the law but introduced him to Governor Francis Fauquier, perhaps the ablest and most popular of Virginia's colonial governors. Forming a *partie quarrée* (a pleasurable party of four), Small, Wythe, Jefferson, and the governor regularly dined at the governor's table and conversed on a variety of topics. There, Jefferson later wrote, he "heard more good sense, more rational and philosophical conversations, than in all my life besides." Fauquier also encouraged Jefferson to play his violin at the concerts he sponsored weekly.

When Small returned to Europe in 1762, Jefferson left William and Mary and returned to Shadwell, where he continued reading law under the direction of Wythe, whom Jefferson considered not only his mentor but his foster father. Jefferson expanded his reading and avidly acquired books for his growing library. He was admitted to the bar in 1767, established a successful and growing practice, doubled his estate to 5,000 acres, and decided to design and build a new house, for he saw Shadwell as his mother's house. He chose a site across the Rivanna River on the summit of a mountain with a commanding view of the Blue Ridge Mountains to the west and overlooking the valley village of Charlottesville. Jefferson called his new home Monticello, Italian for "little mountain."

In 1770 disaster struck when Shadwell burned to the ground and with it Jefferson's library of almost 700 books worth several hundred pounds. Jefferson wished it had been the money that had gone up in flames; that would have cost him not "a sigh."[6] Immediately, however, he started rebuilding his literary treasure, and within three years he had a library of 1,256 volumes.

Although Monticello was far from completed when Shadwell burned down, it was advanced enough to convince Jefferson to abandon "some treasonable thoughts of leaving these my native hills." In November 1770 he moved into a tiny brick cottage at Monticello. "I have here but one room, which, like the cobbler's, serves me for parlor, for kitchen and hall. I may add, for bed chamber and study too." Watching the painfully slow progress on the mansion house, Jefferson could only anticipate "getting more elbow room this summer."[7]

But summer passed, and Jefferson remained in the cottage. He spent much of the year, however, in Williamsburg, where the young lawyer tried cases in the General Court and courted Martha Wayles Skelton, a twenty-three-year-old widow who lived on her father's plantation near Williamsburg. The slender, auburn-haired beauty had been much courted, but she found herself most attracted to the gangly frontier lawyer. The couple married on January 1, 1772, and journeyed the hundred miles west to spend their first winter together in the cozy "honeymoon" cottage on the mountain. In September 1772 their first child, Martha (usually called Patsy), was born. In May 1773 Jefferson's father-in-law died, leaving his daughter about 5,000 acres and fifty slaves, including the Hemings family, but also an enormous debt that plagued Jefferson for years.

❧ The Revolution

In 1769, at the age of twenty-six, Jefferson was elected to the colonial legislature. He proposed but failed to get a bill passed to make it easier for owners to emancipate their slaves. Allied with other young, radical legislators, Jefferson opposed Britain's new imperial policy that attempted to wield greater control over the colonies. The burgesses called for the appointment of committees of correspondence in all of the colonies to coordinate sentiment and activities, and they also called for the appointment of delegates to attend a Continental Congress. Jefferson prepared a petition to the king for Virginia's delegates to Congress, but on the way to take his seat in the House of Burgesses, he was taken ill with dysentery and was unable to attend. He sent copies of his draft petition forward, but the burgesses rejected Jefferson's draft as too radical. Most Americans who opposed British policies argued that Parliament could tax Americans if the tax was primarily aimed at regulating commerce. These "external taxes" were constitutional, but "internal taxes" aimed primarily at raising revenue were blatantly unconstitutional. Jefferson went much further, maintaining that Great Britain and the American colonies were totally separate from each other except in loyalty to the same king. Parliament, therefore, had no authority whatsoever to legislate for the colonies, totally the opposite of Parliament's Declaratory Act (1766), which asserted its authority "to bind Americans in all cases whatsoever."

According to Jefferson, his arguments were "read generally by the members, approved by many, but thought too bold for the present state of things." Several friends, however, arranged to have Jefferson's petition printed as a pamphlet under the title *A Summary View of the Rights of British America*. The pamphlet was distributed broadly in America and in Britain and, Jefferson later noted, "procured me the honor of having my name inserted in a long list" of traitors in a bill of attainder that guaranteed his execution.[8]

Jefferson's *Summary View* argued that "history has informed us that bodies of men, as well as individuals, are susceptible of the spirit of tyranny." Parliament and the king's ministers had crossed the line. Since 1763 they had passed a series of acts that threatened American liberty and property. Jefferson declared these acts void because "the British parliament has no right to exercise authority over us." Under previous British rulers, American rights had been endangered only sporadically. Now, however, a rapid succession of dangerous measures had emanated from London. "Scarcely have our minds been able to emerge from the astonishment into which one stroke of parliamentary thunder has involved us, before another more heavy, and more alarming, is fallen on us. Single acts of tyranny may be ascribed to the accidental opinion of a day; but a series of oppressions, begun at a distinguished period, and pursued unalterably through every change of ministers, too plainly prove a deliberate and systematical plan of reducing us to slavery."

Jefferson urged King George to mediate with Parliament "to recommend . . . the total revocation of these acts, which, however nugatory they be, may yet prove the cause of further discontents and jealousies among us." Americans, like any free people, claim "their rights, as deserved from the laws of nature, and not as the gift of their chief magistrate. Let those flatter who fear: it is not an American art." Jefferson told George III "that kings are the servants, not the proprietors of the people. Open your breast, sire, to liberal and expanded thought. Let not the name of George the third be a blot in the pages of history." America, Jefferson stated, did not wish to separate from Britain. But he warned the king: "There are extraordinary situations which require extraordinary interposition. An exasperated people, who feel that they possess power, are not easily restrained within limits strictly regular." Jefferson concluded:

> The God who gave us life gave us liberty at the same time; the hand of force may destroy, but cannot disjoin them. This, sire, is our last, our determined resolution; and that you will be pleased to interpose with that efficacy which your earnest endeavours may ensure to procure redress of these our great grievances, to quiet the minds of your subjects in British America, against any apprehensions of future encroachment, to establish fraternal love and harmony throughout the whole empire, and that these may continue to the latest ages of time, is the fervent prayer of all British America!

In March 1775 the Virginia provincial convention added Jefferson to its delegation to the Second Continental Congress. Before Congress assembled, the first shots of the Revolution were fired at Lexington and Concord, Massachusetts. Congress drafted petitions to Britain seeking reconciliation and justifying why Americans had taken up arms. Jefferson prepared a draft declaration explaining America's position, but it was too strong for many of the delegates. John Dickinson of Delaware wrote the Declaration of the Causes and Necessity of Taking Up Arms in July 1775. Unable to improve upon Jefferson's closing four paragraphs, Dickinson incorporated them into his draft, which Congress accepted. The rhetoric of these paragraphs was characteristically Jefferson's: powerful, eloquent, stirring. It surely angered the king and probably made reconciliation impossible.

The force and beauty of Jefferson's closing paragraphs still have remarkable impact: "We are reduced to the alternative of choosing an unconditional submission to the tyranny of irritated ministers, or resistance by force. The latter is our choice. . . . Honor, justice, and humanity forbid us tamely to surrender that freedom which we received from our gallant ancestors, and which our innocent posterity have a right to receive from us." He forcefully stated: "Our cause is just. Our union is perfect. Our internal resources are great, and, if necessary, foreign assistance is undoubtedly attainable." He thanked God for not permitting the crisis of British domination to occur "until we were grown up to our present strength" and had gained needed experience fighting a previous war. Americans, Jefferson wrote, did not seek independence from Britain. "Necessity has not yet driven us into that desperate measure, or induced us to excite any other nation to war against" Britain. But Americans were determined to protect their rights and their property with an "unabating firmness and perseverance, . . . being with one mind resolved to die freemen rather than to live slaves."

American petitions, resolutions, and declarations never swayed Parliament, the ministry, or King George. Quite the contrary. The king and Parliament declared the colonists in a state of rebellion. Abandoning efforts at reconciliation, the British attacked with overwhelming military power in an attempt to intimidate Americans into submission. Most Americans, too, became convinced that reconciliation was impossible. The necessity for independence absent in July 1775 appeared full blown a year later, but not all of the delegates in Congress were in agreement when Virginia moved on June 7, 1776, that the "United Colonies are, and of right ought to be, free and independent states." It was decided, therefore, to postpone a vote on independence for almost four weeks. Congress appointed committees to seek foreign assistance and alliances, to draft articles of union, and to draft a declaration of independence. The declaration committee consisted of John Adams, Benjamin Franklin, Robert R. Livingston, Roger Sherman, and Thomas Jefferson. The committee chose the thirty-three-year-old Virginian to draft the Declaration.

It is unclear how the committee selected Jefferson to draft the Declaration, how he wrote it, and how it was eventually presented to Congress. A quarter century later Adams remembered that

> Mr. Jefferson had been now about a Year a Member of Congress, but had attended his Duty in the House but a very small part of the time and when there had never spoken in public: and during the whole Time I sat with him in Congress, I never heard him utter three Sentences together . . . . It will naturally be inquired, how it happened that he was appointed on a Committee of such importance. There were more reasons than one. Mr. Jefferson had the Reputation of a masterly Pen. He had been chosen a Delegate in Virginia, in consequence of a very handsome public Paper, which he had written for the House of Burgesses, which had given him the Character of a fine Writer. Another reason was that Mr. Richard Henry Lee was not beloved by the most of his Colleagues from Virginia and Mr. Jefferson was set up to rival and supplant him. This could be done only by the Pen, for Mr. Jefferson could stand no competition with him or any one else in Elocution and public debate. . . . The Committee had several meetings, in which were proposed the Articles of which the Declaration was to consist, and minutes made of them. The Committee then appointed Mr. Jefferson and me, to draw them up in form, and cloath them in a proper Dress. The Sub Committee met, and considered the Minutes, making such Observations on them as then occurred; when Mr. Jefferson desired me to take them to my Lodgings and make the Draft. This I declined and gave several reasons for declining. 1. That he was a Virginian and I a Massachusettsian.
> 2. that he was a southern Man and I a northern one. 3. That I had

been so obnoxious for my early and constant Zeal in promoting the Measure, that any draft of mine, would undergo a more severe Scrutiny and Criticism in Congress, than one of his composition. 4thly and lastly and that would be reason enough if there were no other, I had a great Opinion of the Elegance of his pen and none at all of my own. I therefore insisted that no hesitation should be made on his part. He accordingly took the Minutes and in a day or two produced to me his Draft. Whether I made or suggested any corrections I remember not. The Report was made to the Committee of five, by them examined, but whether altered or corrected in any thing I cannot recollect. But in substance at least it was reported to Congress where, after a severe Criticism, and striking out several of the most oratorical Paragraphs it was adopted on the fourth of July 1776, and published to the World.[9]

Jefferson wrote the Declaration of Independence in the seclusion of his parlor in his small second-floor apartment in a new three-story brick building on Market Street between Seventh and Eighth streets in Philadelphia. One can only imagine what his thoughts were as he stared down at a blank sheet of paper upon his new "writing-box." Charged with writing a document to justify America's attempt to become an independent nation, the Declaration should inspire the American people and obtain support from abroad, within Britain as well as among Britain's enemies. In another sense, Jefferson wanted to address a much broader audience, all of posterity: both those who would seek to live their lives in liberty as well as those who would seek to dominate over others. Only about a year before his death, Jefferson explained what the Declaration of Independence was supposed to do.

When forced, therefore, to resort to arms for redress, an appeal to the tribunal of the world was deemed proper for our justification. This was the object of the Declaration of Independence. Not to find out new principles, or new arguments, never before thought of, not merely to say things which had never been said before; but to place before mankind the common sense of the subject, in terms so plain and firm as to command their assent, and to justify ourselves in the independent stand we are compelled to take. Neither aiming at originality of principle or sentiment, nor yet copied from any particular and previous writing, it was intended to be an expression of the American mind, and to give to that expression the proper tone and spirit called for by the occasion. All its authority rests then on the harmonizing sentiments of the day, whether expressed in conversation, in letters, printed essays, or in the elementary books of public right, as Aristotle, Cicero, Locke, Sidney, &c.[10]

The genius of Thomas Jefferson is that he infused the Declaration with "the proper tone and spirit called for." Jefferson took a huge body of political literature—22,000 pamphlets published in Britain in the seventeenth century and several thousand more published during the eighteenth century in Britain and America—and condensed it into five sentences, a total of 202 words: the introduction to the Declaration of Independence. These five sentences constitute arguably what is the greatest statement in political literature.

We hold these truths to be self-evident, that all men are created equal, that they are endowed by their Creator with certain un-alienable Rights, that among these are Life, Liberty and the pursuit of Happiness,—That to secure these rights, Governments are instituted among Men, deriving their just powers from the consent of the governed,—That whenever any Form of Government becomes destructive of these ends, it is the Right of the People to alter or to abolish it; and to institute new Government, laying its foundation on such principles and organizing its powers in such form, as to them shall seem most likely to effect their Safety and Happiness. Prudence, indeed, will dictate that Governments long established should not be changed for light and transient causes; and accordingly all experience hath shewn, that mankind are more disposed to suffer, while evils are sufferable. But when a long train of abuses and usurpations, pursuing invariably the same Object evinces a design to reduce them under absolute Despotism, it is their right, it is their duty, to throw off such Government, and to provide new Guards for their future security.

Jefferson's truth may be self-evident, but "the pursuit of Happiness" has baffled many. The simplest explanation is that this phrase is a euphemistic synonym for property, similar to John Locke's "life, liberty, and estate." Jefferson, however, meant far more than the right to buy, possess, and dispose of property. He wanted a government that, in the words of John Adams, "communicates ease, comfort, [and] security,"[11] a government that would provide protection from foreign invasion and attack by Indians, from assault by criminals, and from oppressive government rule and taxation. Government, according to Jefferson, should provide an efficient, well-run economic environment as well as a society where contrary religious and political opinions could exist in harmony, where the majority ruled but with due deference to the rights of the minority. After playing its role in leveling the field, government would step aside and interfere no more. In his first inaugural address as president in March 1801, Jefferson explained the role of government in the pursuit of happiness: "A wise and frugal Government, which shall restrain men from injuring one another, shall leave them otherwise free to regulate their own pursuits of industry and improvement, and shall not take from the mouth of labor the bread it has earned. This is the sum of good government, and this is necessary to close the circle of our felicities."[12]

❧ Reformer

While Jefferson was attending Congress in Philadelphia, his mind was on events in Williamsburg where delegates in a provincial convention were drafting and adopting a bill of rights and a new state constitution for Virginia. In fact, the Declaration of Rights, adopted on June 12, 1776, probably informed Jefferson's Declaration of Independence. Three hundred miles away from home, Jefferson drafted his own constitution and sent it to George Wythe. Jefferson's constitution retained the structure of Virginia's colonial government but provided nearly universal adult male suffrage. He wanted both houses of the legislature and the governor elected annually, with the governor, stripped of his veto power, ineligible for reelection for five years. Except for the wording of the constitution's preamble, the convention ignored Jefferson's proposal in favor of a constitution that favored the wealthy tidewater planters. For the rest of his life, Jefferson chafed at Virginia's constitution, but he never realized any meaningful change.

When the first Virginia House of Delegates assembled in October 1776, Jefferson attended. Using the principles espoused in the Declaration of Independence, Jefferson hoped to rid Virginia of the last vestiges of feudalism and aristocratic favoritism. He suggested that the house appoint a committee to revise the state's laws, and two weeks later it appointed a committee of five, chaired by Jefferson, that included George Wythe. The committee took three years to submit its final report — a thorough reformation of the law on republican and liberal principles — by which time Jefferson, no longer in the house, was unable to shepherd the new laws into being.

The legislature considered some reforms immediately. Jefferson, ever the advocate of republicanism and the widespread ownership of property, successfully campaigned for the abolition of entail, the feudal relic that required inherited property to pass intact to heirs. Later, primogeniture (the inheritance of an estate by the eldest son) and the system of quitrents (a lifetime rental system) were disallowed, thus guaranteeing a broader ownership of land.

Jefferson's reforms sought to moderate Virginia's harsh criminal code. He proposed reducing the numerous capital offenses to two — murder and treason — and rejected corporal punishment as well as the new-fangled policy of long-term imprisonment. Instead, Jefferson favored a broad system of public service for criminals, who would wear uniforms and whose heads would be shaved to prevent escape. In the mid-1780s, when Jefferson was in Europe, James Madison supported these modifications in the criminal code, but with little success. It would take another ten years before Jefferson's ideas would be adopted.

Jefferson also supported the complete separation of church and state. Although the Virginia Declaration of Rights provided that "all men are equally entitled to the free exercise of religion, according to the dictates of conscience," and the state constitution discontinued the official establishment of the Anglican Church, Jefferson felt that a more explicit separation of church and state was needed. In 1779 he drafted a Bill for Religious Freedom. Like most of his reforms, it lay dormant. In 1783 Patrick Henry, Edmund Pendleton, and Richard Henry Lee proposed public support for Christian Protestant ministers. James Madison now revived and championed Jefferson's bill in the House of Delegates, and in January 1786 it was adopted. It provided:

that the opinions of men are not the object of civil government, nor under its jurisdiction. . . . that no man shall be compelled to frequent or support any religious worship, place, or ministry whatsoever, nor shall be enforced, restrained, molested, or burdened in his body or goods, nor shall otherwise suffer, on account of his religious opinions or belief; but that all men shall be free to profess, and by argument to maintain, their opinions in matters of religion, and that the same shall in no wise diminish, enlarge, or affect their civil capacities.

Jefferson was most proud of this act. He also greatly admired the way in which religious freedom was protected in the First Amendment of the U.S. Constitution. In an address to the Baptist Association of Danbury, Connecticut, on January 1, 1802, President Jefferson reiterated his support for "a wall of separation between Church & State."[13]

Jefferson was also a staunch advocate for reform in public education. He submitted a Bill for the More General Diffusion of Knowledge in 1779, which called for a three-tiered system of public education: elementary, general, and university. All free children would be educated for three years at public expense. The best students—the state's "natural aristocracy" of merit and virtue—would advance from one level to the next with public support. Other children could continue their education, but without public support. Jefferson told Wythe that "by far the most important bill in our whole code is that for the diffusion of knowledge among the people. No other sure foundation can be devised, for the preservation of freedom and happiness."[14] Neither Jefferson nor Wythe could get the educational reforms adopted. Support for comprehensive public education in Virginia would have to wait until after the Civil War.

In May 1779 the Virginia legislature elected Jefferson governor. He did not want the job but believed that "in a virtuous government, and more especially in times like these, public offices are, what they should be, burdens to those appointed to them which it would be wrong to decline, though foreseen to bring with them intense labor and great private loss."[15] It was the worst time to be governor of a southern state. The British had abandoned their strategy of separating New England from New York and had transferred their military initiatives to the South, capturing Savannah in December 1778 and Charleston in May 1780. Several amphibious assaults against Virginia took place during this time commanded by Benedict Arnold, and the British army, commanded by General Charles Cornwallis, relentlessly marched northward toward Virginia. On May 20 Cornwallis captured Richmond, Virginia's new capital, forcing the Patriot government to evacuate to Charlottesville. Cornwallis sent a detachment of rangers to capture the government. Warned just in time, government officials hastily fled across the Blue Ridge Mountains to Staunton. At Monticello, Jefferson also was warned and escaped to a nearby mountaintop where he watched the British in Charlottesville through his telescope. The British left Monticello undamaged but wreaked destruction on other property, including Jefferson's farm at Elk Hill.

Although Jefferson's term as governor had expired on June 2, he was blamed by those who looked for a scapegoat for the British devastation because there was no adequate defense. Former governor Patrick Henry, who had led the opposition to Jefferson's reform program, called for an investigation. Finding no evidence of either wrongdoing or cowardice, the House of Delegates passed a resolution affirming "the high opinion which they entertain of Mr. Jefferson's Ability, Rectitude, and Integrity as chief Magistrate of this Commonwealth, and mean by thus publicly avowing their opinion, to obviate and remove all unmerited Censure." The charges against him, however, had done severe damage to Jefferson's reputation and to his attitude about public service. Jefferson vowed never to serve in public office again. He also never forgave Patrick Henry for his attempt to censure Jefferson, referring to Henry as a man with "all tongue, and no head or heart."[16]

And Slavery

Throughout his life Jefferson wrestled with the problem of slavery.[17] He, like most Americans, denounced the foreign slave trade that captured free men, women, and children in Africa, forcibly transported them in the most inhumane fashion to the Western Hemisphere, and sold them as property into lifelong bondage. As a first-year legislator in 1769 and in drafting the Declaration of Independence seven years later, Jefferson had denounced the foreign slave trade. Not until 1782, when Jefferson was temporarily retired from public service, did Virginia prohibit the foreign slave trade. Then, as president in December 1806, Jefferson proposed that Congress prohibit the foreign slave trade as of January 1, 1808, the earliest allowable date for a congressional prohibition under the Constitution. Congress enacted such a bill on March 2, 1807, and President Jefferson signed it the next day.

Jefferson also consistently denounced the institution of slavery in principle. His attitude toward emancipation and toward blacks was more complex. In 1781, as the Revolution neared its conclusion, Jefferson pointed out the incongruity of fighting a revolution for liberty while keeping a race of people in bondage. "Indeed," Jefferson wrote, "I tremble for my country when I reflect that God is just: that his justice cannot sleep for ever." Jefferson deplored not only the injustice done to blacks but the unhealthy effects—political, social, moral, and economic—that slavery had on whites. "There must doubtless be an unhappy influence on the manners of our people produced by the existence of slavery among us. The whole commerce between master and slave is a perpetual exercise of the most boisterous passions, the most unremitting despotism on the one part, and degrading submissions on the other." White children learned to be despotic by observing their parents' behavior toward slaves. The industriousness of whites also suffered from the presence of slaves. "In a warm climate, no man will labour for himself who can make another labour for him."

Agreeing with the scientific theories of the day, Jefferson believed that blacks were naturally and profoundly inferior to whites. In color, the most obvious difference, "the fine mixtures of red and white" produced far more beauty and sensitivity to different expressions of passions than the "eternal monotony" of black that emanated from the blood, the bile, or some other secretion. Their flowing hair and elegance of form also favored whites over blacks and made black men desire white women in the same way that male "Oranootans" favored "black women over those of their own species." The glands and secretions of blacks gave off "a very strong and disagreeable odour." They seemed to need less sleep. They were more "ardent after their females," but "love seems with them to be more an eager desire, than a tender delicate mixture of sentiment and sensation. Their griefs are transcient." Although blacks were observed to be courageous, their bravery seemed unrelated to any forethought but rather merely responsive to immediate dangers. Blacks seemed to be the equal of whites in memory but inferior in reasoning and imagination. Blacks showed no talent for painting, sculpture, or oratory but seemed "more generally gifted than whites" in music.[18]

In the mid-1780s Jefferson saw the institution of slavery as a conflict between "justice" and "avarice & oppression." He looked to the youth of Revolutionary America who "have sucked in the principles of liberty as it were with their mother's milk" to abolish the evil institution.[19] After his presidency Jefferson continued to denounce slavery. "The love of justice and the love of country plead equally the cause of these people, and it is a mortal reproach to us that they should have pleaded it so long in vain, and should have produced not a single effort, nay I fear not much serious willingness to relieve them & ourselves from our present condition of moral & political reprobation."[20]

When asked to participate in several plans for emancipation, Jefferson reiterated his eagerness to end slavery. "There is nothing," he wrote, "I would not sacrifice to a practicable plan of abolishing every vestige of this moral and political depravity." But he saw many obstacles to emancipation. Metaphorically he described slavery as having "the wolf by the ear, and we can neither hold him, nor safely let him go." Now he saw the dilemma as "Justice . . . in one scale, and self-preservation in the other."[21] He refused either to be an active participant or even a silent, behind-the-scenes supporter of emancipation. That was for a future generation.

Jefferson saw emancipation happening only if three parts of a coordinated plan could be implemented: (1) gradual and compensated emancipation in which slave owners would be paid from public funds for their financial loss; (2) colonization of free blacks, preferably in Africa, but more likely in some Caribbean island nation; and (3) replacement of the black labor force with a free alternative, most likely Protestant Germans similar to those who had immigrated to Pennsylvania. Jefferson felt that colonization was required because of racism. His belief in the inferiority of blacks convinced him that the intermingling of blood should be avoided at all costs. Furthermore, blacks would forever hate whites for the evils perpetrated against them. Conflict was thus inevitable if the two races lived close together. But because the practicalities of such a plan prohibited it from being implemented when most slaves remained in the South, Jefferson came to advocate the "diffusion" of slavery throughout America, especially to the West. Only in this way could a similar nationwide attitude and appreciation for the problem be realized. Until his death, Jefferson hoped that this terrible problem could be solved. "The abolition of the evil is not impossible; it ought never therefore to be despaired of. Every plan should be adopted, every experiment tried, which may do something towards the ultimate object."[22] But Jefferson himself would not participate in any such plan.

Sally Hemings

When Jefferson became president in 1801, he freed all the imprisoned printers convicted under the Sedition Act of 1798. James Thomson Callender, an Irish immigrant who had been a publicist for both the Federalist and the Republican parties, was among those liberated. A couple years later, Callender sought appointment as postmaster of Richmond. Jefferson's selection of someone else embittered Callender, who attacked Jefferson in print, accusing him of having an ebony concubine at Monticello who had borne him several children. As customary when publicly attacked, Jefferson denied the report once and ignored all future references.

Over the years the charge of a relationship between Thomas Jefferson and Sally Hemings, a slave at Monticello, occasionally surfaced. The Jefferson family and Jefferson biographers categorically denied the report, suggesting that someone else fathered Sally's children. Peter Carr, one of Jefferson's nephews, was often suggested as the most likely father. The controversy persisted, sometimes intensifying on the written page and between the Jefferson and Hemings families. In 1998 a test of the DNA of several members of the Hemings and Jefferson families took place. The test results, plus the written, oral, and circumstantial history, were interpreted by some as conclusive. Some scholars such as Joseph Ellis and Andrew Burstein, who had denied that a relationship between Jefferson and Sally had existed, now made a dramatic change. Some members of the Jefferson family, many important scholars, the administration at Monticello, and most Americans now accepted Callender's charges that Thomas Jefferson had a longtime sexual relationship with Sally and had sired her children.

The scientists who had conducted the DNA test and other Jefferson scholars criticized the complete acceptance of Thomas Jefferson as the father of Sally's children. The original report issued after the DNA test conclusively proved that Jefferson could not have fathered a child who was said to have been Sally's firstborn. The report also stated that Jefferson or a couple dozen other men in the Jefferson family could have fathered Eston Hemings, Sally's last child, whose descendants' DNA was used in the test. No DNA was available for Sally's four remaining children. A scholarly committee supported by other members of the Jefferson family issued a report suggesting that the likely father was Randolph Jefferson, Thomas's younger brother, who lived twenty miles south of Monticello. With no definitive scientific answer, the controversy continues.

❧ At Home

Jefferson returned home in September 1781 "to my farm, my family and books from which I think nothing will evermore separate me."[23] Immediately visitors started descending on Monticello. Major General the marquis de Chastellux visited the former governor for four days.

> Let me describe to you a man, not yet forty, tall, and with a mild and pleasing countenance, but whose mind and understanding are ample substitutes for every exterior grace. An American, who without ever having quitted his own country, is at once a musician, skilled in drawing; a geometrician, an astronomer, a natural philosopher, legislator, and statesman. A senator of America, who sat for two years in that famous Congress which brought about the revolution; and which is never mentioned without respect, though unhappily not without *regret;* a governor of Virginia, who filled this difficult station during the invasions of Arnold, of Philips, and of Cornwallis; a philosopher, in voluntary retirement, from the world, and public business, because he loves them, inasmuch only as he can flatter himself with being useful to mankind; and the minds of his countrymen are not yet in a condition either to bear the light, or to suffer contradiction. A mild and amiable wife, charming children, of whose education

he himself takes charge, a house to embellish, great provisions to improve, and the arts and sciences to cultivate; these are what remain to Mr. Jefferson, after having played a principal character on the theater of the new world, and which he preferred to the honorable commission of Minister Plenipotentiary in Europe. The visit which I made him was not unexpected, for he had long since invited me to come and pass a few days with him, in the center of the mountains; notwithstanding which I found his first appearance serious, nay even cold; but before I had been two hours with him we were as intimate as if we had passed our whole lives together; walking, books, but above all, a conversation always varied and interesting, always supported by that sweet satisfaction experienced by two persons, who in communicating their sentiments and opinions, are invariably in unison, and who understand each other at the first hint, made four days pass away like so many minutes.[24]

On May 8, 1782, Martha Jefferson gave birth to their sixth child, Lucy Elizabeth (three of their six children had died in infancy). Martha Jefferson never recovered from the childbirth. Perhaps anemia sapped her strength as she steadily weakened before Jefferson's eyes. For four months she languished as Jefferson watched over her almost constantly. For almost three months he did not write a letter. Finally, on September 6 she died. Jefferson collapsed in her bedroom. A period of deep mourning followed. He destroyed his entire correspondence with Martha. His three daughters were sent away, and friends feared that Jefferson too might die. For weeks he incessantly paced in his library, then started riding around his farms on horseback for hours at a time. A concerned James Madison saw that "perhaps this domestic catastrophe may prove in its operation beneficial to his country by weaning him from those attachments which deprived it of his services."[25] Madison convinced Congress to add Jefferson to the ongoing peace negotiations in Paris. Jefferson, who had always wanted to visit Europe, leaped at the chance to leave Monticello. He went to Baltimore to await transport on a French warship, but before it departed word arrived that a preliminary peace treaty had been signed, and Congress rescinded his appointment. Jefferson went back to Monticello and worked on a revision of the Virginia constitution, cataloged his library of 2,640 books, and supervised the education of his two older daughters and a nephew.

❧ Congressional Leader

In June 1783 the Virginia legislature appointed Jefferson a delegate to Congress beginning in November. Jefferson decided to take Patsy, his eldest daughter, with him to Philadelphia so that she could acquire "a little taste and execution in such of the fine arts as she could not prosecute to equal advantage in a more retired situation." They arrived in Philadelphia in early November only to find that Congress intended to move to Annapolis. Jefferson arranged for Patsy's accommodations and "procure[d] for her the best tutors in French, dancing, music & drawing."[26] Jefferson left Philadelphia on November 22; three days later he arrived in Annapolis eager to begin the work of a new country.

Immediately Jefferson became a leader in Congress. In acknowledgment of his literary skills, he was chosen to write Congress's response to George Washington when the commander in chief surrendered his commission on December 23, 1783. During the five-month session, Jefferson wrote reports for at least thirty-one committees. One report proposed a radical new national system of coinage, abandoning the familiar English system in favor of a decimal system based upon the dollar. This report served as the model for the system that was eventually adopted in 1794.

In 1781 Governor Jefferson was instrumental in getting Virginia to cede its huge territory north and west of the Ohio River to Congress. Such a cession benefited Congress, placated other states (especially those with no western lands), and, under the prevailing theory of the baron de Montesquieu that republics could not survive in large territories, would help assure the liberties of Virginians. Now in Congress, Jefferson drafted resolutions (often called the Land Ordinance of 1784) that provided for the administration of the Northwest Territory and the admittance of new states into the Union on an equal basis with the original thirteen states. By the vote of a single delegate, Congress removed Jefferson's prohibition of slavery and indentured servitude from the Northwest Territory, but such prohibitions would be reestablished in the Northwest Ordinance of 1787.

Jefferson also had an interest in the western lands beyond the borders of the United States. According to the recently adopted Treaty of Peace, the Mississippi River served as America's western border. Although Spain claimed the territory west of the Mississippi, information had been received that "a very large sum of money" had been raised in England to explore the land between the Mississippi and the Pacific Ocean. Ostensibly the proposed expedition had only scientific goals, but Jefferson feared that the British "have thoughts of colonizing into that quarter." Jefferson and others began raising funds for an American expedition of discovery. Although he feared that Americans did not possess "enough of that kind of spirit to raise the money," he sounded out fellow Virginian George Rogers Clark, the Revolutionary War hero of battles in Illinois and Indiana, to see if he would be willing "to lead such a party."[27] Jefferson's interest in the West never waned. Twenty years would pass before President Jefferson purchased this expansive territory, thus doubling the size of the United States. He then chose Meriwether Lewis and George Rogers Clark's younger brother William to lead an expedition to the Pacific.

While in Annapolis, Jefferson took an active role in directing the education of his daughter in Philadelphia and Peter Carr, his nephew, in Virginia. As always, Jefferson believed that education had academic, vocational, physical, and moral components. To Peter, he sent a copy of Homer along with the admonition to obey his teacher and not to waste time. "You are now old enough to know how very important to your future life will be the manner in which you employ your present time. I hope therefore you will never waste a moment of it." Jefferson would repeat this advice continually to youth studying under his direction. "Consider how little time is left you, and how much you have to attain in it, and that every moment you lose of it is lost for ever." "Time is now the most pressing and precious thing in the world to you, and the greatest injury which can possibly be done you is to waste what remains."[28]

To Patsy, he outlined her daily schedule: wake up at sunrise and eat breakfast, from 8:00 to 10:00 practice music, from 10:00 to 1:00 dance one day and draw another, from 1:00 to 2:00 draw on the day you dance and write a letter the next day, from 2:00 to 3:00 dine, from 3:00 to 4:00 read French, from 4:00 to 5:00 exercise to music, and from 5:00 till bedtime read English and write. In writing, Jefferson told his daughter, "take care that you never spell a word wrong." If uncertain of the spelling, "turn to a dictionary." It was important to present a proper image in correspondence as well as in person. He told Patsy to keep his letters and refer to them "that you may always have present in your mind those things which will endear you to me."[29]

Jefferson advised Patsy to be wary of religious zealots in Philadelphia who predicted the imminent destruction of the earth.

> The almighty has never made known to any body at what time he created it, nor will he tell any body when he means to put an end to it, if ever he means to do it. As to preparations for that event, the best way is for you to be always prepared for it. . . . never to do nor say a bad thing. If ever you are about to say any thing amiss or to do any thing wrong, consider before hand. You will feel something within you which will tell you it is wrong and ought not to be said or done: this is your conscience, and be sure to obey it. Our maker has given us all, this faithful internal Monitor, and if you always obey it, you will always be prepared for the end of the world: or for a much more certain event which is death. This must happen to all: it puts an end to the world as to us, and the way to be ready for it is never to do a wrong act.[30]

Service Abroad

After the war for independence, Congress wanted to establish diplomatic and commercial relations with all countries. It appointed a three-man commission to negotiate commercial treaties with European and North African countries. Benjamin Franklin and John Adams, both still in France, were obvious appointments. Needing a southerner to round out the commission, Congress appointed Jefferson on May 7, 1784. Jefferson wrote letters to friends and family to provide for the supervision of his plantation and the safekeeping of his two daughters in Virginia. On May 11 Jefferson left Annapolis for Philadelphia and gathered up Patsy. They traveled through New England where Jefferson learned as much as he could about commercial matters. On July 5 the Jeffersons set sail from Boston on the merchant ship *Ceres*. Despite all the horror stories told about Atlantic crossings, their nineteen-day voyage was uneventful. Patsy likened it to floating down a river. Not so the harrowing thirteen-hour crossing of the tempestuous English Channel.

Arriving in Paris in August 1784, both father and daughter shed their provincial attire and purchased new wardrobes fashionable for Paris. Patsy, enrolled in an exclusive Catholic convent school in which religion was excluded from the curriculum, adjusted easily, but her father struggled. His lack of conversational French hampered his ability to communicate, and the dampness of the weather and unwholesomeness of the water caused him considerable suffering during the seasoning process.[31] In January 1785 Jefferson's anguish heightened when he learned of the death of two-year-old Lucy. The awful news sent him into a deep depression for several months. With the warmth of spring, Jefferson felt well enough to resume his duties. He wrote his brother-in-law to ask that Polly, now eight years old, be sent to Europe as soon as practicable.

In late February 1785 Congress appointed John Adams minister plenipotentiary to Great Britain, and in early May, John and Abigail Adams left France. Abigail hated to leave "Mr. Jefferson, he is one of the choice ones of the Earth," and "the only person with whom my Companion could associate; with perfect freedom, and unreserve."[32]

In May 1785 Congress approved Benjamin Franklin's request to return to America and unanimously elected Jefferson to replace him as U.S. minister to France. Franklin returned to America in July. Because of the veneration the French had for Franklin, Jefferson knew that the transition could be difficult. He described it "as an excellent school of humility." When presented as the new American minister, the usual question was, "C'est vous, Monsieur, qui remplace le Docteur Franklin?" Jefferson generally answered, "No one can replace him, Sir: I am only his successor."[33]

Jefferson worked tirelessly to improve commercial relations with France, its Caribbean colonies, and other countries. Treaties were signed with Prussia and Morocco. The marquis de Lafayette greatly assisted Jefferson in commercial matters, not only in France but in Spain as well. According to Jefferson, the young Frenchman's zeal was unbounded; he was "a most valuable auxiliary." Lafayette was equally praising of Jefferson. "No better minister could be sent to France. He is everything that is good, upright, enlightened, and clever, and is respected and beloved by everyone that knows him." To George Washington, Lafayette wrote that "words cannot sufficiently express to you how much I am pleased with Mr. Jefferson's public conduct—He unites every ability that can recommend him with the ministers, and at the [same] time possesses accomplishments of the mind and the heart which cannot but give him many friends." Lafayette was delighted to be Jefferson's "Aid de Camp." "His abilities, His Virtues, His temper, Every thing of Him Commands Respect and Attracts Affection. He Enjoys Universal Regard, and does the Affairs of America to perfection. It is the Happiest choice that Could Be Made."[34]

In addition to opening new markets for American exports in both Europe and the Caribbean, Jefferson sent exotic plants back to America: upland rice and beans from Italy to South Carolina, olive trees and shoots to Baltimore, and Spanish merino sheep and grapevines to George Washington. The introduction of a new crop to a country was, in Jefferson's opinion, "worth more to them than all the victories of the most splendid pages of their history."[35] To his friends Madison and Monroe, as well as others, he sent books—food for the mind—on a wide variety of subjects. Two decades later a good friend from the Jardin des plantes in Paris returned the favor when he sent Jefferson over 700 different species of flowers.

At the request of Adams, Jefferson visited England in March and April 1785 to assist in negotiating commercial treaties with the Portuguese minister to England and a diplomatic agent from Tripoli. Adams arranged to have Jefferson presented to the king and queen at one of their levees. As Adams and Jefferson approached the monarchs, George III turned his back on them. Jefferson wrote that "it was impossible for anything to be more ungracious." In this instant Jefferson clearly saw "the ulcerations in the narrow mind of that mulish being." Jefferson felt that free trade and "peace and friendship with all mankind is our wisest policy; . . . but the temper and folly of our enemies may not leave this in our choice."[36]

Difficult negotiations took place between the United States and the Barbary States of North Africa: Morocco, Algiers, Tripoli, and Tunis. No longer under the protection of the British navy, American merchant vessels were preyed upon by pirates sanctioned by the governments of these countries. Several American ships had already been seized and their crews and passengers enslaved by the Moroccans and the Algerines. Through the good graces of the Spanish, the Moroccans signed a treaty and released the hostages and the ship *Betsy.* Algiers, however, rejected all American overtures and refused to lessen its exorbitant ransom demands. John Adams advised paying the ransom as the cheapest way to handle the problem; Jefferson favored war as the best means of obtaining a lasting peace. Jefferson proposed a confederation of small countries to oppose the Algerines. He also recommended that Congress create a small navy of 150 guns that would cruise the Mediterranean to protect American merchantmen. Such a policy would promote justice by punishing the aggressor, provide honor and respect (which would safeguard future American interests), and produce the least internal danger to the rights of Americans from an empowered Confederation government. (Jefferson, like most Americans of this period, feared that a standing army would endanger liberties.) Furthermore, a just war against so weak an opponent was opportune to show American strength.[37] Congress, however, opposed war, negotiations dragged on, and American hostages remained enslaved for over ten years.

After seven weeks in England, Jefferson returned to Paris, where he enjoyed the architecture, museums, and formal gardens in and around the city. He became so fond of French cuisine that he brought one of his slaves, John Hemings, to Paris to be trained as a French chef. Jefferson came to have a real affection for France and the French people. He felt that France was "the only nation on earth on whom we can solidly rely for assistance till we can stand on our own legs." He told Abigail Adams that Frenchmen "have as much happiness in one year as an Englishman in ten." To others he explained that it was "impossible to be among a people who wish more to make one happy, a people of the very best character it is possible for one to have. We have no idea in America of the real French character." It was hard, he readily admitted, to understand the French. "A Frenchman never says *No:* and it is difficult for a stranger to know when he means it. Perhaps it is the longest to be learnt of all the particularities of the nation." Yet if one asked the seasoned traveler of any nation, "In what country on earth would you rather live?"

they would naturally say their own, but their second choice would always be France.[38]

Jefferson walked four or five miles daily among the tree-lined pathways and fountains of the Bois de Boulogne. It was on one of Jefferson's many sightseeing excursions that he spotted John Trumbull, the young Connecticut painter, whom Jefferson had first met a few months earlier in London. Trumbull introduced Jefferson to Richard and Maria Cosway, fellow painters from London. Immediately Jefferson was smitten with Maria's charm and beauty. She too was taken with the tall, handsome diplomat, who in most ways was the complete opposite of her short, foppish, dissolute husband. When Trumbull left for Germany and Richard Cosway busied himself painting portraits of the French nobility, Jefferson and Maria toured the Parisian countryside by days and half days. Jefferson, now forty-three years old, had been a widower for four years, and he easily succumbed to the twenty-seven-year-old Italian-born beauty. Whether their relationship was consummated or remained merely flirtatious is impossible to know. But Jefferson felt "more dead than alive" when the Cosways left Paris to return to London. Seated by his fireplace "solitary and sad," he wrote one of the great love letters of all time, a dialogue between his head and his heart, in which the head warned against such relationships but the heart rejoiced in all the pleasures and pain of life. A devout Catholic, Maria could never divorce. She did, however, on several occasions leave her husband and reside on the Continent. But travel to America was out of the question: she was deathly afraid of ocean travel. And so when Jefferson planned his return to America in 1789, he wrote Maria that "when wafting on the bosom of the ocean I shall pray it to be as calm and smooth as yours to me." The ardor passed, and their correspondence became intermittent.[39]

Jefferson's instructions to his brother-in-law for arranging Polly's trip to France demonstrate the dangers of eighteenth-century ocean travel. She should come over on a French or British ship to avoid possible capture by the Barbary pirates. The voyage should be made between April and July to avoid the hurricane season as well as the discomfort of a winter crossing. The ship should have made at least one round-trip Atlantic crossing but should be no more than four or five years old.[40]

While Jefferson was touring southern France, he received word that Polly was on her way. He wrote Patsy the good news.

> I have received letters which inform me that our dear Polly will certainly come to us this summer. By the time I return it will be time to expect her. When she arrives, she will become a precious charge on your hands. The difference of your age, and your common loss of a mother, will put that office on you. Teach her above all things to be good: because without that we can neither be valued by others, nor set any value on ourselves. Teach her to be always true. No vice is so mean as the want of truth, & at the same time so useless. Teach her never to be angry. Anger only serves to torment ourselves, to divert others, and alienate their esteem. And teach her industry & application to useful pursuits. I will venture to assure you that if you inculcate this in her mind you will make her a happy being in herself, a most inestimable friend to you, and precious to all the world. In teaching her these dispositions of mind, you will be more fixed in them yourself, and render yourself dear to all your acquaintances. Practice them then, my dear, without ceasing. If ever you find yourself in difficulty and doubt how to extricate yourself, do what is right, & you will find it the easiest way of getting out of the difficulty. Do it for the additional incitement of increasing the happiness of him who loves you infinitely.[41]

Polly's ship stopped in England, and she and her chaperone-companion, the fourteen-year-old slave girl named Sally Hemings, stayed three weeks with John and Abigail Adams. When Polly arrived in Paris, she was enrolled in the same Catholic convent school attended by Patsy.

While in France, Jefferson enjoyed traveling through the countryside observing the people and studying agricultural practices. He wrote Lafayette that "I am never satiated with rambling through the fields and farms, examining the culture and cultivators, with a degree of curiosity which makes some take me to be a fool, and others to be much wiser than I am." Jefferson was appalled by the widespread poverty in such a wealthy, fertile country. He wrote Washington that "I was much an enemy to monarchy before I came to Europe. I am ten thousand times more so since I have seen what they are. There is scarcely an evil known in these countries which may not be traced to their king as its source, nor a good which is not derived from the small fibres of republicanism existing among them."[42]

Jefferson was well aware of the shortcomings of the Articles of Confederation, but his loathing for oppressive governments made him tolerant of troubling events going on in America. "I am sensible that there are defects in our federal government: yet they are so much lighter than those of monarchies that I view them with much indulgence. I rely too on the good sense of the people for remedy, whereas the evils of monarchical government are beyond remedy. If any of our countrymen wish for a king, give them Aesop's fable of the frogs who asked for a king; if this does not cure them, send them to Europe: they will go back good republicans." In Aesop's fable Jupiter tried to convince the frogs of a pond against having a king. When they persisted, Jupiter threw a log into their pond. The big splash awed the frogs initially, but soon they became disenchanted with their motionless sovereign. They asked for another. Jupiter sent them an eel who proved to be good natured. The frogs again wanted a more powerful monarch, whereupon Jupiter sent a heron who devoured the frogs one by one. The few survivors petitioned Jupiter for relief but were told they were being punished for their folly and that they should have left well enough alone.[43]

Divorced from the passion of the unfolding political events in America, Jefferson had few of the anxieties expressed by many of his friends. He saw uprisings like Shays's Rebellion in Massachusetts as nothing to be afraid of, and possibly even a good thing: "They are a proof that the people have liberty enough, and I would not wish them less than they have. If the happiness of the mass of the people can be secured at the expense of a little tempest now & then, or even of a little blood, it will be a precious purchase. *Malo libertatum periculosum quam quietam servitutem* [I prefer dangerous liberty to a quiet servitude]." To James Madison, he wrote: "I hold it that a little rebellion now and then is a good thing, & as necessary in the political world as storms in the physical. Unsuccessful rebellions indeed generally establish the encroachments on the rights of the people which have produced them. An observation of this truth should render honest republican governors so mild in their punishment of rebellions, as not to discourage them too much. It is a medicine necessary for the sound health of government." To Abigail Adams he wrote: "The spirit of resistance to government is so valuable on certain occasions, that I wish it to be always kept alive. It will often be exercised when wrong, but better so than not to be exercised at all. I like a little rebellion now & then. It is like a storm in the Atmosphere." To Abigail's son-in-law he wrote that "the tree of liberty must be refreshed from time to time with the blood of patriots & tyrants. It is its natural manure."[44]

Jefferson fully supported the efforts in America to strengthen the Articles of Confederation. He was proud of his countrymen. "Happy for us, that when we find our constitutions defective & insufficient to secure the happiness of our people, we can assemble with all the coolness of philosophers & set it to rights, while every other nation on earth must have recourse to arms to amend or to restore their constitutions." Jefferson characterized the Constitutional Convention meeting in Philadelphia in the spring and summer of 1787 as "an assembly of demi-gods," even though he severely criticized the delegates for holding their sessions in secret. Nothing, in Jefferson's opinion, "but the innocence of their intentions, & ignorance of the value of public discussions" could justify the "tying up of the tongues of their members." A bit wary of an overreaction to the political, economic, and social instabilities racking the country, Jefferson warned that when making constitutional revisions, "the hole & the patch should be commensurate."[45]

Jefferson admired much of what was in the new Constitution, but the lack of a bill of rights and term limits for the president and the senators concerned him greatly. He felt it best to accept the good in the Constitution and work to amend its shortcomings. When asked if he was an Antifederalist, Jefferson responded that he was "not a Federalist, because I never submitted the whole system of my opinions to the creed of any party of men whatever in religion, in philosophy, in politics, or in anything else where I was capable of thinking for myself. Such an addiction is the last degradation of a free and moral agent. If I could not go to heaven but with a party, I would not go there at all. Therefore I protest to you I am not of the party of Federalists. But I am much farther from that of the Antifederalists."[46] Jefferson was pleased with the outcome of the constitutional revolution in America. There was enough opposition to do good but not enough to do bad.

Jefferson watched the constitutional revolution in America from afar. He was much closer to the beginnings of the cataclysmic events about to explode in France and then in all of Europe. The ideology of the American Revolution had had an impact on many Frenchmen who served during that war and on the French nation as a whole. Men like the marquis de Lafayette led the movement for political, constitutional, economic, and social reform in France. The American ambassador discreetly counseled these early French revolutionaries, cautioning slow steps and pointing to the danger from an uncontrollable mob as well as from a demagogic leader using the mob. Yet Jefferson never wavered in his support of the French people taking control of their own government despite the brutal violence that erupted occasionally. He hoped "that the glorious example" of France would "be but the beginning of the history of European liberty."[47] He espoused the revolutionary movement while in France and continued to support it after he returned to America.

By the fall of 1788 Jefferson started appealing to Congress for a leave of absence. When Patsy announced her intention to convert to Catholicism and perhaps become a nun, Jefferson was convinced of the necessity of returning to America. He wrote President Washington on May 10, 1789, to request a leave of absence, hoping "that I may be able to get back before the winter sets in. Nothing can be so dreadful to me as to be shivering at sea for two or three months in a winter passage."[48] In June the president approved Jefferson's request.

Jefferson and his daughters left Paris on September 26, 1789, and two days later arrived at Le Havre on the French coast where they waited a week and a half before conditions allowed their passage boat to cross the Channel for Cowes on the Isle of Wight. During this ten-day layover, Nathaniel Cutting, a Massachusetts merchant, spent time with the Jeffersons and described them in his journal.

> I found Mr. Jefferson a man of infinite information and sound Judgment, becoming gravity, and engaging affability mark his deportment. His general abilities are such as would do honor to any age or Country. His eldest Daughter is an amiable Girl about 17 years of age, tall and genteel, has been 5 years in France, principally in a convent, for her Education, and though she has been so long resident in a Country remarkable for its Levity and the forward indelicacy of its manners, yet she retains all that winning simplicity, and good humored reserve that are evident proofs of

innate Virtue and an happy disposition.—Characteristics which eminently distinguish the Women of America from those of any other Country. The youngest Daughter is a lovely Girl about 11 years of age. The perfect pattern of good temper, an engaging smile ever animates her Countenance, and the cheerful attention which she pays to the judicious instructions and advice of her worthy Father, the Pertinent queries which she puts to him, and the evident improvement she makes in her knowledge of Foreign Languages, History and Geography, afford a pleasing Presage that when her faculties attain their maturity, she will be the delight of her Friends, and a distinguished ornament to her sex.[49]

Another two-week delay kept them on the island before setting sail aboard the *Clermont* on October 22. Once at sea, the crossing was speedy and uneventful; "through the whole we had nothing stronger than what seamen call a stiff breeze." A relieved Jefferson could say, "I have now passed the Atlantic twice without knowing what a storm is."[50] The *Clermont* reached Norfolk on November 23. A month later the family was home again at Monticello, where Jefferson pondered his future.

❧ Secretary of State

When Jefferson arrived in Virginia, he discovered that President Washington had nominated him as secretary of state and the Senate had already confirmed the appointment. The State Department was to have responsibility not only for foreign affairs but also for many internal matters, such as copyrights and patents, coinage, weights and measures, the census, the federal capital, and certifying amendments to the Constitution. With a budget of $8,000, including $3,500 for the secretary's salary, the department was authorized to have four clerks and a half-time translator. The president wrote Jefferson that his nomination was motivated by both "private regard" and "public propriety." Washington appreciated Jefferson's "talents and disposition" as well as his willingness to serve his country. But the president indicated that he was "desirous to accommodate to your wishes," meaning that if Jefferson preferred to go back to France as U.S. minister, Washington would make that nomination.[51]

In reply Jefferson neither accepted nor rejected the nomination, telling the president that his preference was to remain as minister to France but "it is not for an individual to choose his post. You are to marshal us as may best be for the public good." The final choice was Washington's. "If you think it better to transfer me to another post, my inclination must be no obstacle: nor shall it be." A perplexed and somewhat annoyed Washington responded to Jefferson's ambivalence. He would not oppose Jefferson's "inclinations" to go back to France, but he felt that Jefferson was the best person to handle this difficult new assignment. That was the reason Washington made the nomination in the first place. It was, however, Jefferson's decision to make, not Washington's. In either case, Jefferson should act as quickly as possible. About three weeks later Jefferson unambiguously accepted the appointment but indicated that he would be unable to assume the post until the end of the month. Jefferson's seventeen-year-old daughter Patsy was scheduled to marry Thomas Mann Randolph Jr. on February 25, 1790. Jefferson felt that "the happiness of a child, for life would be hazarded were I to go away before this arrangement is made."[52]

As secretary of state, Jefferson was driven more by realpolitik than by the idealistic theorizing so characteristic of him otherwise. Two main controversies permeated his tenure as secretary of state: America's attitude toward the French Revolution and the conflict between Jefferson and Secretary of the Treasury Alexander Hamilton over the kind of government and economy best suited for the United States.

Jefferson came back from Europe a firm supporter of the French Revolution, which was then at its very beginning. He believed it to be the harbinger of liberty throughout Europe and a valuable support to the still tenuous American experiment in republicanism. Should the French fail to establish a firm, free, republican government, European freedom would suffer a decisive blow, and Americans might find their own Constitution "falling back to that kind of a Half-way house, the English constitution."[53]

As France and Britain came into conflict, Secretary Jefferson lobbied President Washington in support of the French; Secretary Hamilton, in support of the British. The president tried to keep America neutral, believing that the country should not risk the consequences of involvement in a European war. Hamilton strenuously opposed war with

Britain and any discriminatory commercial legislation against Britain even though that country discriminated against America. Hamilton's economic policy was based largely upon revenue derived from duties on goods imported primarily from Britain. Any anti-British policy would endanger that revenue stream. Jefferson also realized that American involvement in a European war would be disastrous, but he did not support neutrality, which violated America's treaty commitments to France. In February 1778 France and America had finalized the treaties of amity and commerce that brought France openly into war with Britain, helping to assure American independence. These treaties were still in force, and Jefferson wanted America to fulfill its commitments to France. Hamilton's supporters argued that the treaties had been signed with Louis XVI's government, not with the revolutionary regime now in power in France. Furthermore, the treaty committed America to defend French territories only if they were attacked by an aggressor; America was not obliged to support France in an offensive war. Jefferson pointed out the importance of France to America in case war broke out with either Spain or Britain. Washington agreed that the United States should cultivate closer relations with France, including the resumption of debt payments, which Hamilton had urged be suspended. This, according to Jefferson, "was the very doctrine which had been my polar star." Jefferson accordingly instructed Gouverneur Morris, U.S. minister to France, that the United States "desire[s] the closest union" with France. "Mutual good offices, mutual affection and similar principles of government seem to have destined the two peoples for the most intimate communion, and even for a complete exchange of citizenship among the individuals composing them." Jefferson advocated the doctrine that the United States would recognize any functioning government: "We surely cannot deny to any nation that right whereon our government is founded." It was imperative, Jefferson believed, to get this principle on the "record in the letter books of my office."[54]

In January 1793 Jefferson wrote his former personal secretary William Short, who had been elevated to chargé d'affaires to France when Jefferson became secretary of state, to stop sending reports vividly describing the brutality of the Reign of Terror in France. Jefferson believed, as he told Lafayette, "We are not to expect to be translated from despotism to liberty in a feather bed." Short's reports were undermining

Jefferson in his struggles with Secretary Hamilton, both in foreign affairs and domestic matters. In dramatic language Jefferson told Short how important the French Revolution was to the world in general and to the United States in particular. The unjust deaths of a few must be weighed against the benefits to be derived.

> In the struggle which was necessary, many guilty persons fell without the forms of trial, and with them some innocent. These I deplore as much as any body, & shall deplore some of them to the day of my death. But I deplore them as I should have done had they fallen in battle. It was necessary to use the arm of the people, a machine not quite so blind as balls and bombs, but blind to a certain degree. A few of their cordial friends met at their hands the fate of enemies. But time and truth will rescue & embalm their memories, while their posterity will be enjoying that very liberty for which they would never have hesitated to offer up their lives. The liberty of the whole earth was depending on the issue of the contest, and was ever such a prize won with so little innocent blood? My own affections have been deeply wounded by some of the martyrs to this cause, but rather than it should have failed, I would have seen half the earth desolated. Were there but an Adam & Eve left in every country, & left free, it would be better than as it is now.[55]

Jefferson believed that Hamilton sought to reestablish monarchy in America and that Hamilton's economic plan would create a favored class dominated by northern merchants and speculators. Jefferson opposed the creation of the Bank of the United States ostensibly on constitutional grounds. In reality, his objection was more pragmatic. Modeled on the Bank of England, the Bank of the United States would ally the federal government with wealthy, largely northern shareholders who would reap windfall dividends when the bank loaned its capital at high rates of interest to large merchants in preference to small farmers. The payment of the federal debt (most of it now held by northern speculators) at face value and the assumption of the states' wartime debts by the federal government also would bountifully benefit this favored class. Hamilton's *Report on the Subject of Manufactures,* which proposed bounties and subsidies to private individuals, was even more blatantly unconstitutional and corrupt in the sense of favoring only one part of society.

To counteract Hamilton's policies, which Jefferson said had given rise to the formation of a political party, Jefferson and James Madison led the movement to create an organized opposition. "Our citizens are divided into two political sects. One which fears the people most, the other the government." Jefferson justified the creation of the Republican Party and his involvement in it by arguing: "The same political parties which now agitate the U.S. have existed thro' all time. Whether the power of the people, or that of the aristocrats should prevail, were questions which kept the states of Greece & Rome in eternal convulsions; as they now schismatize every people whose minds and mouths are not shut up by the gag of a despot." But unlike the political parties of Great Britain, the Republican Party was not created out of "a greediness for office. . . . Where the principle of difference is as substantial and as strongly pronounced as between the republicans & the Monocrats of our country I hold it as honorable to take a firm & decided part, and as immoral to pursue a middle line, as between the parties of Honest men, & Rogues, into which every country is divided."[56]

As secretary of state, Jefferson continued the difficult negotiations with Spain over the right of Americans freely to navigate the Mississippi River and to transfer their agricultural produce from flat-bottom riverboats to oceangoing vessels. Writing to the American chargé d'affaires in Madrid, Jefferson used the threat of western violence for leverage. "It is impossible to answer for the forbearance of our Western citizens. We endeavor to quiet them with the expectation of an attainment of their rights by peaceable means. But should they in a moment of impatience hazard others, there is no saying how far we may be led; for neither themselves nor their rights will ever be abandoned by us." Spain heightened tensions between the two countries by arming and inciting the Creeks and other Indians in the Southwest Territory. Jefferson felt that by not meddling in European politics, America could avoid hostilities. But if provoked, America would respond with "firmness," regardless of the cost. If Spain persisted in inciting the Creeks, America would annihilate them and go to war with Spain as well, "with regret, but without fear."[57]

Jefferson also denounced the British policy of arming and inciting the Indians of the Old Northwest Territory. United tribes had badly defeated an American military expedition in 1789. Jefferson expected that a new expedition under Governor Arthur St. Clair in the summer of 1791 would "give them a thorough drubbing." After that, Jefferson believed the U.S. government should "bribe them into peace, and to retain them in peace by eternal bribes."[58] St. Clair's expedition was almost annihilated in November 1791, but Anthony Wayne defeated the Indians at Fallen Timbers in 1794. British intrigue continued with the Indians in the Northwest Territory, contributing to the western states' demand for war with Britain in 1812.

Jefferson had long believed that "the two principles on which our conduct towards the Indians should be founded are justice & fear. After the injuries we have done them, they cannot love us, which leaves us no alternative but that of fear to keep them from attacking us. But justice is what we should never lose sight of, & in time it may recover their esteem." Eventually Jefferson came to believe that the only choice for Indian peoples was to assimilate into the white man's society. "In truth, the ultimate point of rest & happiness for them is to let our settlements and theirs meet and blend together, to intermix and become one people, incorporating themselves with us as citizens of the U.S. This is what the natural progress of things will of course bring on, and it will be better to promote than to retard it. Surely it will be better for them to be identified with us, and preserved in the occupation of their lands, than be exposed to the many casualties which may endanger them while a separate people."[59]

Second Retirement

Soon after Washington was elected to a second term as president, Jefferson announced his intention to resign. He delayed his departure once, but at the end of 1793, after spending nearly half of his life in public service, the fifty-year-old Jefferson retired to Monticello for a second time, hoping this time to remain forever a private citizen. His debt of service had "been fully & faithfully paid." He admitted that there was a time when perhaps the esteem of the world was of higher value in my eye than everything in it. But age, experience & reflection, preserving to that only its due value, have set a higher on tranquility. The motion of my blood no longer keeps time with the tumult of the world. It leads me to seek for happiness in the lap and love of my family, in the society of my neighbors & my books, in the wholesome occupations of my farm & my affairs, in an interest or affection in every bud that opens, in every breath that blows around me, in an entire freedom of rest or motion, of thought or incogitancy, owing account to myself alone of my hours & actions.

He wrote Vice President Adams that "I return to farming with an ardor which I scarcely knew in my youth, and which has got the better entirely of my love of study. Instead of writing 10 or 12 letters a day, which I have been in the habit of doing as a thing of course, I put off answering my letters now, farmer-like, till a rainy day, & then find it sometimes postponed by other necessary occupations." To Secretary of War Henry Knox he wrote: "I am become the most ardent farmer in the state. I live on my horse from morning to night almost."[60]

The plantation—both fields and buildings—were dilapidated and needed his full attention. Jefferson reorganized his holdings into six rotation patterns. Because the farming was temporarily a financial drain, Jefferson started a nailery employing a dozen young male slaves. The factory soon produced a ton and a half of nails a month, which Jefferson sold to storekeepers and planters or used for his own projects. Supervising the business himself, it yielded "a profit on which I can get along till I can put my farms into a course of yielding profit." Ever experimenting, he applied "mathematical principles" to a new design for a moldboard plow that brought added efficiencies to farming and won awards for him from various agricultural societies at home and abroad. He continued collecting and compiling the ancient and modern laws of Virginia, hoping that a new printed compilation would preserve this valuable legal and historical heritage. He immediately set to work "repairing, altering & finishing" his residence, a structure already twenty-five years in the making with another twenty-five years of work still to come.[61]

But Jefferson could never totally abandon the outside world. Although he canceled his newspaper subscriptions and read few pamphlets, national and international news still flowed to Monticello through the rivers of correspondence from abroad and from politically active friends in America who wanted him back in the fray. Jefferson became increasingly convinced that the central government's policies were more than ever under the control of the monarchist Hamilton. When, in September 1796, President Washington announced his decision to retire after the completion of his second term, it became obvious to Republicans that they needed a candidate to run for president who would combat the dangerous tendency of amassing power in the central government and the growing subservience to Great Britain. At first Jefferson was determined not to run: "I would not give up my own retirement for the empire of the universe."[62] He wanted James Madison to do it, but everyone knew that only Jefferson stood a chance to defeat John Adams. Jefferson relented. Hoping to preserve republicanism in America from the machinations of Alexander Hamilton and other monarchists and lovers of Britain, he agreed not to decline the presidency.

Jefferson's candidacy did not come as a surprise to many of his opponents. They distrusted him and felt that his retirement from the State Department was politically motivated. Years later Adams described the attitude of Jefferson's rivals in the mid-1790s.

Jefferson resigned his office as Secretary of State and retired, and his friends said he had struck a great stroke to obtain the presidency. . . . The whole anti-Federal party at that time considered this retirement as a sure and certain step towards the summit of the pyramid and, accordingly, represented him as unambitious, unavaricious, and perfectly disinterested in all parts of all the states in the union. When a man has one of the two greatest parties in a nation interested in representing him to be disinterested, even those who believe it to be a lie will repeat it so often to one another that at last they will seem to believe it to be true. Jefferson has succeeded; and multitudes are made to believe that he is pure benevolence; that he desires no profit; that he wants no patronage; that if you will only let him govern, he will rule only to make the people happy. But you and I know him to be an intriguer.[63]

Alexander Hamilton felt that it was critical that Washington's "successor shall be a safe man." It was less important who that person was, as long as "it shall not be Jefferson. We have every thing to fear if this man comes in." Federalists must work together, must set aside all "personal and partial considerations . . . to give to the great object of excluding Jefferson."[64]

As was the custom of the day, neither Adams nor Jefferson campaigned. With the country sorely divided, many, including Jefferson, thought that no candidate would receive a majority of the electoral votes and that the election would then revert to the House of Representatives. In such a case, Jefferson preferred that Adams be elected because of his seniority. "He has always been my senior, from the commencement of our public life, and the expression of the public will being equal, this circumstance ought to give him the preference." Jefferson wrote to Madison that "there is nothing I so anxiously hope, as that my name may come out either second or third." The electoral vote was close, and both Adams and Jefferson received majorities of the electoral vote: 71 to 68. Adams would be president and Jefferson vice president. Jefferson was pleased. He hoped that Adams could "be induced to administer the government on its true principles, & to relinquish his bias to an English constitution." Furthermore, it might be beneficial for the country if Adams and the Republicans would work together in future elections. "He is perhaps the only sure barrier against Hamilton's getting in."[65]

As vice president Jefferson believed that he would not be an executive officer. He would not attend cabinet meetings but would only preside over the Senate. Jefferson wrote that "the second office of this government is honorable & easy, the first is but a splendid misery." Jefferson thanked Benjamin Rush "for your congratulations on the public call on me to undertake the second office in the United States, but still more for the justice you do me in viewing as I do the escape from the first. I have no wish to meddle again in public affairs. . . . If I am to act however, a more tranquil and unoffending station could not have been found for me. . . . It will give me philosophical evenings in the winter, and rural days in summer."[66]

❧ The Reign of Witches

When John Adams became president in 1797, he faced a crisis in foreign affairs. The recently adopted Jay Treaty did little to improve Anglo-American relations, but it convinced France that America, with its pro-British president, was siding with its inveterate enemy. France refused to accept America's new minister, and French warships began seizing American merchantmen.

In his opening speech to the Senate, Jefferson praised Adams as an American patriot. Adams suggested to Jefferson that James Madison might be appointed minister to France to repair the diplomatic damage; but before Jefferson could deliver Madison's refusal of the appointment, the president had already taken the advice of his cabinet and withdrawn the offer. From this moment Adams turned a cold shoulder to Jefferson, never seeking his advice.

Adams called a special session of Congress and delivered what Republicans perceived as a war message that elevated the country's passions against France. Another American peace initiative failed when France refused either to accept America's ambassador or to negotiate unless a bribe was first provided. France and America went to war at sea. Congress voted to expand the navy and provide for a provisional army of 25,000 to defend against a potential French invasion. President Adams asked George Washington to come out of retirement and be commander in chief of the army; Washington accepted on the condition that Alexander Hamilton be second in command. Reluctantly Adams accepted Washington's terms. Jefferson perceived the danger of a powerful, oppressive army led in the field by a power-hungry monarchist like Hamilton.

With war raging in Europe, many Europeans emigrated to America. Most were sympathetic to the Republicans. In an effort to silence the ever-growing criticism of the administration, Congress passed and the president signed a new Naturalization Act, Alien Acts, and the Sedition Act. The Naturalization Act and the Alien Acts made it harder to become citizens and easier for the president to deport aliens from both friendly and enemy countries; Adams never used the Alien Acts. The Sedition Act provided that anyone who criticized the president or Congress (the vice president was not mentioned) could be prosecuted and, if found guilty, fined and imprisoned. The federal judiciary—all Federalists—enthusiastically enforced the Sedition Act, and several Republican printers and even a congressman were imprisoned and fined.

Republicans were convinced of the unconstitutionality of the alien and sedition laws. Secretly, Jefferson wrote a series of resolutions condemning the acts. In them he asserted that the states had united and formed a compact creating a central government with strictly limited powers. The Sedition Act went far beyond the federal government's power, he argued, and thus could be nullified by the states. In December 1798 the Kentucky legislature adopted Jefferson's resolutions but only after making significant modifications eliminating the reference to nullification. James Madison wrote a similar resolution, though not going so far as to advocate nullification, and the Virginia legislature adopted it in November 1798. No other state endorsed the states' rights position espoused in the Virginia and Kentucky resolutions.

Despite various appeals for a division of the Union, Jefferson cautioned against such extremes. Federalist and New England domination were only temporary. The popularity of Washington and "the cunning of Hamilton" had deceived men who normally would be Republicans. "Time alone would bring around an order of things more correspondent to the sentiments of our constituents." War, taxes, and violations of the Constitution would have their impact. "A little patience, and we shall see the reign of witches pass over, their spells dissolve, and the people, recovering their true sight, restore their government to its true principles." Who could say whether a divided America would be an improvement. Better to maintain the Union and separate totally from Europe. If Americans felt European power just enough "to hoop us together, it will be the happiest situation in which we can exist."[67]

Realizing that war with America was terribly unwise, the French government sent out peace feelers. Although President Adams was riding a wave of popularity because of the war hysteria, he responded positively to the French overtures by sending a new diplomatic delegation to France to avert war, much to the disgust of many fellow Federalists. This effort to achieve peace exposed the deep fissure among Federalists. The Hamilton wing of the party condemned the president and hoped to defeat both Adams and Jefferson in the upcoming presidential election of 1800.

❧ The Revolution of 1800

In 1800 Republicans sensed a real opportunity to win control of the presidency and both houses of Congress. The country was so evenly divided that it seemed likely the presidential election would be determined by whoever received the electoral votes of New York. That state's legislature, which chose the electors, was so evenly divided that whichever party won the New York City election would have a majority, and with that would control all of the state's electoral votes.

Aaron Burr, who had been the Republican candidate for vice president in 1796, developed a masterful strategy for the election of New York City assemblymen, and in the spring of 1800 the Republicans elected their assembly candidates. It was widely assumed that unless something unforeseen happened, Jefferson would be elected president in the fall. When November came, the New York legislature chose presidential electors committed to Jefferson. For his efforts Burr expected and received the endorsement of the Republican congressional caucus as vice president. Remembering that the 1796 Virginia presidential electors had cast their ballots for the old patriot Samuel Adams instead of for the young New York intriguer, Burr demanded that no electoral votes should be diverted away from him in 1800. A grateful Jefferson, Madison, and the rest of the Republican leadership agreed.

The presidential election of 1800 was unbelievably virulent. Jefferson was vilified as a Jacobin who would plunge America into a reign of terror, as an atheist slave owner who would destroy the country's morals, and as an ally of France who would involve America in the carnage of European war. Federalists saw Jefferson as "too theoretical & fanciful a statesman to direct with steadiness & prudence the affairs of this extensive & growing confederacy."[68] Hamilton outwardly supported the Federalist ticket of President Adams and Charles Cotesworth Pinckney of South Carolina but secretly campaigned for Pinckney to unseat Adams.

Jefferson and Burr each received 73 electoral votes, while Adams received 65 votes and Pinckney 64. Republicans decisively won almost a two-thirds majority of the new House of Representatives. But with Jefferson and Burr tied (and having a majority of the electoral votes), the choice between the two Republican candidates was to be decided by the lame-duck House of Representatives controlled by Federalists. Voting by state delegations, the House was split with eight states favoring Jefferson, six for Burr, and two divided. Neither Jefferson nor Burr made any quid pro quo deals, but neither did Burr explicitly renounce a willingness to be elected president. Hamilton vigorously supported Jefferson, indicating in his correspondence with Federalist representatives that the *"profligate"* Burr had no scruples and could never be trusted to fulfill any promise. Hamilton also discounted much of the Federalist campaign rhetoric about Jefferson. As much as Hamilton personally disliked Jefferson, he recognized that the Virginian would accept certain practical political constraints. He wrote to Delaware's lone representative, James A. Bayard, who leaned toward Burr:

> Nor is it true that Jefferson is zealot enough to do anything in pursuance of his principles which will contravene his popularity, or his interest. He is as likely as any man I know to temporize—to calculate what will be likely to promote his own reputation and advantage; and the probable result of such a temper is the preservation of systems, though originally opposed, which being once established, could not be overturned without danger to the person who did it. To my mind a true estimate of Mr. J's character warrants the expectation of a temporizing rather than a violent system. That Jefferson has manifested a culpable predilection for France is certainly true; but I think it a question whether it did not proceed quite as much from her *popularity* among us, as from sentiment, and in proportion as that popularity is diminished his zeal will cool. Add to this that there is no fair reason to suppose him capable of being corrupted, which is a security that he will not go beyond certain limits.[69]

The House began voting on February 16, only three weeks before the anticipated inauguration. Finally, after thirty-six ballots, Bayard submitted a blank ballot, removing Delaware from the Burr column. South Carolina also voted blank, and the only Republican in the Vermont delegation cast the state's vote for Jefferson. Ten states voted for Jefferson, four for Burr, and two voted blank. Jefferson was elected without a single Federalist vote. Years later Jefferson referred to the election as "the revolution of 1800 ... as real a revolution in the principles of our government as that of 1776 was in its form."[70]

❧ President

March 4, 1801, is an important day in American history, in the history of freedom. On this day power was transferred peacefully from one political party to an opposing party. The fifty-seven-year-old president-elect walked from his boardinghouse to the unfinished Capitol virtually indistinguishable from his fellow citizens. At Jefferson's request Chief Justice John Marshall (a distant cousin and staunch political opponent) administered the oath of office. The luster of the event was tarnished only slightly because of the absence of the outgoing president; John Adams had left the city at 4:00 that morning. Although Jefferson and Adams would live another quarter century, they would never see each other again. In fact, for the next ten years they remained estranged.

Jefferson's inaugural address, spoken in his soft, almost inaudible voice in the Senate chamber overcrowded with 1,000 people, is one of the great documents in American political literature. Knowing that reconciliation was desperately needed, the new president offered an outstretched open hand. "Every difference of opinion is not a difference of principle. We have called by different names brethren of principle. We are all Republicans, we are all Federalists." Though the "sacred principle" of majority rule "is in all cases to prevail, that will to be rightful must be reasonable; that the minority possess their equal rights, which equal law must protect, and to violate would be oppression." He pleaded with his countrymen to "unite with one heart and one mind" to restore "harmony and affection" to their social intercourse. "The honor, the happiness, and the hopes of this beloved country" were dependent on their actions. In a brief two-minute statement, he outlined "the essential principles of our Government," which would be the general policies of his administration.

Equal and exact justice to all men, of whatever state or persuasion, religious or political; peace, commerce, and honest friendship with all nations, entangling alliances with none; the support of the State governments in all their rights, as the most competent administrations for our domestic concerns and the surest bulwarks against antirepublican tendencies; the preservation of the General Government in its whole constitutional vigor, as the sheet anchor of our peace at home and safety abroad; a jealous care of the right of election by the people—a mild and safe corrective of abuses which are lopped by the sword of revolution where peaceable remedies are unprovided; absolute acquiescence in the decisions of the majority, the vital principle of republics, from which is no appeal but to force, the vital principle and immediate parent of despotism; a well-disciplined militia, our best reliance in peace and for the first moments of war till regulars may relieve them; the supremacy of the civil over the military authority; economy in the public expense, that labor may be lightly burthened; the honest payment of our debts and sacred preservation of the public faith; encouragement of agriculture, and of commerce as its handmaid; the diffusion of information and arraignment of all abuses at the bar of the public reason; freedom of religion; freedom of the press, and freedom of person under the protection of the habeas corpus, and trial by juries impartially selected.[71]

Jefferson wanted to establish a new, more republican image as president. His wardrobe as president might best be described as frumpy. Like Washington, he understood the importance of image and precedent. He chose to cultivate a more common image. He hated the tapestry of monarchy and through dress and action attempted to abandon the old ways in favor of the new.

At his inauguration he wore no sword. For two weeks after the inauguration, he resided and dined in a public boardinghouse. He rode around the city of Washington not in a coach but on horseback. He wore no powdered wig, and he sometimes answered the door of the president's house in his robe and slippers or in "old-fashioned clothes, which were not in the nicest order, or of the most elegant kind." At state dinners guests sat pell-mell instead of according to the rigid standards of diplomatic protocol. He replaced the weekly formal levees with informal dinners three or four times a week with a dozen or so members of Congress at a time. He stopped holding celebrations of his birthday and sent his annual messages to Congress in writing rather than presenting it personally. He made himself accessible to and familiar with the people. In personal meetings he was "a little awkward in his first address, but you are immediately at ease in his presence. His manners are inviting and not uncourtly; and his voice flexible and distinct. He bears the marks of intense thought and perseverance in his countenance. . . . His smile is very engaging and impresses you with cheerful frankness. His familiarity, however, is tempered with great calmness of manner and with becoming propriety. Open to all, he seems willing to stand the test of inquiry, and to be weighed in the balance only by his merit and attainments."[72] This lack of formality and openness was not merely a matter of style or political expediency. This was how Jefferson liked to live.

But when the occasion required, Jefferson could present a completely different, more formal image. Federalist senator William Plumer of New Hampshire described one of Jefferson's congressional dinners composed of two senators, ten representatives (including Jefferson's two sons-in-law), and his private secretary. The president "was well dressed—A new suit of black—silk hose—shoes—clean linen, & his hair highly powdered." The dinner "was elegant & rich—his wines very good—there were eight different kinds of which there were rich Hungary, & still richer *Tokay*." No toasts were made either during or after dinner so that guests could limit their consumption. Jefferson also had "on the table two bottles of water brought from the river Mississippi, & a quantity of the Mammoth cheese. This cheese, was one made by some Democrats in Massachusetts two or three years since, & presented to Mr. Jefferson. It weighed 1200 lb. & is very far from being good." The mammoth cheese (four feet wide in diameter, fifteen inches thick, and weighing 1,235 pounds) was made in the summer of 1801 by the Baptist congregation of Cheshire, Massachusetts, allegedly from the milk of 900 Republican cows. It was transported down the Hudson River on a sloop to Baltimore and then by a wagon drawn by six horses and was presented to Jefferson as part of the customary New Year's Day gifts. It was inscribed: "The greatest cheese in America—for the greatest man in America." Because Jefferson opposed this monarchical custom of giving gifts, he made a $200 donation to the congregation (considerably more than the retail price of the cheese). Plumer noted that the president's table had "a great variety of pies, fruit & nuts." He also served ice cream balls placed between warmed pastry. Jefferson "performed the honors of the table with great facility—He was reserved—appeared rather low spirited—conversed little—he is naturally very social & communicative." Plumer noticed that when dinner was announced the president "directs the company to walk, & he is the last that enters the dining room." Another frequent dinner guest, New York senator Samuel L. Mitchill, wrote that Jefferson "is tall in stature and rather spare in flesh. His dress and manners are very plain; he is grave, or rather sedate, but without any tincture of pomp, ostentation, or pride, and occasionally can smile, and both hear and relate humorous stories as well as any other man of social feelings."[73]

Jefferson's determination to be conciliatory was tested immediately. Federalists feared that the president would yield to the demands of partisan Republicans who wanted all Federalist officeholders replaced with Republicans. Instead, Jefferson vowed to retain qualified officeholders who were doing a good job. Only incompetent officials, those who were overtly partisan, and those appointed by President Adams during his lame-duck last two months would be removed. For the most part Jefferson stuck to his policy, and therefore he satisfied neither Federalists nor the more ardent wing of his own party. With the aim of redressing the imbalance in federal service, Jefferson filled all vacancies with Republicans.

Within weeks of taking office, Jefferson developed a policy of not responding to office seekers. The answer to a job solicitation would "be found in what is done or not done." Applicants would be informed "by the fact": if he received a commission, an applicant would know he got the appointment; with no commission, he could be assured that someone else had been nominated. Toward the end of his presidency, Jefferson explained the difficulty of making appointments. Throughout his tenure he found that

> solicitations for office are the most painful incidents to which an Executive magistrate is exposed. The ordinary affairs of a nation offer little difficulty to a person of any experience; but the gift of office is the dreadful burden which oppresses him. A person who wishes to make it an engine of self-elevation, may do wonders with it; but to one who wishes to use it conscientiously for the

public good, without regard to the ties of blood or friendship, it creates enmities without number, many open, but more secret, and saps the happiness and peace of his life.

His policy was "to make the best appointment my information & judgment enable me to do, & then fold myself up in the mantle of conscience & abide unmoved by the peltings of the storm."[74]

Jefferson's policy of retaining most officeholders did not extend to the "midnight appointments" made by President Adams during his lame-duck months. The outgoing Federalist Congress passed the Judiciary Act of 1801, which created sixteen new circuit courts, one for each state, each with its own lifetime judge as well as the whole panoply of court officials, including clerks, bailiffs, marshals, and reporters. All of Adams's appointments were Federalists, many of them overtly partisan. Because federal judges could not be removed, Jefferson worked with Congress to repeal that act and replace it with the Judiciary Act of 1802, which dismissed no judge directly but simply eliminated the courts. The Supreme Court wrestled with the constitutionality of this action and reluctantly acquiesced.

Jefferson's conflict with the federal judiciary continued. When the Constitution was first proposed, Jefferson opposed the omission of a bill of rights because he wanted such a declaration to be used by judges as a "legal check" in defense of liberty. The independence of the judiciary, Jefferson told Madison, "merits great confidence for their learning and integrity." However, judges in the 1790s had not protected rights but had become instruments of partisan oppression, especially in prosecuting cases under the Sedition Act. One of Jefferson's first acts as president was to pardon all those convicted under that act. He then encouraged the House of Representatives to impeach New Hampshire federal judge John Pickering, who was alcoholic, insane, and partisan while presiding over cases. The Senate then convicted and removed Pickering. According to Senator Plumer, the difficulty of this process of impeaching and convicting judges led Jefferson to favor a constitutional amendment to remove judges by address: removal by the president upon the request of both houses of Congress. When that amendment failed to move forward, Jefferson encouraged the House to impeach Samuel Chase, an associate justice of the U.S. Supreme Court. For whatever reason,

Jefferson seems not to have pursued the impeachment, possibly because Secretary of State James Madison and Secretary of the Treasury Albert Gallatin convinced him of the impropriety of making the judiciary subservient to the other two branches of government. A majority of the Senate voted to convict Chase on only two of the eight charges against him, not the two-thirds majority needed for removal. The full-scale attack on judges ended here, although Jefferson would have a lifelong animosity for the federal courts, led by Chief Justice Marshall. After Marshall's decision in *M'Culloch v. Maryland* (1819), Jefferson complained that "the constitution . . . is a mere thing of wax in the hands of the judiciary, which they may twist and shape into any form they please." According to Jefferson, "the germ of dissolution of our federal government is in the constitution of the federal judiciary; an irresponsible body (for impeachment is scarcely a scare-crow), working like gravity by night and by day, gaining a little to-day & a little to-morrow, and advancing its noiseless step like a thief, over the field of jurisdiction, until all shall be usurped from the states, & the government of all be consolidated into one."[75]

Chief Justice Marshall had his own theory to explain Jefferson's attitude toward the judiciary. "The great Lama of the mountains," as Marshall called Jefferson, "is among the most ambitious, & I suspect among the most unforgiving of men. His great power is over the mass of the people & this power is chiefly acquired by professions of democracy. Every check on the wild impulse of the moment is a check on his own power, & he is unfriendly to the source from which it flows. He looks, of course, with ill will at an independent judiciary." Marshall declared "that in a free country with a written constitution, any intelligent man should wish a dependent judiciary, or should think that the constitution is not a law for the court as well as the legislature, would astonish me if I had not learnt from observation that, with many men, the judgment is completely controlled by the passions." By the 1820s, according to Marshall, there was

A deep design to convert our government into a mere league of States. . . . The attack upon the judiciary is in fact an attack upon the union. The judicial department is well understood to be that through which the government may be attacked most successfully, because it is without patronage, & of course without power, and it is equally well understood that every subtraction from its jurisdiction is a vital wound to the government itself. The attack upon it therefore is a marked battery aimed at the government itself. The whole attack, if not originating with Mr. Jefferson, is obviously approved & guided by him.[76]

Jefferson felt that his most important action as president would be to pay off the federal debt. Secretary Hamilton believed that a national debt was a blessing in that it tied the interest of the creditors to the central government; Jefferson believed that a national debt was a source of corruption and an evil that required high taxes to pay interest and principal to a favored class of citizen.

Albert Gallatin, Jefferson's secretary of the treasury, devised a program to retire the entire federal debt in sixteen years. After eliminating virtually all federal domestic taxes, Gallatin estimated annual revenue at $9 million from duties on imported goods and the sale of government land. He proposed that $7 million annually be earmarked to paying off the debt. This left $2 million for the annual cost of government. The army was reduced to garrison duty on the frontier, much of the navy was decommissioned and sold off, and the civil list was held stable. When Jefferson took office the federal government employed a mere 127 people in the capital. When he retired in 1809, even with the doubling of the size of the country, only 123 people served in Washington, D.C. With commerce greatly expanding, Gallatin's revenue estimates were regularly exceeded, and by 1806 the government was running a surplus beyond its scheduled payment of the debt. To assist Gallatin, Jefferson pragmatically kept the Bank of the United States functioning because it served a useful purpose in handling the government's money. Gallatin, however, did sell all of the government's stock in the bank.

Foreign affairs threatened Jefferson's austerity program. In 1801 the pasha of Tripoli, one of the Barbary States, again attacked and captured American merchantmen. As in the mid-1780s, Jefferson felt that the best way to handle this attack was with a show of military force. Unsanctioned by Congress, he sent a small fleet to the Mediterranean with instructions to search for and destroy the enemy's ships and blockade their ports. Such measures would be less expensive than convoying

American merchantmen with naval escorts. After some initial successes the war with Tripoli bogged down. Jefferson's opponents said, "It is his war." They blamed the president for, in Jefferson's own words, sending "the *least* possible competent force"; excessive frugality had prolonged the conflict and endangered American lives. Senator Plumer of New Hampshire thought "it *bad policy, & base wickedness,* for a President to send brave men where they must inevitably be destroyed for the want of an adequate force. Had he sent a sufficient number of men & ships it would have been expensive—it might have endangered his reputation for economy & lessened his popularity with the rabble but would most probably have saved the lives of deserving men. He ought to have sent something more than a sufficiency—enough to inspire the men with confidence—to guard against accidents—& to insure success."[77] However, by 1805 the pasha realized the war with America was counterproductive, and he signed a peace treaty. Treaties were also signed with Algiers and Tunis. The United States became the only commercial nation whose ships could sail safely in the region without paying tribute.

A more serious diplomatic problem arose when in October 1802 Spain announced the closing of the port of New Orleans to American trade. Under President Washington a treaty with Spain had formally opened the Mississippi River and the port of New Orleans to American navigation. Unbeknownst to Americans, Spain and France, now allies fighting Great Britain, had agreed secretly to transfer all of the Louisiana territory from Spanish to French control. Napoleon dreamed of recreating the French Empire in the Western Hemisphere, and the Spanish saw the French possession as an effective buffer separating Spain's lucrative Mexican colonies from the dangerous, ever-expanding American settlements. Jefferson viewed the transfer of Louisiana from a weak and ineffective Spanish rule to France as a danger. Writing to Robert R. Livingston, America's new minister to France, without the benefit of secret code, Jefferson indirectly let Napoleon know that a French acquisition of Louisiana would lead to an American alliance with Britain.

Jefferson then authorized Livingston to purchase New Orleans and West Florida for $10 million. As these diplomatic negotiations were transpiring, war fever raged in the American West, and a grand French army sent to protect the new French holdings was decimated by rebellious slaves and fever in Saint-Domingue. In need of money to carry on his European wars, Napoleon offered to sell America the entire Louisiana territory, stretching over 1,000 miles from the Mississippi River to the Rocky Mountains, for $15 million. Uncertain of the constitutionality of buying territory from another country, Jefferson thought about seeking a constitutional amendment to authorize the purchase, but he realized that the opportunity had to be seized. He agreed to the purchase, creating for America an "empire for liberty." Minor opposition to the purchase arose in Congress, especially from New England Federalists who saw their region's relative strength in the Union weakened by such an immense acquisition of territory in which slavery might be permitted. The Senate ratified the treaty by a vote of 24 to 7. Already planning a scientific and military expedition to the Pacific Ocean, Jefferson now appointed his secretary Meriwether Lewis and William Clark to lead an indomitable corps of discovery across the continent.

With these major accomplishments, Jefferson was easily reelected. To avoid a repetition of the political and constitutional crisis posed by the election of 1800, the newly adopted Twelfth Amendment to the Constitution provided that candidates for president and vice president would run together as a ticket. With New York's elder statesman George Clinton replacing Aaron Burr as Jefferson's vice president, the Republican ticket resoundingly defeated the Federalist ticket of Charles Cotesworth Pinckney and Rufus King by an electoral vote of 162 to 14. Jefferson was popular not only with the general public but with Congress as well. Vermont senator Stephen Roe Bradley said "that Mr. Jefferson's influence in Congress was irresistible—that it was alarming—That if he should recommend to us to repeal the Gospels of the Evangelist, a majority of Congress would do it."[78]

When Jefferson's popularity was at its greatest and reelection was imminent, personal disaster struck. On April 17, 1804, Jefferson's younger daughter Polly died shortly after delivering her third child. With only Patsy surviving, Jefferson felt that he had "lost even the half of all I had."[79]

Jefferson's second administration was nearly as dismal as his first had been triumphal. As the European war intensified, both Britain and France preyed on American shipping. Wanting to avoid war at almost any cost, Jefferson and Secretary of State Madison used an embargo on commerce as diplomatic leverage to moderate French and British naval aggression against neutral shipping. Nothing was achieved except economic hardship within America, large-scale smuggling of American goods outside of the country, and political opposition soaring to new heights in New England. Mathew Carey, a prominent Philadelphia printer, reported that had Jefferson been a Nero and Madison a Caligula, they could not have been "more completely abhorred & detested" than they were in New England.[80]

Shortly after his reelection Jefferson let it be known that he would not seek a third term; he would follow the two-term precedent set by Washington. Senator Plumer considered this disclosure "as one of the most imprudent acts of Mr. Jefferson's public life," for as a lame-duck president, Jefferson lost political leverage. Several state legislatures and various private and public groups asked Jefferson to seek a third term, and for a while he did nothing to suppress these overtures, thus regaining some of his power. But by 1807 he announced publicly that he would not seek reelection. At this point he stepped back and refused to make decisions that would affect his successor. His opponents said "the President wants nerve—he has not even confidence in himself . . . he has been in the habit of trusting almost implicitly in Mr. Madison. Madison has acquired a complete ascendancy over him." Federalists viewed Madison as "too cautious—too fearful & timid to direct the affairs of this nation," and many in the country agreed that there was no proper leadership. After Madison was elected president in the fall of 1808, Jefferson offered only opinion while the president-elect made all final decisions that Jefferson clothed "with the forms of authority."[81] In many ways the last year of Jefferson's presidency was rudderless as the nation drifted between war and peace. Senator Plumer condemned the president. "Mr. Jefferson is too timid—too irresolute—too fickle—he wants nerve—he wants firmness & resolution. A wavering doubtful hesitating mind joined with credulity is oftentimes as injurious to the nation as a wicked depraved heart."[82]

Last Retirement

Jefferson looked forward to retirement. On nearly the last day of his presidency, he wrote an old friend about retiring "to my family, my books & farms." Others now would be buffeted by political storms, and he would not envy them. "Never," he wrote, "did a prisoner, released from his chains, feel such relief as I shall on shaking off the shackles of power. Nature intended me for the tranquil pursuits of science, by rendering them my supreme delight. But the enormities of the times in which I have lived, have forced me to take a part in resisting them, and to commit myself on the boisterous ocean of political passions."[83]

Jefferson attended the inauguration of his successor but tried to be as inconspicuous as possible, knowing that the day belonged to James Madison. After taking a week to settle his affairs and pack his belongings, Jefferson sent three wagons overland and a number of trunks via water to Monticello. He himself traveled by carriage until the roads became so "excessively bad" on the last three days that he rode on horseback alone, the final eight hours "through as disagreeable a snow storm as I was ever in."[84]

Patsy and her eight children greeted him. She and her husband lived on a neighboring plantation, but she regularly moved to Monticello when her father visited. She and her children, including another three born after 1809, would live at Monticello for the remaining seventeen years of Jefferson's life. Patsy would outlive her father by ten years.

Supervising his gardens and fields and rearing his grandchildren took up much of Jefferson's time. He established a large vegetable garden and enjoyed planting flowers and trees. The latter were not for his own "gratification" but for "posterity"; "a Septuagenary," he wrote, "has no right to count on anything beyond annuals." The former president loved trees. As secretary of state in Philadelphia, he had lived in a house that was "entirely embosomed in high plane trees, with good grass below, & under them I breakfast, dine, write, read, & receive my company. What would I not give that the trees planted nearest round the house at Monticello were full grown." While hosting one of his dinner parties as president, Jefferson had exclaimed, "How I wish that I possessed the power of a despot." The guests sat astonished before Jefferson finished his idea. "Yes, I wish I was a despot that I might save the noble, the beautiful trees that are daily falling sacrifices to the cupidity of their owners, or the necessity of the poor."[85] Now that he was retired, he would plant trees on his own mountain. Jefferson loved to work in the garden. If he were to relive his life, "it should have been on a rich spot of earth, well watered, and near a good market for the productions of the garden. No occupation is so delightful to me as the culture of the earth, & no culture comparable to that of the garden. Such a variety of subjects, some one always coming to perfection, the failure of one thing repaired by the success of another, & instead of one harvest, a continued one thro' the year. Under a total want of demand except for our family table. I am still devoted to the garden. But tho' an old man, I am but a young gardener."[86]

Visitors streamed into Monticello, many making the somewhat arduous three-day journey from Washington City. Perhaps typical was Margaret Bayard Smith and her husband William, editor of the influential Washington newspaper the *National Intelligencer,* both close friends of the former president.[87] The Smiths arrived at Monticello on July 29, 1809, only five months after Jefferson had retired. After crossing the Rivanna, described by Mrs. Smith as "a wild & romantic little river," they wound their way up Jefferson's little mountain. The "untamed woodland," undeveloped by Jefferson's "superintending care," surprised Mrs. Smith. "Winding upwards" over a seemingly "endless road," they finally spied a cornfield, but the road continued "wild & uncultivated." After two miles they reached the summit. Overcome with emotion, Mrs. Smith gazed upon the magnificent vista stretching for over sixty miles all around with the majestic "blue mountains, in all their grandeur." As their carriage approached the house, Jefferson appeared on horseback, returning from his "morning ride." He welcomed the Smiths and brought them through the main hall of the manor house into a drawing room where they relaxed and enjoyed refreshments with Jefferson and Patsy.

At 5:00 p.m. the first of two bells rang, calling the family and guests to assemble for dinner. The second bell signaled that seats should be taken at the cloth-covered table as dinner was ready to be served. The Smiths joined a dozen family members, including Jefferson, his daughter and son-in-law, the grandchildren, and a young man resident at Monticello studying law with Jefferson. "The table was plainly, but genteely & plentifully spread." Jefferson's French and Italian wines were followed by Madeira and "a sweet ladies wine." After dessert the company stayed seated in conversation. Because Jefferson withdrew after breakfast either to his chambers for writing or riding throughout the plantation, this after-dinnertime was reserved for the family. When the conversations ended, the company separated, and some took walks throughout the maze of mountaintop roads and pathways. They passed by Jefferson's vegetable garden, which was not yet completely established. It consisted of a plot of leveled land terraced on the south side of the mountain stretching 800 by 40 feet. A second similarly sized terraced garden was scheduled to be erected slightly below the first one. After the walk the adults reconvened in the drawing room where at 9:00 p.m. tea and fruit were served. Jefferson usually retired after the tea, not partaking of the fruit. The rest of the company retired within an hour.

Mrs. Smith awakened early the next morning to view the sunrise. She gazed down upon a vast ocean of fog punctured only intermittently by the tops of forested mountains looking like islands. Often the morning was tinctured with showers or mists during which the clouds threw large masses of shade onto the mountains interspersed with a variety of spots lit by the sunshine. Rainbows often plunged downward to the river 500 feet below. On rare occasions a moonlight rainbow appeared. Like dinner, breakfast was announced with two bells and consisted of tea, coffee, muffins, wheat and corn bread, butter, and cold ham. After breakfast the family dispersed. Jefferson "went to his apartments, the door of which is never opened but by himself." The seclusion seemed so sacred that Mrs. Smith told Jefferson "it was his sanctum sanctorum." Jefferson's son-in-law left to ride over to his plantation, not usually returning till the evening. Charles Bankhead, the law student and recent husband of Patsy's oldest daughter, went off to his study in an adjoining building, while Patsy's oldest son, Jefferson Randolph, left to survey a tract of woodland. Patsy took her younger children to the nursery where she cared for them. She also served as their tutor when not occupied with the supervision of the housekeeping chores. After breakfast visitors either retired to their rooms or took walks or rides throughout the grounds. Those who read filled their time with books from Jefferson's extensive library. Then, between 4:00 p.m. and 5:00 p.m., the dinner bells would ring again.

Jefferson greatly enjoyed his early years of retirement. Soon, however, the country was at war with Great Britain, and some of President Madison's advisers put forward a plan that called for Jefferson's return to government service. John Mason, superintendent of Indian trade, Richard Rush, in the State Department, and Gabriel Duvall, long-time comptroller of the treasury and recently appointed associate justice of the Supreme Court, all conversed and addressed the president separately suggesting that Secretary of State James Monroe be named as the army's field commander and that Jefferson fill the cabinet vacancy. Duvall wrote that "altho' Mr. Jefferson has already attained the pinnacle of political fame, his condescension to fill the office of Secretary of State would evince such genuine & disinterested patriotism that it could not fail to increase the veneration with which the people of the present age regard his character, & to perpetuate it with posterity."[88]

Rush told the president that Monroe's military commission would only be half the remedy.

> Who will fill the chasm he would leave? To deprive the nation of the hopes to which it clings in this quarter as to part of the wisdom required in its councils; to deprive you, too, Sir, of such services at such a time would not do! Where, then, is the substitute? Shall I presume to suggest one? not impracticable I trust, effectual—more than heart could wish—I am sure: Where, Sir, is the illustrious Jefferson? I, indeed, can be no stranger, more than all others, to his great age, to his long, useful, arduous, services; to his love of retirement, to his claims to be now exempt from toil. But, Sir, might he not still be prevailed upon to lend the mighty weight of his name—of his venerable years—yet a little longer, to the service of his country when a new crisis addresses itself, as it now would; to his feelings of constant devotion to her cause? May not his venerable and now almost canonized form be seen to step forth to this post; to leave the shades of his secluded and beloved mansion at such a time, at such a call? The sacrifice would, indeed, be great; but, to him, what sacrifice would be too great when his country was in question, her benefit, her highest interests, the stake? Then, Sir, I speak, I am sure, the language of millions when I say, depression would give place to joy, confidence rise to enthusiasm! Then would the great republican family of the union be one—feel with but one heart, rise up in its whole strength! Such an event, Sir, and the best hopes of the patriot are made sure! Such an event, and the glory of the setting days of the then greatest of patriots is more than ever crowned![89]

Mason, who forwarded Rush's letter to the president, entirely agreed with the plan. The army desperately needed Monroe, and the objection to his leaving your Cabinet, at this time, can be overcome in no way but by Mr. Jefferson in person to supply his Place—and may not the Friends throughout the Continent, of that great and good Man hope, he will, on such an occasion, make the Sacrifice?

His Country would hail him with enthusiastic Joy as Secretary of State! and I even will venture to hope that his lofty mind will consider it no Condescension to aid your councils with his Wisdom and his virtue, at such a time.[90]

Jefferson quickly stifled such suggestions. He was no longer capable of serving. As each year passed he noticed various faculties diminishing. "Last year it was the sight, this it is the hearing, the next something else will be going, until all is gone." He began wearing spectacles at night and when reading small print during the day. His hearing in a group gave him difficulty. He had a little rheumatism in his left hip, and the aching in his wrists caused by dislocations many years before made his writing slow and painful. But fortunately he retained good health, which he ascribed partly to his temperate living—Diet: primarily vegetarian; drink: coffee or tea for breakfast, wine, beer, malt liquor, and cider at other times, but never ardent spirits; exercise: walking a mile winded him but riding a horse six to eight miles a day (and sometimes thirty to forty miles) invigorated him—and partly to a sixty-year ritual of bathing his feet in cold water every morning. In an age of poor dental care, he was proud that he had lost no teeth to age. He slept five to eight hours nightly, "according as my company or the book I am reading interests me." No matter how many hours he slept, he rose with the sun.[91]

Jefferson found "delight" in corresponding with old and intimate friends, especially Benjamin Rush and John Adams, with whom Rush arranged a reconciliation in 1812. On hearing that the two retired presidents had started writing to one another, Rush wrote Adams that "I rejoice in the correspondence which has taken place between you and your old friend Mr. Jefferson. I consider you and him as the North and South Poles of the American Revolution. Some talked, some wrote, and some fought to promote and establish it, but you and Mr. Jefferson *thought* for us all."[92]

Adams tended to write three letters to Jefferson for every one he received from him. But if Jefferson enjoyed writing to friends, the great burden of his retirement was answering the hundreds of letters from strangers who wrote "civilly" and made it "hard to refuse them civil answers." Although this "drudgery of the writing table" denied him the pleasure of reading as much as he would like, yet he still made it a point never to "go to bed without an hour, or half hour's previous reading of something moral, whereon to ruminate in the intervals of sleep."[93]

One of the happiest and yet saddest events in Jefferson's life occurred in 1815. After the British burned the Capitol in Washington during the dark days of the War of 1812, Jefferson offered to replace Congress's library with his own for whatever Congress was willing to pay. Having spent fifty years gathering his magnificent collection of 6,500 volumes, he had "spared no pains, no opportunity or expense, to make it what it is." On his free afternoons in Paris he had searched the bookstores, and he had standing orders at the "principal book-marts" in the major cities of Europe. He acquired "everything which related to America, and indeed whatever was rare and valuable in every science." Most of the volumes were well bound; many elegantly so. It was, quite simply, a literary treasure. Congress paid $23,000 for the library. Ten wagons hauled the books away nailed shut in Jefferson's original bookcases. Jefferson immediately felt the emptiness, the void at Monticello and, unable to restrain himself, started to acquire another library. "I cannot live without books," he told John Adams. He would need fewer now, only those necessary for his own "amusement."[94]

Throughout his life Jefferson wanted to reform education in Virginia. In retirement he again considered the problem and decided to propose something that might be attainable: a publicly supported university. Georgia and North and South Carolina had already established such universities. Jefferson obtained a charter from the state legislature, selected the site, served on the board of visitors and as the first rector, raised the necessary public and private funds, drafted the curriculum, recruited the faculty, designed the plan of the academic village, and drew the architectural plans for the buildings, including the Rotunda, the grand central building modeled after the Pantheon in Rome. About a year before Jefferson's death, after more than a decade of hard work, the University of Virginia opened with its first class of about thirty students.

In December 1824 Daniel Webster spent five days visiting Jefferson at Monticello. The young man took extensive notes describing his remarkable host and their conversations on a myriad of topics.

Mr. Jefferson is between 81 & 82—over 6 ft. high—an ample long frame—rather thin & spare. His head which is not peculiar in its shape is set rather forward upon his shoulders & his neck being long when he is in conversation, or walking, there is a considerable protrusion of his chin.—His head is still well covered with hair, which having been once red & now turning to white, is of an indistinct, light, sandy colour—His eyes are small, & very light & now, neither striking, nor brilliant—His chin is rather long & not sharp. His teeth are still good. His mouth well formed & generally compressed with an expression of benevolence & contentment. His skin formerly light, and freckled, is now rough & bears the marks of age & cutaneous affections. His limbs are uncommonly long & his wrists of extraordinary size. His walk is not precise & military, but easy & swinging. He stoops a little, not so much from age, as from constitutional formation—When sitting he seems short & low, partly from not sitting erect & partly from the disproportionate length of his limbs. He wears a dark grey surtout coat—a yellow kersimere waist coat, with an under one faced with a dingy red. His pantaloons are very loose, long & of the same material with his coat. His hose are grey woolen & his shoes those which bear his name. His whole dress not slovenly, but neglected. He wears a common round hat & when he rides on horseback, a grey strait bodiced coat, & a long spencer of the same material both fastened with pearl buttons. When we first saw him riding, he wore round his neck, instead of a cravat, a white woolen tippet & to guard his feet, black velvet gaiters under his pantaloons. His general appearance indicated an extraordinary degree of health, vivacity & spirits for his age. His sight is still good, as he needs spectacles only in the evening. His hearing is not much impaired, but a number of voices in animated conversation around him, seems to confound it.

He rises in the morning, as soon as he can see the hands of his clock & examines his thermometer immediately, for he keeps a regular meteorological diary. Until breakfast, he employs himself chiefly in writing. He breakfasts at nine. From that hour till dinner, he is employed in his study; excepting that on every fair day he rides from 7 to 14 miles on horseback. He dines at 4; retires to the drawing room about 6, passes the succeeding hours in conversation & goes to bed at nine—His habit of retiring early is so strong that it has become essential to his health. His breakfast is made up of tea & coffee & bread in all the good Virginia varieties of which he does not seem afraid however new & warm. He enjoys his dinner well, taking with his food a large proportion of vegetables. With regard to wine, he may be said to excell both in the knowledge & the use—His preference is for wines of the continent of which he has many sorts of excellent quality. His dinners are in the half French, half Virginia style, in good taste & abundant. No wine served before the cloth is removed. Tea & coffee in the saloon between 7 & 8—His conversation is easy & natural & apparently not ambitious—It is not loud as challenging general attention, but usually address[ed] to the person next to him—The topics, when not selected with regard to the character & feelings of his auditors, are those subjects with which his mind seems now particularly occupied. And these at present may be justly said to be first science & letters & especially the University of Virginia, which will rise it is to be hoped to usefulness & credit under his continued care. When we were with him, his favorite literary subjects were Greek & Anglo-Saxon, & secondly historical recollections of the times of the Revolution & of his residence in France, from 1783 to 89.[95]

As Jefferson got old, he experienced the pain of seeing friends die. He wondered whether it was desirable "to witness the death of all our companions, and merely be the last victim?" He doubted it. Why he asked, would one choose to remain "as a solitary trunk in a desolate field, from which all its former companions have disappeared?" But the survivors have "the traveller's consolation. Every step shortens the distance we have to go; the end of our journey is in sight." He wrote to John Adams that "there is a ripeness of time for death, regarding others as well as ourselves, when it is reasonable we should drop off, and make room for another growth. When we have lived our generation out, we should not wish to encroach on another."[96]

When Abigail Adams died in 1818, Jefferson wrote her spouse John a letter of condolence, as someone who had lost a beloved wife and children.

> Tried myself, in the school of affliction, by the loss of every form of connection which can rive the human heart, I know well, and feel what you have lost, what you have suffered, are suffering, and have yet to endure. The same trials have taught me that, for ills so immeasurable, time and silence are the only medicines. I will not therefore, by useless condolences, open afresh the sluices of your grief nor, altho' mingling sincerely my tears with yours, will I say a word more, where words are vain, but that it is of some comfort to us both that the term is not very distant at which we are to deposit, in the same cerement, our sorrows and suffering bodies, and to ascend in essence to an ecstatic meeting with the friends we have loved and lost and whom we shall still love and never lose again. God bless you and support you under your heavy affliction.[97]

Two years later, facing their own mortality, Jefferson again wrote Adams. "We . . . have done for our country the good which has fallen in our way, so far as commensurate with the faculties given us. That we have not done more than we could cannot be imputed to us as a crime before any tribunal. I look therefore to that crisis, as I am sure you also do, as one 'qui summum nec metuit diem nec optat' [who neither fears the final day nor hopes for it]."[98]

In one of the great coincidences of history, Jefferson and Adams both died only hours apart on July 4, 1826, the fiftieth anniversary of the Declaration of Independence. Recognizing the importance of the symbolism for the new country, both men valiantly held on to life until that glorious anniversary arrived. It was their final gift to a grateful country. On hearing of Jefferson's death, James Madison, his friend for fifty years, wrote that "he lives and will live in the memory and gratitude of the wise & good, as a luminary of Science, as a votary of liberty, as a model of patriotism, and as a benefactor of the human kind."[99]

James Madison

CHAMPION OF LIBERTY & JUSTICE

Preface

The American political system is a complex labyrinth that has survived for over 200 years. Surprisingly, it was a short, shy, soft-spoken, studious man who, more than any other person, laid the foundations of this complicated system. For his contributions James Madison has been called the Father of the Constitution. Madison, however, always shared credit for writing the Constitution. He always regarded it as the work of many heads and many hands, not the offspring of a single mind.

Born in 1751, Madison called himself "a child of the Revolution." Although commissioned a colonel in the Virginia militia, he never served in the military. His battlefields were the legislative and convention chambers. His weapons were not muskets and sabers but words and ideas. In *Federalist* No. 37 Madison wrote of the importance of words in expressing ideas. "The use of words is to express ideas. Perspicuity therefore requires not only that the ideas should be distinctly formed, but that they should be expressed by words distinctly and exclusively appropriated to them. But no language is so copious as to supply words and phrases for every complex idea, or so correct as not to include many equivocally denoting different ideas." Even "when the Almighty himself condescends to address mankind in their own language, his meaning, luminous as it must be, is rendered dim and doubtful, by the cloudy medium through which it is communicated." Madison's object was not to win a particular battle or defeat a specific enemy but to champion liberty and justice whenever they were endangered.

Throughout his lifetime, and throughout American historiography, Madison has been accused of inconsistency: of being an arch nationalist in the 1780s, of opposing and then advocating a federal bill of rights, of being a states' rightist during the 1790s, of being a pragmatist while in power during the first two decades of the nineteenth century, and finally of opposing states' rightists during the last decade and a half of his life. In reality, however, Madison was consistent. His focus was never on a particular type of government. Whenever he saw liberty and justice threatened by a "change of circumstances," he sought means to limit or eliminate the danger.

Madison first saw the danger to liberty and justice in colonial Virginia when Baptist ministers were imprisoned "for publishing their religious Sentiments." He strongly opposed such oppression publicly, and as a political neophyte he worked in the Virginia convention of June 1776 to broaden the religious toleration advocated by George Mason to full freedom of religion. He strongly opposed the new British imperial policy implemented by various ministries after 1763 and joined the movement for independence in the early 1770s. When he saw the danger posed by the states to liberty and justice, he advocated the reduction of state power and the enhancement of federal authority under the Articles of Confederation. When the vices of the state and Confederation governments became apparent and seemingly incapable of being changed within the existing federal arrangement, he sought, through the construction of a new system of government, to achieve liberty, justice, and happiness for his fellow citizens. When Secretary of the Treasury Alexander Hamilton and later the Federalist Party and the federal judiciary threatened liberty and justice through a "forced construction" of the Constitution, Madison argued in the Virginia Resolution of 1798 for a reduction of federal authority and the empowerment of state legislatures in their relationship with the federal government. When the Jeffersonian Republicans assumed power after the Revolution of 1800, Madison adopted a more pragmatic attitude toward the federal government. Finally, during his retirement years Madison opposed the neo-Antifederalists who supported states' rights as a means of preserving their slavery-based culture and economy.

Throughout the 1780s Madison looked to the state courts for protection from oppressive state legislatures. During the debate over ratifying the new U.S. Constitution, Madison predicted that the federal judiciary would protect liberty and justice from oppression from both state and federal governments. In 1789 he proposed the bill of rights as a weapon to be used by federal courts to defend liberty and justice. In the late 1790s, however, Madison looked to the states for protection from the federal judiciary, which was being used as a partisan instrument of oppression. But Madison believed that the Supreme Court under Chief Justice John Marshall "naturally and liberally" interpreted the Constitution to give the federal government the kind of power envisioned by the Federal Convention of 1787 and by Federalists in the ratification debate that followed. Only in the 1819 case of *M'Culloch v. Maryland* did Madison believe that Marshall's court had gone too far with a "forced construction" in expanding the implied powers of the Constitution.

Throughout his long years of service, James Madison worked to defend liberty and justice. Sometimes this required him to emphasize local or state power, sometimes federal power. But he always wanted power to serve the cause of freedom. Thus, in looking at Madison's defense of liberty and justice from wherever danger appeared, we see a remarkable consistency.

Introduction

James Madison entered the national political scene at the end of the War for Independence. Throughout the 1780s he steadily advocated increased powers for Congress under the Articles of Confederation, America's first federal constitution. When it became evident that amendments to the Articles could not be obtained, Madison worked outside of the normal political and constitutional arenas to obtain change.

At the Federal Convention that met in Philadelphia from May through September 1787, Madison was arguably the most influential delegate. He advocated radical alterations both in the structure of the country's constitution and in the relationship between the central government and the states. Madison based his proposals upon (1) his own comprehensive study of the history of confederacies and why they had always failed, (2) his thorough analysis of the weaknesses of Congress and the vices of the states under the Articles of Confederation, (3) his years of studying history, political science, and human nature, and (4) his years of service in Congress and the Virginia House of Delegates.

Madison's contribution to the American political system did not end with the promulgation of the Constitution in September 1787. He became the most important Federalist in the struggle to ratify the Constitution, serving as a clearinghouse of information in New York City, as a coauthor of the monumental *Federalist Papers*, and as the Federalist champion in the Virginia ratifying convention in June 1788, where he successfully battled the renowned Patrick Henry and the revered George Mason.

Denied election to the first U.S. Senate by Patrick Henry's dominance in the Virginia legislature, Madison was elected to the first U.S. House of Representatives. He wrote President George Washington's first inaugural address and for two years served as de facto prime minister, leading the First Congress in putting muscle and fiber on the skeletal Constitution. Hearing the many calls for adding a bill of rights, he introduced the amendments and steered them through the First Congress.

After two years, however, Madison and his longtime political collaborator and friend Secretary of State Thomas Jefferson became increasingly disenchanted with the policies of Secretary of the Treasury Alexander Hamilton. To combat the pro-British, pro-northern, monarchical tendencies of Hamilton, Madison and Jefferson organized an opposition political party. The first American political party system emerged, and a loyal opposition arose to defend liberty from perceived threats.

Contemporaries recognized Madison's political genius, but they disagreed on whether he was pragmatic or impractical. Massachusetts representative Fisher Ames felt that Madison was "too much attached to his theories, for a politician." Although choosing politics as his profession, Madison, according to Ames, thought of it as "rather a science, than a business with him. He adopts his maxims as he finds them in books, and with too little regard to the actual state of things." Hamilton referred to Madison as "a clever man" but too "little Acquainted with the world."[1]

Madison left Congress in 1797. Working from Virginia, he helped Jefferson to achieve the "Revolution of 1800" in which President John Adams and the Federalist Party were defeated. Madison served as Jefferson's secretary of state for eight years during which he experienced the highs of acquiring the vast Louisiana Territory that doubled the size of the United States and the lows of an increasingly hostile domestic response to the administration's inability to combat British and French depredations on the high seas. Madison succeeded Jefferson as president and stumblingly led the country to war with Britain. Peace found the beleaguered president riding a wave of nationalistic pride that raised his popularity. As the country united and partisanship waned, Madison retired to Montpelier, his Virginia piedmont plantation, where he lived until 1836, as one of the last surviving leaders of the Revolutionary era.

Early Life

James Madison was born in the Virginia tidewater at Port Conway, King George County, on March 16, 1751, on his maternal grandmother's ancestral plantation. Four generations earlier his father's ancestors had emigrated to Virginia, acquiring a sizable tract of land through Virginia's generous headright system. Madison's paternal grandfather, Ambrose Madison, moved his family to Orange County in the piedmont. His plantation of over 3,000 acres was perfectly situated. The virgin red soil was rich, the temperatures moderate, and, unlike the tidewater, the location was healthy. Located between the Southwest Mountains and the majestic Blue Ridge Mountains, about thirty miles to the west, the plantation had gently rolling fertile, arable land, good pasture, valuable timber stands, and numerous streams and springs. Mount Pleasant, re-named Montpelier around 1780, was the only home that James Madison would ever know.

Ambrose Madison died in 1732 and left his estate to his son, who was only nine years old. The plantation was run by Ambrose's widow, Frances Taylor Madison, until her son, James Madison Sr., reached age eighteen. James Sr. married Nelly Conway in September 1749. Just seventeen, Nelly was the youngest daughter of a merchant-planter of Caroline County. By 1757 the Madison plantation had grown to over 4,000 acres, and James Sr. was among the most prominent planters in Orange County. By 1782 the family owned at least 118 slaves. James Sr. built a new mansion house at its present location in 1759 and presided over Montpelier until his death in 1801 at the age of seventy-eight. His widow, James Madison Jr.'s mother, resided at Montpelier until her death at the age of ninety-eight in 1829.

Like most children in colonial America, James Jr. learned to read and write from his mother and grandmother. His early education at home probably included instruction from the local Anglican minister. A major turning point in James's life occurred when in June 1762 he was sent seventy miles away to a boarding school in King and Queen County operated by Donald Robertson, a forty-five-year-old Scottish immigrant who had been educated at Aberdeen and the University of Edinburgh. Madison was resident in the school for five years. He would later write of Robertson, "All that I have in life I owe largely to that man."[2]

Madison left Robertson's school at the age of sixteen. He returned to Montpelier where he was given more advanced personal instruction by the Reverend Thomas Martin, the newly appointed rector of Madison's home church. Martin had graduated from the College of New Jersey in 1762 and now took up residence at Montpelier where he instructed all of the Madison children. It was through Martin's influence that Madison decided to attend the College of New Jersey (now Princeton University) instead of the College of William and Mary, the customary choice of young Virginia gentlemen. The location of William and Mary in the sickly tidewater and the recent arrival of the Reverend John Witherspoon from Scotland to be the president of the Presbyterian institution in New Jersey also helped Madison decide to go north.

In the summer of 1769 the frail, bookish eighteen-year-old James Madison arrived in Princeton, and for the next three years he lived in Nassau Hall, the "convenient, airy, and spacious" three-story stone building that served as both a residence hall and classroom building. Madison easily passed the freshman exam and accelerated through the three-year program in two years, graduating in September 1771. He was a serious student. His mentor, President Witherspoon, said of him that "during the whole time he was under [my] tuition, [I] never knew him to do nor to say an improper thing." His studies consumed most of his time and energy. "His only relaxation from study consisted in walking and conversation."[3] After graduating and still unclear as to what his future career would be, Madison continued studying with Witherspoon. Throughout his years at Princeton, but especially during the last eighteen months, Madison was immersed in the history and literature of seventeenth-century England with its epic struggle between king and Parliament, as the debate between the American colonies and Parliament became increasingly angry. Witherspoon taught Madison to be a deep-thinking scholar. Madison left Princeton never wanting to "intoxicate his brain with Idleness & dissipation."[4] Witherspoon, a revolutionary who signed the Declaration of Independence for New Jersey, taught Madison to be a patriot, supporting America's cause against Parliament.

Madison remained frail, suffering periodically from the bilious lax, an intestinal disorder that probably would be diagnosed today as irritable bowel syndrome. This chronic ailment also aggravated his serious condition of hemorrhoids. Since his early youth he also seemed to be plagued by what was called epileptoid hysteria. Madison described the condition as "a constitutional liability to sudden attacks, somewhat resembling Epilepsy, and suspending the intellectual functions. They continued thro' life, with prolonged intervals." It was this ailment that kept him off ships for fear that sailing would bring on attacks. Throughout his youth Madison looked pale, feeble, and chronically ill. As a young man, he expected not to have "a long or healthy life."[5] This sense of foreboding pervaded his thinking as he finished his formal education and returned to Virginia.

Revolutionary Public Servant

Although Madison thought about political matters, he did "not meddle with Politicks." He determined "to read Law occasionally and . . . procured books for that purpose." He pictured the law, medicine, and commerce as "honorable and usefull professions," but he remained uncertain about his future. The law, he wrote, "alone can bring into use many parts of knowledge . . . & pay you for cultivating the Arts of Eloquence. It is a sort of General Lover that wooes all the Muses and Graces. This cannot be said so truly of commerce and Physic." He found himself fascinated by "the principles & Modes of Government [which] are too important to be disregarded by an Inquisitive mind and I think are well worthy [of] a critical examination by all students that have health & Leisure." He spent much of his time reading and thinking, what he called "my customary enjoyments [of] Solitude and Contemplation."[6] Teaching his younger siblings took up only a small amount of his time.

One of Madison's first forays into politics occurred in January 1774 after he heard about the imprisonment of several Baptist ministers in adjacent Culpeper County. They were charged with "publishing their religious Sentiments" without getting a license from the established Anglican Church. Appalled at these violations of the free exercise of religion, Madison "squabbled and scolded, abused and ridiculed so long about it, to so little purpose that I am without common patience." He was pleased that petitions "were forming among the Persecuted Baptists and I fancy it is in the thoughts of the Presbyterians also to intercede for greater liberty in matters of Religion." Madison, however, was pessimistic about liberalizing the official government policy toward dissident religions. "Incredible and extravagant stories" about religious "Enthusiasm" had been propagated in the legislature, making any kind of reform doubtful. That was indeed unfortunate for Virginia, Madison firmly believed, because "religious bondage shackles and debilitates the mind and unfits it for every noble enterprize, every expanded prospect."[7] This early encounter with religious persecution inspired Madison. Throughout his life he would be an enemy to violations of personal rights. His outrage now energized him and perhaps gave a turn to his career.

In April 1774 Madison accompanied his younger brother William to Princeton to enroll him in Princeton's prep school. While in Philadelphia, Madison heard about Parliament's draconian response to the Boston Tea Party. The merciless closing of the port of Boston, the suspension of the colony's charter, the suspension of the civil government, and the appointment of a military governor seemed to be disproportionately harsh and a gross attack on the liberty of the colony. Madison and other Virginians joined with Americans from every colony in denouncing this outrageous, despotic legislation. Virginians, Madison wrote, "are willing to fall in with the Other Colonies in any expedient measure, even if that should be the universal prohibition of Trade."[8] They all sensed that someday Parliament's tyranny might be applied to their own colony.

Madison advocated immediate action, instead of waiting for the British response to American petitions protesting the imperial policies. "Would it not be advisable," he argued, "as soon as possible to begin our defence & to let its continuance or cessation depend on the success of a petition to his majesty. Delay on our part emboldens our adversaries and improves their schemes, whilst it abates the ardor of the Americans inspired with recent Injuries and affords opportunity to our secret enemies to disseminate discord & disunion." Madison felt that "the frequent Assaults that have been made on America, Boston especially, will in the end prove of real advantage."[9]

The Intolerable Acts, as Americans referred to them, were but the final actions in the new imperial policy aimed at gaining greater control over Britain's American colonies. Madison and other colonists saw the dispute with Parliament as a confrontation over the principle of self-government, the essence of liberty. Americans since their settlement had exercised a significant amount of self-rule. But according to Parliament, any authority exercised by the colonies was a grant from the king and Parliament that could be revoked at the will of the imperial authority. The Declaratory Act, passed in 1766 a day after Parliament repealed the hated Stamp Act, proclaimed Parliament's unalterable position that it could bind Americans "in all cases whatsoever." Much of Madison's future career would center over these very same issues of the division of power between federal and state governments.

In December 1774 Madison was elected to the Orange County Committee of Safety, which was charged with enforcing the Continental Association established by the First Continental Congress. The Association prohibited most colonial exportations and importations in an attempt to pressure British economic interests to lobby Parliament to change its policies toward America. Madison described the Revolutionary fervor mounting in Virginia.

> The proceedings of the Congress are universally approved of in this Province & I am persuaded will be faithfully adhered to. A spirit of Liberty & Patriotism animates all degrees and denominations of men. Many publicly declare themselves ready to join the Bostonians as soon as violence is offered them or resistance thought expedient. In many counties independent companies are forming and voluntarily subjecting themselves to military discipline that they may be expert & prepared against a time of Need. I hope it will be a general thing thro'ought this province. Such firm and provident steps will either intimidate our enemies or enable us to defy them.[10]

In October 1775 Madison was commissioned a colonel in the Orange County militia. His poor health, however, kept him from military service.

In the spring of 1776, Madison was elected to the Virginia provincial convention, the effective ruling authority in Virginia since the royal government had collapsed almost a year earlier. Here Madison came into contact with some of Virginia's most prominent statesmen. On May 15, 1776, the convention voted, with Madison in the majority, to instruct its delegates to the Second Continental Congress to propose a declaration of independence.

A backbencher throughout all of his convention service, Madison's passionate belief in religious freedom informed his service on the committee to draft a declaration of rights and a new state constitution. George Mason, a prominent Fairfax County planter, drafted a declaration of rights which declared that "all men should enjoy the fullest Toleration in the Exercise of Religion, according to the Dictates of Conscience." At first Madison attempted to win a complete disestablishment of the Anglican Church. After this effort failed, he was able to replace Mason's draft advocating mere toleration of dissenters with the positive statement that "all men are equally entitled to the free exercise of religion, according to the dictates of conscience."[11]

The Virginia convention adjourned on July 5, 1776, unaware that the Second Continental Congress had carried out its instruction to declare independence. In October 1776 the convention reassembled. It was at this time that Madison met Thomas Jefferson. The two served on a committee on religion. Jefferson also advocated a complete separation of church and state. But like Madison's proposal, it was as yet too radical to be adopted.

In April 1777 Madison announced his intention to stand for election to the House of Delegates under the new state constitution of June 1776. The custom of the time called for candidates for public office to provide voters with "spirituous liquors, and other treats" on election day; "swilling the planters with Bumpo" it was called. Madison was a righteous young man who thought such practices "equally inconsistent with the purity of moral and of republican principles." His opponent, a tavern keeper, had no such qualms. The voters thought Madison was motivated by either "pride or parsimony," and he lost the election,[12] but in the process he learned a valuable lesson for he never lost another popular election in his long political career.

On November 15, 1777, the House of Delegates elected Madison to the eight-man council of state, which shared executive power with the governor. His election to the council suggests that he was a well-respected young politician. Madison's two years of service were momentous. Much of the day-to-day operation of government had been transferred from the occasionally sitting legislature to the council, which sat daily except for the sickly season stretching from mid-July to mid-November. The Continental Congress and the states faced desperate financial conditions as their paper money depreciated to worthlessness. Raising supplies to keep the army in the field became a struggle. As Madison took on more and more responsibility on the council, Governor Patrick Henry gave way to Benjamin Harrison and then to Thomas Jefferson. When the British army opened a new theater of action in the South, the situation became dangerous for Jefferson and Virginia.

Madison impressed Jefferson and the legislature with his hard work in one committee after another. His diligence was rewarded in December 1779, when the legislature elected Madison to represent Virginia in the Continental Congress. Madison informed Governor Harrison that he accepted the appointment and gave his "assurances that as far as fidelity and zeal can supply the place of abilities the interests of my Country shall be punctually promoted."[13] Madison eagerly embraced this new challenge, a difficult and arduous assignment for most.

In Congress the First Time

Madison had few of the hesitancies that other men had about going to Congress. Unmarried, he left no wife and children behind when he traveled to far-off Philadelphia. Because his father, in his late fifties, still managed the family plantation, Madison did not have to rely on an overseer and worry how the plantation and other affairs were being handled. While many other delegates needed their salaries to meet their considerable expenses while in Philadelphia, Madison's family wealth provided him with financial security. Delegates from rural areas often found the urban life of Philadelphia unpleasant, but Madison looked forward to escaping from his "Obscure Corner" of the world and returning to "the Fountain-Head of Political and Literary Intelligence." He had long wanted to breathe the "free Air" of Philadelphia again: "it will mend my Constitution [that is, his health] & confirm my principles."[14]

The work of Congress was primarily carried on in dozens of committees; the most active delegates had twenty to thirty committee assignments. Mornings and afternoons were spent either in formal congressional sessions or in committees, while in the evenings delegates frequently socialized in taverns, inns, and boardinghouses with fellow committee

members, often discussing the difficult issues confronting their committees. Most members of Congress hated this committee drudgery as well
as the monotony of Congress when it was actually in session. Madison
reveled in it and wrote huge numbers of committee reports.

Seemingly Madison did not make a favorable first impression. He
was always suspicious of "those impertinent fops that abound in every
City to divert you from your business and philosophical amusements.
You may please them more by admitting them to the enjoyment of your
company but you will make them respect and admire you more by
showing your indignation at their follies and by keeping them at a becoming distance." These fops, Madison felt, "breed in Towns and populous places, as naturally as flies do in the Shambles, because there they
get food enough for their Vanity and impertinence." Although almost
thirty years old, Madison still looked like a teenager. Thomas Rodney of
Delaware, only seven years older than his colleague, described Madison
as a young man "who with some little reading in the Law is Just from
the College, and possesses all the Self conceit that is Common to youth
and inexperience in like cases—but is unattended with that graceful-
ness & ease which Sometimes Makes even the impertinence of youth
and inexperience agreeable or at least not offensive." Outside of Congress, Madison fared no better. Martha Dangerfield Bland, the wife of
Congressman Theodorick Bland of Virginia, described the young man
as "a gloomy, stiff creature. They say he is clever in Congress, but out of
it, he has nothing engaging or even bearable in his Manners—the most
unsociable creature in Existence." This was perhaps the last time anyone would say unkind things about Madison's personality. He must have
changed considerably during his Philadelphia years. In the future, even
his political enemies would comment favorably on Madison's charm
and social graces. As he left Philadelphia to return home in December
1783, Eliza House Trist, the daughter of the proprietor of Madison's
boardinghouse, commented on Madison. "He has a Soul replete with
gentleness, humanity and every social virtue." Surely, Trist felt, he could
be elected governor of Virginia, but he "is too amiable in his disposition
to bear up against a torrent of abuse. It will hurt his feelings and injure
his health."[15]

Madison again left Virginia for Congress in March 1780 and did
not return home until December 1783. Throughout this federal service

Madison advocated additional powers for Congress. During his first year he led the movement to cede to Congress Virginia's claims to the land north and west of the Ohio River. He served on the Board of Admiralty and drafted Congress's instructions to U.S. Minister to Spain John Jay, calling on him to assert America's right to navigate the Mississippi River. Described as "a Young Gentleman of Industry and abilities," Madison already was considered one of the leading candidates for the new position of secretary for foreign affairs.[16]

By his second year in Congress, Madison had established a reputation as a diligent, effective legislator, a man who could write legislation and, through compromise, obtain consensus. In many respects he mirrored the image of what George Washington thought a good young legislator ought to be. "If you mean to be a respectable member, and to entitle yourself to the Ear of the House," speak "on important matters—and then make yourself thoroughly acquainted with the subject. Never be agitated by more than a decent warmth, & offer your sentiments with modest diffidence—opinions thus given, are listened to with more attention than when delivered in a dictatorial stile. The latter, if attended to at all, altho they may force conviction, is sure to convey disgust also."[17]

Madison was appointed to a three-man committee charged with drafting an amendment to the Articles of Confederation giving Congress coercive power over the states and their citizens. Madison premised the committee's report on the last of the Articles, which provided "that every State shall abide by the determinations of the United States in Congress assembled on all questions which by this Confederation are submitted to them. And that the Articles of this Confederation shall be inviolably observed by every State." According to Madison, these provisions meant that Congress was vested with "a general and implied power . . . to enforce and carry into effect all the Articles of the said Confederation against any of the States which shall refuse or neglect to abide by such their determinations." Despite the specific limitation in Article II providing that Congress had only those powers that were "expressly delegated" to it, Madison proposed to broaden the powers of Congress over the states and their citizens enormously. If the states failed to pay their requisitions, Congress could use the army and navy to force any delinquent states "to fulfill their federal engagements" by laying an embargo by land and sea on all trade between the delinquent state and other states and foreign countries. Congress's military forces could seize the ships and goods of any delinquent state or any citizen thereof. If Madison had his way, the whole federal relationship would be reversed. States would no longer retain their "sovereignty, freedom and independence." Congress would be supreme. Such a proposal was far too radical for most members of Congress. Consequently, Madison's report was referred to a grand committee (one member from each state), which proposed a far milder report that was submitted to a series of small committees before being allowed to die without any final congressional action.[18]

During Madison's last year in Congress, he served on a committee that proposed a comprehensive financial program for the country. Largely melded together by Madison, the plan called for (1) a 5 percent impost on most imported goods for a maximum of twenty-five years earmarked exclusively to pay the interest and principal on the wartime debt, (2) an annual requisition of $1.5 million apportioned among the states, and (3) an encouragement of western land cessions to Congress by those states that had not yet ceded their western claims. In writing the address that accompanied the financial proposal to the states in April 1783, Madison argued that the success or failure of the Revolution and the future of republican forms of government depended upon how the states responded to the economic proposal.

> The plan thus communicated and explained by Congress must now receive its fate from their Constituents. All the objects comprised in it are conceived to be of great importance to the happiness of this confederated republic, are necessary to render the fruits of the Revolution, a full reward for the blood, the toils, the cares and the calamities which have purchased it. . . . If justice, good faith, honor, gratitude & all the other Qualities which ennoble the character of a nation, and fulfill the ends of Government, be the fruits of our establishments, the cause of liberty will acquire a dignity and lustre, which it has never yet enjoyed; and an example will be set which can not but have the most favorable influence on the rights of mankind. If on the other side, our Governments should be unfortunately blotted

with the reverse of these cardinal and essential Virtues, the great
cause which we have engaged to vindicate, will be dishonored
& betrayed; the last & fairest experiment in favor of the rights
of human nature will be turned against them; and their patrons
& friends exposed to be insulted & silenced by the votaries of
Tyranny and Usurpation.[19]

Madison also played a key role in drafting an amendment to the Articles
to apportion federal expenses based upon population.

In June 1783, while Madison served in Congress, disgruntled soldiers
from the Pennsylvania Line mutinied, descended on Philadelphia, sur-
rounded the statehouse, and sent an ultimatum to the Pennsylvania
Supreme Executive Council meeting there demanding their back pay.
Congress, which was also meeting in the statehouse, felt threatened and
asked Pennsylvania president John Dickinson to call out the state militia. Dickinson refused, and Congress adjourned to Princeton. Madison
grievously felt Congress's embarrassment at not being able to defend
itself. Ashamed for his country, he realized how important it was for
Congress to have coercive authority of its own territory and not to depend on any state for its protection.

Years later Madison remembered some of the amusing aspects of
Congress's exile in the tiny community of Princeton. The lack of hous-
ing forced Madison to share a single small room with fellow Virginian
Joseph Jones. The room had but one bed that the two congressmen
shared. The bed so filled the room "that one was obliged to lie in bed
while the other was dressing." It was a way, Madison joked, of "bringing
members of Congress into close quarters."[20]

In December 1783 Madison, accompanied by Thomas Jefferson,
briefly returned to Philadelphia and then traveled to Annapolis, yet another new residence for Congress. Just as Madison became the most
prominent member of Congress, his federal career ended. The Articles
of Confederation provided that congressional delegates could serve
only three years in any six-year period. Madison had committed himself to the war effort and to acquiring increased power for Congress. He
had become the most important member of Congress through his hard
work in the federal cause. He was now forced to return to Montpelier
and an uncertain future.

❧ Back in Virginia

For the next three years, Madison compartmentalized his life. Each year in the early fall he traveled north to New York and Philadelphia. Each spring, beginning in April 1784, Orange County electors sent him to the House of Delegates in Richmond. The last spring legislative session was held in 1784; thereafter the legislature met only once annually in October, usually adjourning sometime in January. When not traveling north or resident in Richmond, Madison resided at Montpelier.

Madison viewed Montpelier as both a haven and a prison. This was his home. As the eldest son he could be expected to take the lead in operating the plantation, but farming did not interest Madison at this time. His father and brothers recognized Madison's devotion to politics and government and seem willingly to have supported his career. But Madison's dependence on his family made him uncomfortable. Searching for an independent source of income for himself, he approached a number of people with land speculation schemes, but nothing materialized except a small venture with James Monroe along the Mohawk River in New York. Perhaps Madison's dependence on his father, who lived until 1801, when Madison was fifty years old, had a psychological impact on why Madison wanted Congress to be financially independent of the states.

When at Montpelier, Madison divided his time between family affairs and professional activities. He rose with the sun, busied himself with correspondence, and then had a light breakfast. Sequestered again, he read law, did research in his ever-growing library, prepared for the upcoming legislative session, and read newspapers, political tracts, and scientific works. Madison's correspondence expanded with prominent Virginians at home, serving in Congress, and abroad. His favorite correspondent was Thomas Jefferson, then serving as U.S. minister to France. Beginning in 1786, Madison's correspondence with George Washington increased significantly. Madison made time in the day for exercise, walking and riding around the estate. After dinner at 3:00 or 4:00, he spent time with the family and visitors talking about politics and business. Often the evenings ended playing whist, a card game, for half bits until bedtime.

In September and October 1784 he participated in his most ambitious journey north. Linking up with the marquis de Lafayette and
French consul general Barbé-Marbois, he traveled to Fort Stanwix (at
present-day Rome, New York) for a treaty conference with the Iroquois.
Madison and his companions went deep into the wilderness, ford-
ing streams to visit the chief village of the Oneida. It was thrilling but
exhausting, and the trip bonded Madison and Lafayette for life. In 1785
and 1786 Madison spent time in Philadelphia and New York City, meeting with members of Congress and old friends in both cities. He also
took the opportunity to buy books for his library.

In May and November 1784 and October 1785 and 1786, Madison
served in the Virginia House of Delegates. His remarkable service in
Congress had created a reputation for excellent legislative work, and
much was expected of him, though he had never served in the state legislature. In mid-May 1784 William Short, soon to be Jefferson's private
secretary in Paris, reported that "the Assembly have not yet proceeded
to active Business. They have formed great Hopes of Mr. Madison,
and those who know him best think he will not disappoint their most
sanguine Expectations." Edmund Randolph, with whom Madison had
served in Congress, characterized him "as a general of whom much has
been preconceived to his advantage."[21]

Madison did not disappoint. He quickly became one of several leaders in the house, advocating an agenda of reform, economic recovery,
and stabilization at home and nationally, increased powers for Congress,
and a defense of the rights of individuals. In particular, Madison hoped
to enact the revised code of laws drafted by Thomas Jefferson, George
Wythe, and Edmund Pendleton in 1777–79. To ensure success, Madison sought the support of Patrick Henry, but soon it was obvious that
Henry would oppose everything that Madison favored. Henry's election as governor removed his powerful personality and oratory from
the floor of the house, but Henry's opposition from outside was still a
mighty force for Madison to overcome. Nevertheless, over the course
of three years, Madison succeeded in getting over 40 of the remaining
117 revised laws enacted. Archibald Stuart, one of Madison's legislative
allies, praised his efforts. "Can you suppose it possible that Madison
should shine with more than usual splendor [in] this Assembly. It is
sir not only possible but a fact. He has astonished mankind & has by

means perfectly constitutional become almost a Dictator upon all subjects, that the House have not so far prejudged as to shut their Ears from
Reason & armed their minds from Conviction. His influence alone has
hitherto overcome the impatience of the house & carried them half
thro the Revised Code." Madison failed, however, to enact two of the
most important reforms, a bill establishing a public school system and
a bill revising the state's penal code. Madison was also unsuccessful at
getting a reform of the state's judiciary and a revision of the state constitution. Jefferson could only console him from Europe by saying, "What
we have to do I think is devoutly to pray for [Henry's] death."[22]

Probably the most important action of the legislature during Madison's three-year tenure was the enactment of Jefferson's bill for religious
freedom. In 1784 Patrick Henry, Richard Henry Lee, and Edmund Pendleton introduced legislation to allow public funds to be used to support
Christian ministers. Through a series of adroit delaying tactics and his
anonymously written "Memorial and Remonstrances against Religious
Assessments," Madison was able not only to kill the general assessment
act but in January 1786 to win approval for Jefferson's bill. Madison
wrote Jefferson that they had "extinguished for ever the ambitious hope
of making laws for the human mind."[23]

And Slavery

James Madison, like many other southern leaders of the Revolutionary era, abhorred the institution of slavery. In time, it was expected that
slavery would wither and die. But in the meantime, in the southern culture slavery was looked upon as the norm. Slaves were necessary in the
southern economy and to serve their masters. Madison was born and
raised in this kind of society. When he was eight years old, his grandmother deeded him in trust an infant slave to be raised alongside Master
Jemmy, and he and Billey grew up almost as brothers. But then, at a
certain age, both of them realized that there was a difference: one was
black, the other white; one was a slave, the other master.

To complicate matters further, the Revolutionary rhetoric preached
the doctrine of liberty and freedom while denouncing the new British
imperial policy that, if left unchecked, would enslave Americans. Both
white and black Americans saw the incongruity of Patriots struggling for

their freedom from potential enslavement while keeping a whole race of men, women, and children in bondage. Slave owners' self-interest vied with their philosophical antipathy for slavery, while the specter of slave insurrections always haunted southern planters.

While serving in Congress in 1783, Madison participated in the debate over how to apportion federal expenses among the states. The provision in the Articles of Confederation basing the requisition of federal taxes among the states on the value of land simply did not work. Most states did not submit their estimated valuations of lands, and those states that did submit valuations naturally undervalued their land. Congress agreed that an amendment to the Articles of Confederation should apportion federal expenses among the states based upon population. The debate ultimately focused on whether or not to count slaves as part of the population for apportioning the taxes. Delegates from northern states argued that slaves, as people, should be counted; southern delegates, however, argued that slaves were property and therefore should not be counted. Various delegates suggested compromises. Madison proposed that three-fifths of the slaves be counted in apportioning federal taxes. Congress accepted Madison's proposal and thus was established the "federal ratio." Although the New Hampshire and Rhode Island legislatures did not adopt it, the population amendment with the three-fifths clause was used by the Confederation Congress in the requisitions of 1786 and 1787.[24] It was adopted by the Federal Convention of 1787 as the ratio for counting slaves for purposes of both representation and direct taxation, the infamous three-fifths clause of the Constitution.

When Madison finished his congressional service, he wrote to his father that he would be home soon but that Billey would not return with him. "On a view of all circumstances I have judged it most prudent not to force Billey back to Virginia even if [it] could be done." Billey's mind, according to Madison, was "too thoroughly tainted to be a fit companion for fellow slaves in Virginia." Madison did not blame Billey "for coveting that liberty for which we have paid the price of so much blood, and have proclaimed so often to be the right, & worthy the pursuit, of every human being." Instead of freeing Billey, Madison sold him into indentured servitude for seven years, the maximum allowable time under Pennsylvania law. He knew that he would not "get near the worth of him" from the transaction, but this was a way for Billey to learn a trade that could sustain him as a free man.[25]

Out of national politics, Madison continued reading law. He did not, however, wish to make the law his full-time profession. But, he wrote, "another of my wishes is to depend as little as possible on the labour of slaves." In the Virginia House of Delegates, Madison observed the hostile response to the Methodist ministers' petition campaign to abolish slavery. "The pulse of the House of Delegates was felt on Thursday with regard to a general manumission by a petition presented on that subject. It was rejected without dissent. . . . A motion was made to throw it under the table," a sign of contempt. Counterpetitions were offered opposing "any step towards freeing the slaves, and even praying for a repeal of the law which" made manumissions by individuals easier.[26] Slavery could not be abolished by law or in the immediate future.

When Madison acknowledged that the great division in the Federal Convention was not between large and small states but "between the Northern & Southern" states, he meant those states "having or not having slaves." Feeling strongly that the interests of both the slave states and nonslave states needed to be protected, he suggested that instead of using the federal ratio of three-fifths of the slaves in computing representation in both houses of Congress, one house be apportioned "according to the number of free inhabitants only; and in the other according to the whole number counting the slaves as if free. By this arrangement the Southern Scale would have the advantage in one House, and the Northern in the other." Madison felt uneasy about making such a proposal because of "his unwillingness to urge any diversity of interests on an occasion when it is but too apt to arise of itself" and because of "the inequality of powers that must be vested in the two branches, and which would destroy the equilibrium of interests."[27] Madison's proposal never received serious consideration.

Madison and most of his fellow convention delegates wanted an immediate close of the African slave trade. He and George Mason spoke out strenuously against the provision that would prohibit Congress from closing the African trade before 1808. "Twenty years," Madison pleaded, "will produce all the mischief that can be apprehended from the liberty to import slaves. So long a term will be more dishonorable to the American character than to say nothing about it in the Constitution." Madison also strove to keep any mention of the word *slavery* out of the Constitution, thinking "it wrong to admit . . . the idea that there could be property in men."[28]

One of the most important actions of the First Congress under the Constitution was to provide revenue for the new government, most of which was expected to come from a 5 percent tariff on imports. Toward the end of the debate over the tariff in May 1789, Madison had a proposal introduced to levy a $10 tax on every slave brought into America, the maximum tax allowed under Article I, section 9 of the Constitution. He supported the duty from "the dictates of humanity, the principles of the people, the national safety and happiness, and prudent policy." "It is hoped," he said, "that by expressing a national disapprobation of this trade, we may destroy it, and save ourselves from reproaches, and our posterity the imbecility ever attendant on a country filled with slaves." The danger of slave insurrections that the federal government might have to suppress led Madison to make a rare statement in support of a broad interpretation of the Constitution. He suggested that "it is a necessary duty of the general government to protect every part of the empire against danger, as well internal as external; every thing therefore which tends to encrease this danger, though it may be a local affair, yet if it involves national expence or safety, becomes of concern to every part of the union, and is a proper subject for the consideration of those charged with the general administration of the government."[29] (This was dangerously close to the interpretation of the Constitution that Patrick Henry had made in the Virginia ratifying convention in warning about the possibility of a federal abolition of slavery.) After a vehement debate over the tax on imported slaves that threatened the entire tariff bill, Madison agreed to withdraw the proposal to be resubmitted as a separate bill later in the session. Such a bill was proposed in September 1789 but postponed until the next session. No further consideration of a tax on imported slaves occurred until 1804 when South Carolina reopened its foreign slave trade.

In response to petitions from the abolition societies of Pennsylvania and New York and from Quakers from Pennsylvania to Virginia, the U.S. House of Representatives debated whether Congress could (1) immediately prohibit the African slave trade, (2) regulate the African slave trade, (3) emancipate slaves throughout the United States, and/or

(4) regulate the condition of slaves throughout the country. The debate was vehement and continued from late February through late March 1790. The petitions were referred to a committee chaired by Madison which concluded that Congress could not prohibit the African slave trade before 1808 (as specified in Article V of the Constitution) and could not abolish or interfere with the institution of slavery where it existed. Congress could, however, regulate the African slave trade under its power to regulate commerce. Madison wanted these conclusions to be entered on the House journals "for the information of the public." Such a public statement would show that Congress would act whenever it could constitutionally. It would also satisfy those southern representatives who had been so ardent in the debate, and it would "tend to quiet the apprehensions of the Southern states, by recognizing that Congress had no power whatever to prohibit the importation of slaves prior to the year 1808, or to manumit them at any time."[30]

In June 1791 Robert Pleasants, a prominent Quaker merchant from Henrico County, Virginia, asked Madison to submit a memorial to Congress from the Virginia Abolition Society that condemned slavery and asked for an amelioration of the conditions of the African slave trade. Pleasants also asked Madison to submit a petition to the Virginia legislature calling for the gradual abolition of slavery in the state that would end "an Evil of great Magnitude." Living "in an enlightened age, when liberty is allowed to be the unalienable right of all mankind," Pleasants felt that "it surely behooves us of the present generation, and more especially the Legislature, to endeavour to restore one of the most valuable blessings of life, to an injured and unhappy race of people."[31]

Madison turned down both requests. He replied that his constituents were "greatly interested in that species of property" and "it would seem that I might be chargeable at least with want of candour, if not of fidelity, were I to make use of a situation in which their confidence has placed me, to become a volunteer in giving a public wound, as they would deem it, to an interest on which they set so great a value." Madison also believed that the Quaker memorial would have little chance of success in Congress no matter who introduced it. In fact, though Madison in 1790 had argued that Congress could regulate the foreign slave trade, Congress never enacted any regulations to ameliorate the atrocious conditions under which slaves were transported from Africa to America.

Madison felt that the petition to the Virginia legislature seeking a gradual abolition of slavery was a matter "of great delicacy and importance." The consequences of such a petition "ought to be weighed by those who would hazard it." In all likelihood, Madison wrote, the petition would "do harm rather than good." Perhaps the legislature would make it more difficult to manumit slaves and might even enact a law requiring freedmen to leave the state within a year of their manumission.[32]

Madison, like Jefferson, denounced slavery but believed that blacks were inherently inferior to whites. Unlike Jefferson, he never actually wrote such a statement about black inferiority, but Madison's racism deepened as he grew older and profoundly affected his attitude toward emancipation. He came to believe that abolition of slavery could take place only in a three-step process: (1) a gradual system of emancipation with public compensation for slave owners had to be accompanied by (2) the colonization of free blacks apart from white society and (3) the introduction of an alternative workforce to replace the freed slaves.[33] Madison did little to implement this difficult process. When asked to lead, he declined; and as years passed he despaired that much could be done to rid the country of this terrible injustice. Madison and his southern brethren were willing to risk their all for their own independence; they refused to take similar risks for the liberty of enslaved blacks.

Changing the Constitution

A decade after declaring their independence, most Americans felt dissatisfied with their governments, both state and federal. Infused with the optimism of Enlightenment philosophy and with a sense of mission for all of mankind, Americans had confidently crafted state and federal constitutions between 1776 and 1780. When these written constitutions failed to answer all their needs, Americans worried that the Revolutionary principles they had fought so hard to preserve might be lost as republican governments succumbed to one form or another of despotic rule. The Federal Convention of 1787 seemed to offer the last hope that the people actually could determine their own forms of government through reflection and choice rather than tamely submitting to governments imposed by force or chance.

Throughout his tenure in the Virginia House of Delegates, Madison had sought to strengthen the powers of Congress. He hoped that Virginia would lead the way, and during the October 1785 session, he worked to have the legislature adopt an amendment to the Articles of Confederation that would give Congress the power to regulate commerce. When that effort failed, a motion was introduced by John Tyler (perhaps at Madison's request) to call a general convention of the states to address commercial concerns. After delaying consideration for almost two months, the house and senate overwhelmingly adopted the measure on January 21, 1786, the last day of the session. Madison had previously opposed such unorthodox methods, preferring to work within the legislature and Congress. Now, however, he felt that though it would "probably miscarry," a commercial convention was "better than nothing, and . . . may possibly lead to better consequences than at first occur."[34]

The legislature appointed Madison and seven other commissioners to attend the convention, a delegation so large that he feared it might "stifle the thing in its birth." The convention was "to consider how far a uniform system" of "commercial regulations may be necessary" for the "common interest and . . . permanent harmony" of the country. The Virginia commissioners decided to hold the convention in September 1786 in Annapolis, Maryland. Madison explained that "it was thought prudent to avoid the neighbourhood of Congress [i.e., New York City], and the large Commercial towns [i.e., Philadelphia], in order to disarm the adversaries to the object, of insinuations of influence from either of these quarters." Madison worried that if the convention failed, it would confirm "Great Britain and all the world in the belief that we are not to be respected, nor apprehended as a nation in matters of Commerce." Although he was pessimistic about the convention's success, "yet on the whole," Madison wrote, "I cannot disapprove of the experiment. Something it is agreed is necessary to be done, towards the commerce at least of the U.S., and if anything can be done, it seems as likely to result from the proposed Convention, and more likely to result from the present crisis, than from any other mode or time. If nothing can be done we may at least expect a full discovery as to that matter from the experiment, and such a piece of knowledge will be worth the trouble and expence of obtaining it."[35]

Nine states elected commissioners to the convention, including Madison and Alexander Hamilton of New York. Before the September meeting, Madison and others got the idea that the convention might be used as a springboard to a more ambitious convention. Madison confided to Jefferson in mid-August that "gentlemen both within & without Congress wish to make this Meeting subservient to a plenipotentiary Convention for amending the Confederation." Some people, particularly in New England, suspected as much. Boston merchant Stephen Higginson wrote that "political," not "commercial," objectives were being sought. The men elected as commissioners were all "esteemed great aristocrats . . . few of them have been in the commercial line, nor is it probable they know or care much about commercial objects."[36]

Twelve commissioners from five states met in Annapolis on September 11. Without waiting for others to arrive, the delegates present, including Madison, hastily wrote a report and adjourned. The convention called for a general convention of the states to meet in Philadelphia in May 1787 "to devise such further provisions as shall appear to them necessary to render the constitution of the Federal Government adequate to the exigencies of the Union." Madison was delighted. He was determined to assure that Virginia would elect the best possible delegation to this new convention.

Before the Annapolis convention assembled, Shays's Rebellion broke out in Massachusetts. Violence or disturbances of one kind or another occurred in a half dozen other states as well. Anxiety filled the country. A crisis loomed. George Washington wrote that "there are combustibles in every State, which a spark might set fire to."[37]

Madison also felt the urgency. With a sense of foreboding, he worked feverishly hard to prepare himself for the upcoming convention. He turned down diplomatic appointments to the Netherlands and Spain, partly because of his fear of ocean travel and partly because he sensed that America was the place for him to be. Between April and June 1786 Madison read widely from his library at Montpelier on ancient and modern confederations. As a man of the Enlightenment, he believed in the utility of history, and Madison hoped to discover the weaknesses of confederacies and how to guard against these fatal flaws. He convinced himself that confederacies were fragile and that they tended either to dissolve or become impotent when they lacked a central controlling power over the people. Because the Annapolis convention adjourned so quickly, Madison was not able to use his findings in that convention's debates. He would further develop his ideas about confederations for use in the next convention and in the public debate that would follow.

The Virginia legislature considered the Annapolis report in November and passed an act authorizing the election of seven delegates to the Federal Convention to meet in Philadelphia in May. Madison wrote the act, a powerful piece of political propaganda that was sent to all of the state governors and legislatures encouraging them to appoint delegates to the convention. Like the Declaration of Independence a decade earlier, it stated the "necessity" of America's situation. No one could

> doubt that the crisis is arrived at which the good people of America are to decide the solemn question, whether they will by wise and magnanimous efforts reap the just fruits of that Independence, which they have so gloriously acquired, and of that Union which they have cemented with so much of their common blood; or whether by giving way to unmanly jealousies and prejudices, or to partial and transitory interests, they will renounce the auspicious blessings prepared for them by the Revolution, and furnish to its enemies an eventual triumph over those by whose virtue and valour it has been accomplished.

Changes were necessary that would "render the United States as happy in peace as they have been glorious in war."[38] The document was in essence a declaration of independence from the states.

On December 4, 1786, the legislature elected Madison, George Washington, Patrick Henry, Edmund Randolph, George Mason, George Wythe, and John Blair as delegates to the upcoming convention. Even without Henry, who refused the appointment, it was the most prestigious of the state delegations. Washington was by far the most important delegate from any state, and without the ongoing pressure from Madison and Randolph, he would not have attended the convention. Madison told Washington, "The advantage of having your name in the front of the appointment as a mark of the earnestness of Virginia, and an invitation to the most select characters from every part of the Confederacy, ought at all events to be made use of." On the day the delegation was elected, Madison wrote to Jefferson that there had been a "revolution of sentiment which the experience of one year has affected in this Country."[39] The time was ripe to make a serious change in the Articles of Confederation.

In Congress a Second Time

On November 7, 1786, the Virginia legislature elected Madison to return to Congress. His three-year "exile" from national politics was over. Madison returned to Montpelier from Richmond on January 11 and four days later left for New York City. David Stuart, a legislative colleague, wrote Washington that "I have no doubt Mr. Madison's virtues and abilities make it necessary that he should be in Congress, but from what I already foresee, I shall dread the consequences of another Assembly without him."[40]

Madison attended Congress on February 10, 1787, and immediately resumed his position of leadership. With Shays's Rebellion suppressed, Charles Pinckney of South Carolina moved that Congress suspend the enlistment of troops authorized in October to combat "Indian uprisings" on the frontier. Madison, without addressing the propriety or constitutionality of raising an army to suppress an internal insurrection within a state, strongly opposed Pinckney's motion because he was uncertain "that the spirit of insurrection was subdued" and because the mobilization of troops by Lord Dorchester in Canada might allow the British "to take advantage of events in this Country." Madison also endorsed a report by Secretary for Foreign Affairs John Jay that condemned the states' repeated violations of the Treaty of Peace and unequivocally proclaimed Congress's "exclusive right and power" over foreign affairs.[41] Finally, Madison joined other southerners in condemning Congress's alteration of its instructions to Secretary Jay that would allow him, if necessary, to cede the American right to navigate the Mississippi River in exchange for a commercial treaty with Spain. The intense debate over this sectionally divisive issue convinced everyone that such a cession would never be allowed; it also shook the unity of those who espoused giving more power to the federal government. Sectionalism was now an additional factor endangering the Confederation.

❧ Preparing for the Convention

Madison continued to prepare himself and his state's delegation for the Philadelphia convention. He wrote a memorandum on the "Vices of the Political System of the United States" and drafted the outline of a new constitution that would replace—not simply revise—the Articles of Confederation. Drawing upon theory and America's experience since 1776, Madison demonstrated the weaknesses of the Articles and the "multiplicity," "mutability," and "injustice" of state laws, innumerable laws that were often repealed by subsequent legislatures and that sometimes violated the rights of individuals. He acknowledged and endorsed the basic feature of republican government—that the majority should rule—but denounced the tendency of majorities to tyrannize over minorities. Without a coercive authority, Congress under the Articles of Confederation could not collect taxes, regulate commerce, enforce treaties, defend states against internal insurrections, or prevent states from encroaching on Congress's power, trespassing on the rights of other states, or violating the liberties of their citizens. According to Madison, these "vices" required a fundamental alteration in the country's constitution.

Madison outlined his plan for a new constitution in a remarkable series of letters to George Washington, Edmund Randolph, Thomas Jefferson, and Edmund Pendleton from February through April 1787. As the convention neared, he felt the pressure mount. Madison believed that the responsibility for success or failure rested on his shoulders. Virginia would be expected to take the lead, and he would have to be the driving force on the Virginia delegation. The convention was perhaps America's last chance freely and rationally to choose its government. Madison was convinced that "unless the Union be organized efficiently & on Republican Principles, innovations of a much more objectionable form [such as monarchy or aristocracy] may be obtruded, or in the most favorable event, the partition of the Empire into rival & hostile confederacies will ensue." He wrote his friend and mentor Edmund Pendleton that "the nearer the crisis approaches, the more I tremble for the issue. The necessity of gaining the concurrence of the Convention in some system that will answer the purpose, the subsequent approbation of Congress, and the final sanction of the States, presents a series of chances, which would inspire despair in any case where the alternative was less formidable." What made matters particularly difficult was the necessity of augmenting Congress's power and reducing the power of the states and then getting the state legislatures and the people to agree to such monumental changes.[42]

Madison's letter to Governor Edmund Randolph is particularly revealing. As delicately as he could, Madison disagreed with Randolph's plan to revise the Articles of Confederation by jettisoning the bad provisions and adding new ones in their place. Madison preferred creating a completely new constitution and incorporating only "the valuable articles into the new System." "An explanatory address" should accompany the new constitution when it was sent to the people, who would have to accept or reject the whole new system. Adoption of only some provisions would be unacceptable.[43]

As a fundamental belief Madison felt that the American Union— "the idea of an aggregate sovereignty"—could not survive if the states retained their "sovereignty, freedom and independence" as provided in Article II of the Articles of Confederation. At the same time he realized that consolidating the states "into one simple republic" was not only "unattainable" but also "inexpedient." A "middle ground" had to be found "which will at once support a due supremacy of the national authority, and leave in force the local authorities so far as they can be subordinately useful."

The first principle that had to be changed was representation. The unicameral Confederation Congress, where each state had one vote regardless of population or wealth, had to give way to a bicameral Congress in which representation in both houses was apportioned according to population or by contributions (payment of taxes). The large states had accepted equal state voting under the Confederation because Congress had no authority over individuals—it could act only upon states—and no coercive power to enforce acts that the large states disliked and chose to violate. But under a government that acted directly on the people as individuals, "the case would be materially altered." The states and their populations would have to be fairly represented in Congress.

The national government would have to "be armed with a positive & complete authority in all cases where uniform measures are necessary." This meant that Congress should retain all the powers that it had under the Confederation but also be given the power to regulate commerce, to levy and collect taxes, to raise an army and navy, etc. Congress must also have the power (as the king in council had before the Revolution) to veto "in all cases whatsoever" any and all acts passed by the state legislatures. Madison said that he conceived this power "to be essential and the least possible abridgement of the State Sovereignties. Without such a defensive power, every positive power that can be given on paper will be unavailing." He also believed that this kind of congressional control over state legislation would "give internal stability to the States" and protect the rights of people.

A federal judiciary would also have to be created to which people could ultimately appeal. "If the judges in the last resort depend on the States & are bound by their oaths to them and not to the Union, the intention of the law and the interests of the nation may be defeated by the obsequiousness of the Tribunals to the policy or prejudices of the States. It seems at least essential that an appeal should lie to some national tribunals in all cases which concern foreigners, or inhabitants of other States."

Congress, Madison argued, should have two houses. One should be elected directly by the people or by the state legislatures for a short term. A second, smaller chamber with a longer term should be elected by a different constituency and might have staggered terms. This chamber might have the veto power over state legislation.

Madison also called for a separate, single executive. He was unclear about exactly what powers this officer would have, but he thought that in combination with some federal judges, it might form a council of revision, which would serve, in essence, as a third branch of the legislature. Every bill passed by Congress would need the approval of this council. This would be a far more effective method of bringing the authority and experience of judges into legislation than judicial review. New York had such a council in its 1777 constitution, and Madison seemed to think it functioned well. The legislature could override council vetoes by a two-thirds vote of both houses.

The new constitution should "expressly guarantee the tranquility of the States against internal as well as external dangers." To give this new constitution "proper energy," it should be adopted "by the authority of the people, and not merely by that of the [state] Legislatures."

Madison realized that these might seem to be "extravagant" and "unattainable" proposals, and thus "unworthy of being attempted." But he believed that they went "no further than is essential" and that at this time of crisis, they were attainable.

❧ The Constitutional Convention

Madison left Congress in New York City on May 2 and arrived in Philadelphia three days later before any other non-Pennsylvania delegate had arrived and three weeks before the convention formed a quorum. His fellow Virginia delegates also arrived early, and for a week they caucused "two or three hours every day, in order to form a proper correspondence of sentiments."[44] They agreed upon the Virginia Plan, primarily a compilation of Madison's ideas, and selected Governor Randolph, an eloquent speaker, to present it at the outset of the convention. Randolph presented Virginia's proposal on May 29, the first day of debate. It stunned everyone as a revolution in government. On June 16 supporters of minimal amendments to the Articles presented their plan. Then, in what was either a brilliant piece of strategy or a completely fortuitous event, Alexander Hamilton on June 18 presented an even more radical proposal than Virginia's outlining a strong national government that some saw as veering toward monarchy. Suddenly the Virginia Plan did not look so radical; in fact it was now the centrist plan. The convention voted on June 19 to reject the plan to amend the Articles and to continue with the Virginia Plan as the basis for debate.

Madison had three primary goals in the convention: (1) he wanted to replace the weak Confederation government that acted upon strong sovereign states with a powerful national government that could act directly on individuals and was dominant over the states; (2) he wanted to replace the equal representation of the states in a unicameral congress with a bicameral congress in which the states were represented proportionally; and (3) he wanted the central government to have a veto power over the legislation of the states "in all cases whatsoever." He succeeded in his first goal but only partially in accomplishing the second and third.

At the convention Madison spoke over 200 times, exceeded only by Gouverneur Morris and James Wilson, both representing Pennsylvania.

He spoke authoritatively on every subject, his knowledge was unsurpassed, and the convention usually adopted the position he espoused. Fellow delegate William Pierce of Georgia explained how this timid, young Virginian came to have such an impact. Madison

> is a character who has long been in public life; and what is very remarkable every Person seems to acknowledge his greatness. He blends together the profound politician with the Scholar. In the management of every great question he evidently took the lead in the Convention, and tho' he cannot be called an Orator, he is a most agreeable, eloquent, and convincing Speaker. From a spirit of industry and application which he possesses in a most eminent degree, he always comes forward the best informed Man on any point in debate. The affairs of the United States, he perhaps, has the most correct knowledge of, of any Man in the Union. He has been twice a Member of Congress, and was always thought one of the ablest Members that ever sat in that Council. Mr. Maddison is about 37 years of age, a Gentleman of great modesty,—with a remarkable sweet temper. He is easy and unreserved among his acquaintance, and has a most agreeable style of conversation.

Echoing Pierce, Thomas Jefferson wrote in his autobiography that Madison had "at ready command the rich resources of his luminous and discriminating mind." Madison's "extensive information rendered him the first of every assembly of which he became a member."[45]

Toward the end of the convention, Madison served on the five-man Committee of Style that wrote the final language of the Constitution. Although he signed the Constitution (with the tiniest cribbed signature of the thirty-nine signers), Madison was sorely disappointed in the final product. Actually, he believed that he had failed. During the four months the convention sat, Madison and Jefferson continued their longtime correspondence. While the convention was in session, the secrecy rule prevented Madison from divulging to his friend the details of the proceedings, but he assured Jefferson that "as soon as I am at liberty I will endeavor to make amends for my silence." Madison predicted that "there can be no doubt but that the result will in some way or other have a powerful effect on our destiny." Shortly before the convention adjourned, he confided to Jefferson his disappointment in how things turned out. He feared that the proposed Constitution "will neither effectually answer its national object nor prevent the local mischiefs which every where excite disgusts against the state governments."[46] It took six weeks for the dejected Madison to explain to his friend the difficulties faced by the convention and how the lack of a congressional veto over state laws would seriously weaken the central government.

One of Madison's most important contributions at the convention was his note-taking. While doing research on ancient and modern confederations a year earlier, Madison was disappointed in finding "very imperfect account[s], of their structure, and of the attributes and functions of the presiding Authority." His "curiosity" was not satisfied "especially in what related to the process, the principles, the reasons, & the anticipations, which prevailed in the formation of them." He thus determined "to preserve as far as I could an exact account of what might pass in the Convention," knowing how grateful future generations would be. He also realized how valuable such a record would be for historians in studying "a Constitution on which would be staked the happiness of a people great even in its infancy, and possibly the cause of Liberty throughout the world." Sometime during the early 1830s, in an essay obviously meant as an introduction to a printed edition of his convention notes, Madison described the procedure he used for taking notes.

> In pursuance of the task I had assumed I chose a seat in front of the presiding member, with the other members, on my right & left hands. In this favorable position for hearing all that passed, I noted in terms legible & in abbreviations & marks intelligible to myself what was read from the Chair or spoken by the members; and losing not a moment unnecessarily between the adjournment & reassembling of the Convention I was enabled to write out my daily notes during the session or within a few finishing days after its close in the extent and form preserved in my own hand on my files. . . . It happened, also, that I was not absent a single day, nor more than a casual fraction of an hour in any day, so that I could not have lost a single speech, unless a very short one.[47]

Madison's experience at taking notes of the debates in Congress during the early 1780s and in the first half of 1787 assisted him in note-taking in the convention.

Although over the years Madison received many requests for information about his notes, he almost always refused access to them except for a very few people, among whom was Thomas Jefferson. When asked for information about what the Federal Convention did, Madison referred inquirers to the printed debates from the state ratifying conventions and the public debate in newspapers, broadsides, and pamphlets. Not until 1840—four years after his death—were his papers published in a three-volume edition. Two of the three volumes contained his convention notes. They remain today the most thorough and reliable record of what transpired in the Federal Convention, a precious gift from Madison to his country.

❧ Ratifying the Constitution

Despite his disappointment with the Constitution, Madison praised the work of the convention and the Constitution itself. In an extraordinary statement by a man who believed in the complete separation of church and state, Madison wrote that the Constitution was divinely inspired. With all the difficulties in drafting a constitution for such a diverse country, "The real wonder is, that so many difficulties should have been surmounted; and surmounted with a unanimity almost as unprecedented as it must have been unexpected. It is impossible for any man of candor to reflect on this circumstance, without partaking of the astonishment. It is impossible for the man of pious reflection not to perceive in it, a finger of that Almighty hand which has been so frequently and signally extended to our relief in the critical stages of the revolution." Madison even praised the fact that the convention had created a constitution different from his original conception. He wrote that it was "wonderful" that the convention was "forced into some deviations from the artificial structure and regular symmetry, which an abstract view of the subject might lead an ingenious theorist to bestow on a Constitution planned in his closet or in his imagination."[48]

Madison left Philadelphia on September 21 to return to Congress in New York City. On September 26–28 he participated in the debate over sending the Constitution to the states for their consideration. Federalists—supporters of the Constitution—in Congress, twenty-seven of the thirty-two delegates present, wanted to send the Constitu-

tion to the states with the endorsement of Congress. Antifederalists—
opponents of the Constitution—wanted to transmit it with criticism of
the convention for exceeding its authority and its delegates for violating their instructions only to revise the Articles. In the course of the
debate, Antifederalists tried to propose amendments. Richard Henry
Lee, Madison's Virginia colleague, proposed a bill of rights and other
amendments changing the structure of the Constitution. Madison opposed Lee vigorously and argued that "a bill of rights [was] unnecessary
because the powers [of Congress] are enumerated and only extend to
certain cases." To add amendments to the Constitution would create in-
surmountable problems. An amended Constitution would be the Confederation Congress's Constitution; and according to the Articles of
Confederation, when Congress proposed changes to the Articles, they
were to be sent to the state legislatures for their unanimous approval.
The convention, on the other hand, had suggested that the Constitution be sent to the states to be considered in specially elected ratifying
conventions and that when nine conventions ratified, the Constitution
would go into effect among the ratifying states. Thus, Madison said,
"there will be two plans. Some [states] will accept one and some another. Confusion would result."[49]

Although they controlled eleven of the twelve state delegations in attendance, Federalists were willing to compromise because they wanted
to preserve the appearance of unanimity. Congress was, as usual, meeting behind closed doors, and Federalists hoped that the discussion, and
especially Lee's suggested amendments, would not become known by
the public. They agreed to transmit the Constitution to the states without endorsement if Antifederalists would agree to strike any dissent
(including Lee's proposed amendments) from the journals. To avoid
congressional endorsement, the outnumbered Antifederalists agreed to
the compromise. Shrewd politicians that they were, Federalists, led by
Madison, cleverly introduced the transmittal resolution with the words
"Resolved unanimously," giving the false impression of unanimous approbation, while Congress was unanimously agreeing only to send the
Constitution to the states for their consideration. When Madison explained to George Washington what had happened in Congress, Washington replied: "I am better pleased that the proceedings of the Convention is handed from Congress by a unanimous vote (feeble as it is) than

if it had appeared under stronger marks of approbation without it. This apparent unanimity will have its effect. Not every one has opportunities to peep behind the curtain; and as the multitude often judge from externals, the appearance of unanimity in that body, on this occasion, will be of great importance."[50]

Except for a week's trip to Philadelphia in early November, Madison stayed in New York City to attend Congress and to serve as an unofficial Federalist clearinghouse of information until early March 1788, when he returned to Orange County to stand for election to the Virginia ratifying convention. Letters from Federalists all over the country streamed in to him. He, in turn, gathered and consolidated this information and relayed it to his correspondents throughout the country. Newspapers and pamphlets were sent to him to forward to Hamilton in New York, to Rufus King in Boston, or to Federalists in Virginia. He transmitted copies of the debates from the Pennsylvania and Massachusetts conventions to correspondents. Only two other Federalists performed similar functions, Secretary at War Henry Knox, who was also in New York, and Washington at Mount Vernon. Until very late in the process, there was no Antifederalist coordination in the campaign against the Constitution.

Antifederalists took the lead in the newspaper debate over whether or not to ratify the Constitution. About a month into the debate, Alexander Hamilton and John Jay decided to write a comprehensive exposition of the Constitution in a series of newspaper essays. They asked Madison to join the enterprise. The purpose of the series was to show the necessity of the Union, the weaknesses of the Articles of Confederation, and the nature and benefits of the new Constitution. The essays were "to give a satisfactory answer to all the objections which shall have made their appearance that may seem to have any claim to the public's attention."[51]

Later in life Madison described how the essays were prepared for publication. They

were written most of them in great haste, and without any special allotment of the different parts of the subject to the several writers. J.M. being at the time a member of the then Congress, and A.H. being also a member, and occupied moreover in his profession at the bar, it was understood that each was to write as their respective situations permitted, preserving as much as possible an order & connection in the papers successively published. This will account for deficiency in that respect, and also for an occasional repetition of the views taken of particular branches of the subject. The haste with which many of the papers were penned, in order to get thro the subject whilst the Constitution was before the public, and to comply with the arrangement by which the printer was to keep his newspaper open for four numbers every week, was such that the performance must have borne a very different aspect without the aid of historical and other notes which have been used in the Convention and without the familiarity with the whole subject produced by the discussions there. It frequently happened that whilst the printer was putting into type the parts of a number, the following parts were under the pen, & to be furnished in time for the press.

In the beginning it was the practice of the writers, of A.H. & J.M. particularly to communicate each to the other, their respective papers before they were sent to the press. This was rendered so inconvenient, by the shortness of the time allowed, that it was dispensed with. Another reason was, that it was found most agreeable to each, not to give a positive sanction to all the doctrines and sentiments of the other; there being a known difference in the general complexion of their political theories.[52]

Madison wrote twenty-nine of the eighty-five essays in the series: Nos. 10, 14, 18–20, 37–58, 62–63. His first essay is the most famous of all the eighty-five. In *Federalist* No. 10, published in the New York *Daily Advertiser* on November 22, 1787, Madison dealt with special-interest-group politics and how to preserve liberty in a republic. Madison rejected the commonly held belief espoused by the baron de Montesquieu that republics could survive only in small confined countries with homogeneous populations. Most former republics satisfied these requirements, but they all had collapsed and degenerated into despotism. Madison turned Montesquieu's ideas on their head. He argued that to be viable, republics needed both to expand their territory and to diversify their populations.

Free societies, Madison wrote, always would contain factions—today we call them special-interest groups—that were dedicated to their own interest at the expense of the general good and could be dangerous to the rights of others. But to eliminate factions would require the elimination of liberty. Madison favored creating conditions that would make it difficult for factions to form majorities. The larger the area and the more diversified the population, the greater the difficulty for any majority to be formed or, once formed, to stay together for a long time. "Extend the sphere, and you take in a greater variety of parties and interests; you make it less probable that a majority of the whole will have a common motive to invade the rights of other citizens." Madison expected that under the Constitution there would be struggles among special-interest groups. But they were not to be feared because the Constitution was so constructed that factions would be controlled and prevented from doing harm.

Madison wanted to provide a buffer for federal legislators from the arbitrary and immediate whims of an outraged majority, the most dangerous element in any democratic society. He hoped that America could be ruled by the most meritorious and virtuous citizens, who would compose a "natural aristocracy." He despised government by a hereditary aristocracy, those favored by birth and wealth.

One way to guarantee that only the best people would be elected was to limit the size of Congress. If all the states ratified the Constitution, the first Senate would contain 26 members and the first House of Representatives 65 members. Opponents of the Constitution worried that such small legislative bodies could not adequately represent the American people. After all, tiny Rhode Island had an assembly of 70, while Massachusetts had almost 400 in its House of Representatives. Madison, however, knew that the small number of federal legislators would require large, perhaps even statewide election districts in which only the most meritorious could garner enough support to be elected. The small Congress would also provide the corollary benefit of keeping government expenses down.

To further insulate federal legislators, Madison supported longer terms: six years for senators and two years for representatives as opposed to the standard one-year terms in state legislatures and in the Confederation Congress. In addition, federal legislators should not be subject to recall, term limits, or binding instructions by their constituents. The per diem salaries and expenses of federal legislators also would be paid by the federal treasury as opposed to the individual state treasuries under the Articles of Confederation. Knowledgeable representatives would listen to the debate and use their intellect to make the proper choice for their country as well as for their own districts. In *Federalist* No. 37 Madison defended the terms for representatives and senators.

> The genius of republican liberty, seems to demand on one side, not only that all power should be derived from the people, but, that those entrusted with it should be kept in dependence on the people, by a short duration of their appointments; and that, even during this short period, the trust should be placed not in a few, but in a number of hands. Stability, on the contrary, requires, that the hands, in which power is lodged, should continue for a length of time the same. A frequent change of men will result from a frequent return of electors, and a frequent change of measures, from a frequent change of men; whilst energy in government requires not only a certain duration of power, but the execution of it by a single hand.

In *Federalist* No. 39 Madison showed that the new Constitution was based on republican principles and would create a government that would be partly federal, operating on the states, and partly national, operating directly on the people. Madison defined a republican government as one "which derives all its power directly or indirectly from the great body of the people; and is administered by persons holding their offices during pleasure, for a limited period, or during good behavior." There was no question in Madison's mind that the new federal government should be republican in nature. "No other form," he wrote, "would be reconcilable with the genius of the people of America; with the fundamental principles of the revolution; or with that honorable determination, which animates every votary of freedom, to rest all our political experiments on the capacity of mankind for self-government."

In one of his greatest literary flourishes, in *Federalist* No. 51, Madison concisely stated the problem faced by all governments. "If men were angels, no government would be necessary. If angels were to govern men, neither external nor internal controls on government would be necessary. In framing a government which is to be administered by men over men, the great difficulty lies in this: You must first enable the government to control the governed; and in the next place oblige it to control itself." Seemingly the Articles of Confederation and many of the state constitutions did neither. All agreed that the central government to be created under the new Constitution would have sufficient power to govern the people. The question was whether it would have sufficient checks to be able to control itself.

The primary method of controlling government, Madison wrote, was through a dependence on people through elections. But because experience had shown that elections alone were inadequate, Madison argued that "auxiliary precautions" were needed. These included fundamental structural safeguards built into the Constitution: separation of powers, checks and balances, a bicameral legislature, and the division of power between state and federal governments. "In the compound republic of America," Madison stated, "the power surrendered by the people is first divided between two distinct governments, and then the portion allotted to each, subdivided among distinct and separate departments. Hence a double security arises to the rights of the people. The different governments will control each other, at the same time that each will be controlled by itself." During the debate over the ratification of the Constitution, Madison argued that it was these structural protections that safeguarded rights, not the "parchment barrier" of a bill of rights. Only after the Constitution had been ratified did Madison enlarge his auxiliary precautions to include a bill of rights.

According to Madison, the most serious constitutional problem facing America was the dominance of state governments. Under the Articles of Confederation, states retained their sovereignty, freedom, and independence, and Congress had only those powers expressly delegated to it by the Articles. Congress had no power or authority to restrain what the states did. Madison felt that the states had to be limited so that they could not pass laws that violated the rights of individuals or subverted the authority of the federal government. Article I, section 10 of the Constitution specifically prohibits the states from certain actions, while the supremacy clause in Article VI provides that "this Constitution, and the laws of the United States which shall be made in pursuance thereof; and all treaties made, or which shall be made, under the authority of the

United States, shall be the supreme law of the land; and the judges in every state shall be bound thereby, anything in the Constitution or laws of any State to the contrary notwithstanding." Although the supremacy clause was not so extensive as Madison's proposed congressional veto over any and all state laws, he defended the clause in *Federalist* No. 44. Without it, he wrote, the Constitution "would have been evidently and radically defective. . . . the world would have seen for the first time, a system of government founded on an inversion of the fundamental principles of all government; it would have seen the authority of the whole society every where subordinate to the authority of the parts; it would have seen a monster, in which the head was under the direction of the members."

In one brief sentence in *Federalist* No. 51, Madison explained what the Constitution attempted to do. "Justice," he wrote, "is the end of government." Throughout his writings in the *Federalist,* Madison demonstrated how the Constitution placed restrictions on government so that liberty and justice under a stable government would prevail.

The *Federalist* was recognized at the time as the definitive explication of the Constitution. George Washington wrote that no other work was "so well calculated . . . to produce conviction on an unbiased mind." Thomas Jefferson told Madison that the series was "the best commentary on the principles of government which ever was written."[53]

Virginia Ratifying Convention

The opposition to the Constitution in Virginia was strong. Edmund Randolph and George Mason had refused to sign it at the Federal Convention. Other opposition was expected from three former Virginia governors—Patrick Henry, Benjamin Harrison, and Thomas Nelson—as well as from Arthur and Richard Henry Lee. Against this powerful force Madison would be the Constitution's "main pillar: but tho an immensely powerful one, it is questionable whether he can bear the weight of such a host." Jefferson also knew that Washington would play a minor role, for "it is not in his character to exert himself much in the case."[54]

Actually Madison did not want to serve in the Virginia ratifying convention, for he felt that the final decision on the Constitution "should proceed from men who had no hand in preparing and proposing it." But Madison's fellow Virginia Federalists convinced him that he was needed at the convention. He was the best person to explain what the Federal Convention had done and why. Seeing that other Federal Convention delegates served in their state ratifying conventions also helped persuade Madison to serve. He thus reluctantly agreed to stand for election to the convention from his home of Orange County, but he hoped that he would not have to campaign for a seat. In fact, he expected not to go home from New York for the elections. Friends, however, warned him to return to Virginia. Governor Randolph implored him. "You must come in. Some people in Orange are opposed to your politicks. Your election to the convention is, I believe, sure; but I beg you not to hazard it by being absent at the time." William Moore, a friend and Orange County planter, reminded Madison of "the disadvantage of being absent at Elections to those who offer themselves to serve the Public. I must therefore intreat and conjure you, nay command you, if it was in my Power, to be here in February or the first of March next. If you do, I think your Election will be certain (if not I believe from reports it will be uncertain)."[55]

Because of "the badness of the roads & some other delays," Madison did not reach Orange until March 23, one day before the elections. Much to his chagrin, he found "the County filled with the most absurd and groundless prejudices against the federal Constitution." For the first time in his life, Madison felt compelled "to mount . . . the rostrum before a large body of the people, and to launch into a harangue of some length in the open air and on a very windy day. What the effect might be I cannot say, but either from that experiment or the exertion of the federalists or perhaps both, the misconceptions of the Government were so far corrected that two federalists one of them myself were elected by a majority of nearly 4 to one. It is very probable that a very different event would have taken place as to myself if the efforts of my friends had not been seconded by my presence." Another report indicated that Madison had "converted" the people of Orange "in a speech of an hour & three quarters." Cyrus Griffin, a Virginian and president of the Confederation Congress, wrote Madison that "we all rejoice greatly at your election: indeed, my dear sir, we consider you as the main pillar of the business on the right side."[56] Francis Taylor, Madison's cousin and another Orange County planter, reported that Madison had received 202 votes, while fellow Federalist James Gordon received 187. The two Antifederalist candidates received 56 and 34 votes.

The Virginia convention met in Richmond from June 2 to June 27. Madison was one of five of Virginia's seven delegates to the Federal Convention who served in the state convention. He led the Federalists with strong assistance from Governor Edmund Randolph, George Nicholas, George Wythe, convention president Edmund Pendleton, and John Marshall. Against them was a phalanx of powerful Antifederalists led by Patrick Henry, George Mason, William Grayson, and James Monroe. The stress of combating such dynamic speakers wore heavily on Madison. In fact, for two days, June 9 and 10, he was too sick from stress to attend the convention proceedings. Federalists succeeded in getting the convention to agree to examine the Constitution paragraph by paragraph, a procedure conducive to Madison's scholarly style as a speaker. Despite the convention's rule, Henry used his dynamic oratorical dominance over the delegates to denounce the Constitution in broad, general strokes.

Madison responded to virtually all arguments put forth by the Antifederalists. His "plain, ingenious, & elegant reasoning" was repeatedly praised.[57] He decried Henry's generalities. He demanded specifics. Show us, he said, where the dangers are. "It is urged that abuses may happen.—How is it possible to answer objections against [the] possibility of abuses? It must strike every logical reasoner, that these cannot be entirely provided against." Governments must have coercive power. "There never was a Government without force. What is the meaning of Government?" he asked. It is "an institution to make people do their duty. A Government leaving it to do his duty, or not, as he pleases, would be a new species of Government, or rather no Government at all." "We must limit our apprehensions to certain degrees of probability." Many of the Antifederalist evils were "extremely improbable. Nay, almost impossible."[58] "There must be some degree of confidence put in agents [of government], or else we must reject a state of civil society altogether." "If a possibility be the cause of objection, we must object to every Government in America." "If powers be necessary, apparent danger is not a sufficient reason against conceding them."[59]

Madison argued that the Constitution "increases the security of liberty more than any Government that ever was," despite or perhaps because it had power. The Constitution would "promote public happiness." The militia power of Congress would protect states from domestic insurrections and allow the federal government to guarantee the states republican forms of government.[60] "Governments destitute of energy," he said, "will ever produce anarchy." Freedom was lost more frequently by having too many freedoms, not from having a government with appropriate powers. Madison opposed a bill of rights because the Constitution would create a government of strictly delegated powers, and the powers it had would not endanger rights. It was not possible to list all the rights the people had, and any right not listed would be presumed to be given up.[61]

The new government's powers were appropriate. The power of laying and collecting taxes was indispensable and essential to the existence of any efficient, well-organized system of government. "Voluntary contributions will eventually end in disunion and Union is indispensably necessary."[62] Madison defended the necessary and proper clause, arguing that the legislative powers were limited and defined. Because the Constitution established a government with only delegated powers, "the delegation alone warrants the exercise of any power." "The powers of the General Government relate to external objects, and are but few. But the powers in the States relate to those great objects which immediately concern the prosperity of the people." "The exercise of the power must be consistent with the object of the delegation."[63]

If people would give "a fair and liberal interpretation upon the words," Madison believed that the Constitution would be found safe. The new government would "not become consolidated as a national government." It would be partly federal and partly national.[64]

The great defect of the Articles of Confederation was that Congress could exercise its powers only over states and not individuals. The Confederation was weak, and "foreign nations [were] unwilling to form any treaties with us." The inability of Congress to pay its debts endangered the country's happiness and security. If the Articles of Confederation were not changed, "consequences must ensue that Gentlemen do not now apprehend."[65]

Madison granted that the Constitution was imperfect, but amendments could be made when needed and in fact were easier to make under the Constitution than under the Confederation.[66] Madison strongly

objected to the argument that the Constitution should be amended before Virginia ratified it. This was "but another name" for rejection; such
previous amendments were "pregnant with dreadful dangers," and they
presented "the extreme risk of perpetual disunion." How could amendments be obtained before ratification, Madison argued, when Antifederalists could not agree among themselves. The convention should, like
other state conventions, recommend amendments to be considered in
the first federal Congress after the Constitution was ratified. Madison
asked, "If there be an equal zeal in every State [for alterations], can there
be a doubt that they will concur in reasonable amendments?"[67]

Madison confessed that "from the first moment that my mind was
capable of contemplating political subjects, I never, till this moment,
ceased wishing success to a well regulated Republican Government.
The establishment of such in America was my most ardent desire." He
believed in the "great republican principle, that the people will have
virtue and intelligence to select men of virtue and wisdom." "A change,"
Madison said, was "absolutely necessary." He saw "no danger in submitting to practice an experiment which seems to be founded on the
best theoretic principles."[68] It was time to establish a viable republic
in America.

Madison told the delegates that America was at a crossroads. "It is a
most awful thing that depends on our decision—no less than whether
the thirteen States shall Unite freely, peaceably, and unanimously, for
the security of their common happiness and liberty, or whether every
thing is to be put in confusion and disorder!" "There are uncertainty
and confusion on the one hand, and order, tranquility and certainty
on the other."[69]

For several weeks it was uncertain whether the convention would
adopt the Constitution or reject it. With assurances offered by Madison
that Federalists would support recommendatory amendments, the convention voted by a slim majority of 89 to 79 to ratify the Constitution
without previous amendments. Two days later the convention recommended that Virginia's future representatives in Congress propose forty
amendments, half in the form of a declaration of rights and half structural changes to the Constitution.

Most observers agreed that without Madison, Virginia would not
have ratified the Constitution. One spectator in the convention gallery

reported that Madison spoke "with such force of reasoning, and a display of irresistible truths, that opposition seemed to have quitted the field." Another report said that "Mr. Henry's declamatory powers [were] vastly overpowered by the deep reasoning of our glorious little Madison." Madison was even praised poetically.

> Maddison among the rest,
> Pouring from his narrow chest,
> More than Greek or Roman sense,
> Boundless tides of eloquence.

Of all the speakers, it was Madison who "carried the votes of the two parties. He was always clear, precise and consistent in his reasoning, and always methodical and pure in his Language."[70]

Virginia was the tenth state to ratify. New Hampshire, which ratified four days earlier, had the honor of being the ninth state to ratify and thus implement the Constitution. With Virginia's ratification, New York realized that it must also accept the Constitution and work for amendments within Congress instead of outside of the Union.

☙ First Federal Elections

With the Constitution adopted, attention focused on who would be elected to fill the new federal offices. Virginia Federalists hoped that James Madison, who had returned to Congress in New York after the Virginia ratifying convention adjourned, would be elected one of the state's first U.S. senators. The Constitution provided that senators were to be elected by the state legislatures. The Virginia legislature decided to elect senators in the same manner in which it had elected delegates to the Confederation Congress, by a joint ballot of both houses. Patrick Henry, the acknowledged leader of the dominant Antifederalists in the legislature, worked strenuously to defeat Madison. Henry "publickly said that no person who wishes the constitution to be amended should vote for Mr. Madison to be in the senate." Henry conceded Madison's "talents and integrity" but argued that he was "unseasonable upon this occasion" because his "federal politics were so adverse to the opinions of many" Virginians. Even Madison's friends admitted that "it was doubtful, whether [he] would obey instructions" to support amendments.

"There," said Henry, "the secret is out: it is doubted whether Mr. Madison will obey instructions." Henry Lee wrote Madison that "Mr. Henry on the floor exclaimed against your political character & pronounced you unworthy of the confidence of the people in the station of Senator. That your election would terminate in producing rivulets of blood throughout the land."[71] On November 6 Madison, along with Antifederalists Richard Henry Lee and William Grayson, was nominated for the two Senate seats. Two days later the legislature, under the control of Patrick Henry, voted to elect Lee and Grayson. They received 98 and 86 votes, respectively. Madison received 77 votes.

Federalists throughout the country lamented the loss. A newspaper columnist in Maryland condemned the "misfortune. Mr. Maddison was excluded [from the Senate] who was allowed to be the greatest man in the general convention, though only little more than thirty years of age; his abilities are transcendently great, his integrity unimpeached, and he had the honor of first moving for the appointment of a general convention." A week later the same essayist criticized Patrick Henry for excluding "from the service of his country the ablest statesman in it." Martin Oster, French vice-consul in Richmond and Norfolk, reported that "it is generally regretted that Mr. James Madison, a good federalist, is not one of these representatives, because of his outstanding worth."[72]

A delegate to the assembly from Winchester described how Madison was defeated and what it meant for the country.

Those who know the abilities of Mr. Madison, who know that his whole life has been devoted to the services of the public, and that he has so conducted himself as to avoid every cause of offence in his public speeches and private conversation to any man or description of men — that envy itself, or the jaundiced eye of faction have never imputed to him interested or corrupt motives — might be at a loss to account for such marks of neglect or disapprobation: —But, Sir, the conduct of Mr. Henry on the day of Mr. Madison's nomination, fully explains the mystery — in a well informed speech, he made a pointed attack against him in the House, taking for the ground of his opposition, Mr. Madison's attachment to the Federal Government. I felt much for Mr. Madison, but more for my country—for I considered this as the trumpet of discord—a dæmon which I fear will destroy that domestic peace and happiness which unanimity of sentiment has hitherto secured to us, as well during the late arduous conflict as since its happy conclusion.— Hereafter, when a gentleman is nominated to a public office, it is not his virtue, his abilities or his patriotism we are to regard, but whether he is a federalist or anti-federalist—a distinction which might well take place while the new government was under consideration, but which ought to cease as soon as it was agreed to.[73]

After Madison's rejection as a senator, he and his fellow Virginia Federalists began an effort to get him elected to the U.S. House of Representatives. On November 19 the Virginia legislature created ten election districts throughout the state and called for the election to be held on February 2, 1789. Patrick Henry's influence was again predominant, and he did what he could to defeat Madison's candidacy. The election law provided that candidates had to be residents of the district they represented. Henry thereupon loaded the Fifth District, Madison's home district, with eight counties, half of which were heavily Antifederalist. Antifederalists selected James Monroe, Madison's close friend who had staunchly opposed the ratification of the Constitution in the state convention, as Madison's only challenger. It was expected that Monroe's supporters would be "most active . . . to secure his election."[74]

Madison's friends advised him that his election would not be easy. They strongly advised him to return home and campaign throughout the district, appearing in each county on its monthly court day, or to write a statement for publication outlining his position on amendments to the Constitution. Madison "always despised and wish[ed] to shun" "electioneering appearances." Before he knew what counties formed his district, he felt that "if Orange should fall into a federal district it is probable I shall not be opposed; if otherwise a successful opposition seems unavoidable." But the news from the Fifth District was bad. Antifederalists, encouraged by Patrick Henry, were "making every exertion, however unmanly to exclude" Madison from the House of Representatives. They "propagate an idea that you are wholly opposed to any alteration in the Govt. having declared that you did not think that a single letter in it would admit of a change. This circumstance alone would render your presence necessary for let these reports be denied as often as they may by your friends, there are others among those who oppose you who will as repeatedly revive them and nothing can give them an effectual check but a Denial of them in the face of the people and an avowal of your real Sentiments on the subject of Amendments."[75]

A few Virginia Federalists advised Madison not to make the arduous journey home to campaign. They expected that he would be elected in his home district because they had been told that "the people of both descriptions are much disgusted with all the proceedings of the Anti's here." If Madison was defeated in the Fifth District, Virginia Federalists would run him as a candidate in either the Third or the Tenth District. Although this would violate the state election law, which required that candidates be a "bona fide" resident of the district, Madison's advisers were "of the opinion that such a restriction was not within the power of the Legislature, and that it will avail nothing in Congress, where the qualifications of Members are to be judged of."[76]

Campaigning was heavy in the Fifth District throughout January 1789. Newspapers, broadsides, and personal visits one-on-one got the candidates' messages across. Monroe's supporters advocated that voters "unite in favor of a Gentleman who has been uniformly in favour of Amendments. . . . A man who possesses great abilities, integrity and a most amiable Character who has been many years a member of Congress, of the House of Delegates and of the Privy Council." They said the question voters should ask themselves was: Do you favor amendments to the Constitution? "If you do, who is the most likely to obtain them, the man who has been uniformly in favor of them, or one who has been uniformly against them."[77]

Madison was so concerned about the election that he returned to Virginia late in December to campaign. He attended January court days and met and corresponded with county leaders and influential Baptist ministers. He and Monroe traveled around the district together, and on several occasions they debated. At one such debate on court day in Culpeper County, "in the open air, on a cold, January day . . . in the face of a keen, north-easterly wind," one of Madison's ears suffered frost-bite. Traces of the injury remained throughout his life. He sometimes "playfully pointed to them as the honorable scars he had borne from the battle-field."[78]

Madison wrote several letters that were published to explain his position on amendments. To Baptist minister George Eve, pastor of Blue Run Church in Orange County, he wrote:

> I freely own that I have never seen in the Constitution as it now stands those serious dangers which have alarmed many respectable Citizens. Accordingly whilst it remained unratified, and it was necessary to unite the States in some one plan, I opposed all previous alterations as calculated to throw the States into dangerous contentions, and to furnish the Secret enemies of the Union with an opportunity of promoting its dissolution. Circumstances are now changed. The Constitution is established on the ratifications of eleven States and a very great majority of the people of America; and amendments, if pursued with a proper moderation and in a proper mode, will be not only safe, but may serve the double purpose of satisfying the minds of well meaning opponents, and of providing additional guards in favour of liberty. Under this change of circumstances, it is my sincere opinion that the Constitution ought to be revised, and that the first Congress meeting under it, ought to prepare and recommend to the States for ratification, the most satisfactory provisions for all essential rights, particularly the rights of Conscience in the fullest latitude, the freedom of the press, trials by jury, security against general warrants &c.[79]

"A friend to religious freedom" addressed the freeholders of the district.

> The eyes of all America have been fixed on Virginia, with anxious expectation, that in her late choice of senators, the eminent services and distinguished virtue of Mr. MADISON, would not have been forgot. The eyes of all virtuous in Virginia, are now placed on you, with confident hopes, that you will not frustrate their warmest wish, by following the example of your Legislature. Remember, it is now no novelty for the people to correct the errors of the Assembly, and recal them to a sense of their duty. It

is, indeed, the most valuable prerogative which a free people can
enjoy, and, when manfully asserted, will never fail to prove their
defence against every violation of their rights, arising either from
party spirit, or the overgrown influence of individuals.

. . . Believe me, you were never called on to give your votes
on a matter of such infinite concern. It is not every age, nor every
country, which can furnish a man of equal endowments and
virtues with the one you have it in your power to chuse. Virginia cannot boast his equal. What then must be the anguish of
mind, which the lovers of virtue, morality and religious freedom,
through the state, will suffer, if you disappoint them in a man
whom they revere as the fairest patron of the former, and the firm-
est bulwark of the latter?[80]

Madison's effort paid off. The polls opened on Monday, February 2,
under severe winter conditions. Temperatures fell to −10° below zero
that morning. A few votes trickled in over the next couple days. Madison and Monroe evenly split the eight counties of the Fifth District,
but Madison had a 336-vote majority out of the 2,280 votes cast. Madison's cousin, the Reverend James Madison, president of the College of
William and Mary, expressed the feelings of many Virginians. "I rejoice
that you are in a Situation, which enables you to be extensively useful,
& that, we who are to receive the Law may at least be assured, one Voice
will always utter what Wisdom & Virtue shall dictate." South Carolin-
ian Ralph Izard was "very glad to find that Mr. Madison is elected. . . .
I think highly of his abilities and expect considerable advantages will
be derived from them."[81]

President's Adviser

Madison and George Washington first met in August 1781. Their
correspondence and collaboration increased in the mid-1780s, and
they became close friends. Their "relationship flourished because each
possessed something the other needed. Washington relied heavily on
Madison's advice, pen, and legislative skills. Madison, in turn, found
Washington's prestige essential for achieving his goals for the new nation, especially a stronger federal government."[82] For fifteen years their

careers intertwined: both left federal service to return to Virginia in 1783, both served in the Federal Convention in Philadelphia in 1787, both took office under the new Constitution in 1789, and both retired from public service in 1797, by which time they were estranged and never communicated with each other again.

When Madison came back to Virginia to campaign for a seat in the House of Representatives, he stopped at Mount Vernon for a week of consultations. After the election Madison left Montpelier in mid-February 1789 to attend Congress in New York City. On his way he again stopped at Mount Vernon for ten days. For the next several years, Madison would serve as a special adviser to the president, as a sort of cabinet secretary without portfolio, a floor leader, or almost a prime minister. The president sought Madison's advice on a wide range of issues : on protocol, appointments, speeches, legislation, foreign affairs, western lands, and especially precedent-setting matters. The first service offered by Madison was writing Washington's inaugural address.

Sometime before December 1788 Washington had asked David Humphreys, a former aide-de-camp who had been living at Mount Vernon since October 1787, to write an inaugural address in case it might be needed. In early January 1789, when Madison had only recently arrived in Virginia to campaign, Washington sent him a seventy-three-page handwritten copy of Humphreys's draft. Madison and other confidants confirmed Washington's suspicion that Humphreys's draft ought not to be delivered. Instead, Washington asked Madison to draft a new inaugural address. The two men discussed what should go into the speech.

George Washington took the oath of office as president on the balcony of Federal Hall in New York City on April 30, 1789. After the oath Washington addressed a joint session of Congress in the Senate chamber. He spoke for eleven minutes, far more appropriate than the two hours that it would have taken to deliver Humphreys's version. In the speech Washington expressed his unwillingness and his lack of qualifications to serve as president. However, a sense of duty—one of the themes of the address—forced him to accept the position. "I was summoned by my Country, whose voice I can never hear but with veneration and love." In this his "first official Act," Washington thanked

Heaven for smiling upon America. Americans had set an example of adopting a new form of government peacefully. Washington hoped that the members of Congress would work for the good of the Union, because "the preservation of the sacred fire of liberty, and the destiny of the Republican model of Government, are justly considered as deeply, perhaps as finally staked, on the experiment entrusted to the hands of the American people." The address avoided specific recommendations, with one exception. Washington asked that Congress propose a bill of rights to be added to the Constitution. Such a proposal would demonstrate "a reverence for the characteristic rights of freemen, and a regard for the public harmony."[83]

The two houses broke up and reassembled in their own chambers. Each house appointed a committee to respond to the president's speech. Madison chaired the House committee. The House vowed to work with the president "in a system of legislation, founded on the principles of an honest policy, and directed by the spirit of a diffusive patriotism." Immediately on receiving the House's response, Washington asked Madison to write his response to the House. Madison's response for Washington said that "your very affectionate Address produces emotions which I know not how to express." The president was speechless: yes, Madison was doing all of the writing. The Senate responded to the inaugural address on May 16, and again the president asked Madison if he would write his response, which ended with the statement, "I readily engage with you in the arduous, but pleasing, task, of attempting to make a Nation happy."[84] In fact, it could be said that this was Madison's lifework—"to make a Nation happy."

❧ First Federal Congress

Madison arrived in New York in mid-March 1789, but the House of Representatives did not have a quorum until April 1. Much was expected of the new Congress, and much of Madison personally. Fisher Ames, a young dynamic congressman from Massachusetts, said of Madison, "He is our first man." An older Pennsylvania congressman was pleased to see Ames and Madison "introduced to each other—two young but shining political characters, who cannot fail distinguishing themselves in the Federal legislature."[85]

Ames described Madison as

> a man of sense, reading, address, and integrity, as 'tis allowed. Very
> much Frenchified in his politics. He speaks low, his person is little
> and ordinary. He speaks decently, as to manner, and no more. His
> language is very pure, perspicuous, and to the point. Pardon me,
> if I add, that I think him a little too much of a book politician, and
> too timid in his politics, for prudence and caution are opposites
> of timidity. He is not a little of a Virginian, and thinks that state
> the land of promise, but is afraid of their state politics, and of his
> popularity there, more than I think he should be.

Two weeks later Ames again wrote that

> Madison is cool, and has an air of reflection, which is not very dis-
> tant from gravity and self-sufficiency. In speaking, he never relaxes
> into pleasantry, and discovers little . . . warmth of heart. . . . he
> speaks very slow, and his discourse is strongly marked. He states a
> principle and deduces consequences, with clearness and simplic-
> ity. Sometimes declamation is mingled with argument, and he ap-
> pears very anxious to carry a point by other means than address-
> ing their understandings. He appeals to popular topics, and to the
> pride of the House, such as that they have voted before, and will
> be inconsistent. I think him a good man and an able man, but he
> has rather too much theory, and wants [i.e., lacks] that discretion
> which men of business commonly have. He is also very timid, and
> seems evidently to want manly firmness and energy of character.[86]

Ames had some insight into Madison, and his descriptions of his speaking style are valuable. But he greatly underestimated the steel in Madison and his leadership ability. In the coming years Ames and Madison
were to become leaders of their respective parties in the new, often bitterly partisan party system.

While waiting for a quorum to arrive, Madison read a list of those
elected to Congress. He lamented that there was but "a very scanty proportion who will share in the drudgery of business."[87] As in the old Congress, he knew he would have to take the lead. He did so almost immediately, proposing an impost bill that would provide the primary revenue
for the new government. He opposed a protective tariff that would help

infant American industries, preferring instead a tariff that would raise enough revenue to eliminate the need for other taxes and excises. He also fought strenuously to include a discriminatory provision in the bill that would levy a higher tariff on the goods of those countries that did not have commercial treaties with the United States, a measure aimed primarily at Great Britain. The Senate removed this last provision.

Madison also began the process of creating the government of the United States. He introduced legislation to set up cabinet departments for foreign affairs, the treasury, and war. In debate Madison strongly advocated that the president had the power to remove officials without the need for senatorial approval, a position approved by the House and then by the Senate, with Vice President John Adams casting the tie-breaking vote.

Early in the session Madison announced that he would soon propose amendments to the Constitution. He found little support. Both Federalist and Antifederalist congressmen believed that there were more important matters that needed immediate attention. Undismayed, Madison persevered and on June 8, 1789, presented one of the greatest speeches in congressional history, advocating a series of amendments that would protect rights. Madison preferred that the amendments be incorporated into the text of the Constitution, not collected at its end in the form of a bill of rights.

Madison declared that his purpose in proposing the amendments was to show that Federalists "were as sincerely devoted to liberty and a republican government, as those who charged them with wishing the adoption of this constitution in order to lay the foundation of an aristocracy or despotism." He also wanted to reconcile Antifederalists, the greatest part of whom had opposed the Constitution because it did not contain "those safeguards which they have been long accustomed to have interposed between them and the magistrates who exercised the sovereign powers." He expected that the amendments also might encourage North Carolina and Rhode Island to ratify the Constitution. Madison believed that a bill of rights would "kill the opposition everywhere" and would eliminate any possibility that a second constitutional convention would be called.

Madison reiterated many things that he stated in his published campaign letters. He never saw the Constitution as dangerous without a bill of rights, but he had opposed any effort to amend the Constitution before it was ratified. Now with the Constitution ratified, he supported amendments to protect rights, but he was "unwilling to see a door opened for a re-consideration of the whole structure of government," as might happen in a second general convention.

Madison argued that in republics the legislative branch of government "is the most powerful, and most likely to be abused." The great danger was that through the legislature the majority of the people would abuse the rights of the minority. The legislature could be constrained by bicameralism and by the presidential veto. Another powerful restraint would come from the courts through judicial review. By having rights spelled out in the Constitution, "independent tribunals of justice" would draw upon them and "would become an impenetrable bulwark" against every assumption of power in the legislative or executive branch. The judiciary would strike down as null and void any act of Congress that violated the bill of rights.

Madison always believed that the states had been violating private rights during the Confederation years and likely would continue to do so. He therefore provided in the amendments he introduced that the states could not violate the freedom of conscience, the freedom of the press, and the right to trial by jury in criminal cases. During the debate in the House, the right of freedom of speech was added. Later, when the Senate considered the amendments submitted by the House, the amendments limiting the states were deleted. The Senate—elected by the state legislatures at that time—wanted no restrictions on its constituents. Thus until after the adoption of the Fourteenth Amendment, the Bill of Rights applied only to the federal government. Madison concluded his speech by saying that

> nothing is in contemplation, so far as I have mentioned, that can endanger the beauty of the government in any one important feature, even in the eyes of its most sanguine admirers. I have proposed nothing that does not appear to me as proper in itself, or eligible as patronized by a reasonable number of our fellow citizens; and if we can make the constitution better in the opinion of those who are opposed to it, without weakening its frame, or abridging its usefulness, in the judgment of those who are attached to it, we

act the part of wise and liberal men to make such alterations as shall produce that effect. . . . We should obtain the confidence of our fellow citizens, in proportion as we fortify the rights of the people against the encroachments of the government.

The House debated Madison's amendments for two months, deciding to keep them as an addendum rather than integrating them into the original Constitution. They were thus sent on to the Senate, which modified some amendments and deleted those restricting the states. A conference committee worked out the differences, and the amendments were sent to the states for their consideration. Within two years the required three-quarters of the state legislatures adopted the ten amendments that we now refer to as the Bill of Rights.

Madison was severely condemned for his staunch advocacy of the amendments during the long House debate. Massachusetts Federalist representative Theodore Sedgwick wrote that "Mr. Madison's talents, respectable as they are will for some time be lost to the public, from his timidity. He is constantly haunted with the ghost of Patrick Henry. No man, in my opinion, in this country has more fair and honorable intentions, or more ardently wishes the prosperity of the public, but unfortunately he has not that strength of nerves which will enable him to set at defiance popular and factious clamors." Fisher Ames said that Virginia's "murmurs, if louder than a whisper, make Mr. Madison's heart quake." Federalist Robert Morris, one of Pennsylvania's senators, lamented "Poor Madison took one wrong step in Virginia by publishing a letter respecting Amendments and you, who know every thing, must know what a Cursed thing it is to write a Book. He in consequence has been obliged to bring on the proposition for making Amendments; The Waste of precious time is what has vexed me the most, for as to the Nonsense they call Amendments I never expect that any part of it will go through the various Trials which it must pass before it can become a part of the Constitution."[88]

In the old Congress and in the debate over ratifying the new Constitution, Madison had worked closely with Alexander Hamilton. In the new government it was said that Madison was responsible for Hamilton's being appointed secretary of the treasury. There was every reason to believe that their cooperation would continue, but soon Secretary

Hamilton submitted his economic plans for the nation. They called for the wartime debt largely held by foreign and domestic speculators to be funded at face value, the assumption of the states' wartime debt by the federal government, the creation of a national bank with private and public ownership of bank stock, an excise tax on a variety of commodities including whiskey, and a series of bounties and protections for certain manufactures. Madison opposed all of these proposals, which were extremely unpopular in Virginia and the rest of the South. The bank and the bounties, Madison argued, were unconstitutional because they were not powers specifically enumerated in the Constitution. The funding of the debt and the establishment of the bank were adopted despite Madison's opposition. The assumption of the state debts passed in a compromise brokered by Madison, Jefferson, and Hamilton, exchanging southern votes (though not Madison's) in favor of assumption for northern votes to move the location of the federal capital from New York City to a site along the Potomac River. The support for manufacturing was never enacted.

Madison's opposition to Hamilton's program was severely criticized. He "disgusted many of his friends" as well as his political opponents. According to Theodore Sedgwick,

> Mr. Madison who is the leader of the opposition is an apostate from all his former principles. Whether he is really a convert to anti-federalism—whether he is actuated by the mean and base motives of acquiring popularity in his own state that he may fill the place of Senator which will probably soon be vacated by the death of Grayson, or whether he means to put himself at the head of the discontented in America time will discover. The last, however, I do not suspect, because I have ever considered him as a very timid man. Deprived of his aid the party would soon be weak and inefficient.

Federalist Benjamin Goodhue, a Massachusetts congressman, believed that "Madison would be an excellent politician if he was not so much warped by local considerations, and popular influences, but with those about him he is a dangerous foe, to those measures which soar above trifling objects, and have national advantages for their basis." John Trumbull of Connecticut, also a Federalist, felt that "Maddison's character is

certainly not rising in the public estimation. He now acts on a conspicuous stage and does not equal expectation. He becomes more and more
a Southern Partisan and loses his assumed candor and moderation."
Another Federalist, Gouverneur Morris, a colleague from the Federal
Convention, believed that Madison had really hurt his own reputation.

> I am very sorry indeed to learn that our friend Madison has
> adopted such singular Ideas respecting the public Debt. This
> Thing will prove injurious to him because it will give a Handle
> to those who may wish to call his Judgment in Question and the
> World is so formed that Objections on that Ground are frequently
> more fatal than upon that of Morals. I think that on this Occasion
> he has been induced to adopt the Opinions of others for I can-
> not believe that his own Mind would so much have misled him.
> I am very very sorry for it because I think he is one of those Men
> whose Character is valuable to America.[89]

The Opposition

The politics of the 1790s became increasingly partisan. Thomas Jefferson returned from Paris late in 1789 and accepted Washington's appointment as U.S. secretary of state. Henry Knox served as secretary of
war, and Edmund Randolph was attorney general. With the establishment of the cabinet, President Washington gradually relied more on it
and less on Madison for advice. Madison and Jefferson increasingly felt
that Hamilton's policies would lead either to monarchy or a rapprochement with Great Britain. The French Revolution and the European war
added to the growing partisanship. "Democratic-Republican" societies
sprang up throughout the country criticizing the influence of Hamilton over the president. The 1794 Jay Treaty with Great Britain further
heightened opposition to the Washington administration, especially in
the South.

Washington had wanted to retire from the presidency after one term,
and at his request Madison had drafted a farewell address for him. Washington's advisers all convinced him to stay for another term. By 1796,
however, he decided that he would not seek a third term. By this time
Washington and Madison had become estranged. The president gave

Hamilton Madison's draft 1792 farewell address to recast for publication in September 1796. Both Washington and Madison retired from public service in March 1797 and returned to Virginia.

It was during the beginning of Washington's second term that a major alteration in Madison's personal life occurred. In May 1794 he asked Aaron Burr to introduce him formally to one of Burr's law clients, the attractive twenty-six-year-old widow Dolley Payne Todd. The previous year her Quaker husband and in-laws and her youngest child all died in the terrible yellow fever epidemic that struck Philadelphia. With the estates settled, Dolley, left with one son, was a very eligible widow. Madison was quite smitten with Dolley. She was vivacious, witty, intelligent, and well read. Madison probably also felt more responsibility for Montpelier with the death of his brother Ambrose in 1793 and his father's advancing age. By August 1794 Dolley had accepted Madison's proposal of marriage, and the couple was wed on September 15, 1794. Marriage readily agreed with Madison. Connecticut Federalist Jonathan Trumbull Jr. wrote that "Mr. Madison has been married in the course of last summer—which event or some other, has relieved him of much Bile—and rendered him much more open and conversant than I have seen him before."[90]

Vice President John Adams succeeded Washington as president, but his administration drifted deeper into partisan politics, and the Federalist Party itself divided between supporters of Hamilton and backers of President Adams. An undeclared naval war with France developed after the French, viewing the Jay Treaty as a rapprochement between America and Great Britain, began seizing American merchantmen. The French aggression frightened Federalists, who for several years had pictured Jeffersonian Republicans as Jacobins bent on bringing class warfare and the guillotine to America. Jeffersonians increasingly viewed Federalists as monarchists. War fever increased the Federalists' popularity and their majority in Congress.

Congress authorized a provisional army of 25,000 men. President Adams named Washington commander-in-chief; Washington accepted the position on the condition that Hamilton be put second in command. Republicans feared that the army, with Hamilton commanding in the field, would be used not against an invading French army but against Republicans. The Alien and Sedition Acts of 1798 increased their fears, especially when the administration and the federal judiciary vigorously prosecuted Republican newspaper printers and even one opposition congressman under the Sedition Act.

Madison and Jefferson anonymously wrote resolutions for the Virginia and Kentucky legislatures, both controlled by Jeffersonians, condemning the Alien and Sedition Acts and calling upon other states to join in working for their repeal. Madison had come a long way in the last decade. In 1787–88 he saw the states as the greatest danger to the authority of Congress and the rights of the people. Now, in 1798, he called upon the states to protect the people from the increasingly powerful and despotic federal government.

With war seemingly inevitable, President Adams made one last effort at peace. Although this effort ultimately avoided all-out war, it bitterly divided the Federalist Party; and as the threat of war subsided, Federalist war measures, including new taxes, became very unpopular. Jeffersonians strenuously campaigned in 1800 and were highly successful at the state and federal levels. Jefferson and Aaron Burr defeated Adams and Charles Cotesworth Pinckney for the presidency. Although Jefferson was the assumed candidate for president and Burr for vice president, the two men each received 73 electoral votes. Because of the tie vote, the election went to the Federalist-dominated lame-duck House of Representatives, where it took thirty-six ballots before Jefferson was elected president.

❧ Secretary of State

A couple of weeks before the House of Representatives elected Jefferson president, Jefferson asked Madison to come to Washington, D.C., to be his secretary of state. Madison felt such a journey would be premature. Furthermore, after a year during which both Madison and his father were often ill, Madison's father died on February 27, 1801. As executor of the estate, Madison struggled to fulfill his father's wishes. The settlement was complicated by the fact that since his father wrote his will years before, two of Madison's siblings had died. Several scraps of paper and a number of oral statements made by James Madison Sr. also had to be considered. Then, as Madison was about ready to leave Montpelier, he was bedridden for four days by a severe attack of rheumatism. Madison finally arrived in the capital on May 1, 1801. Although nearly half of the country felt that Jefferson was unqualified to be president, "the virtuous, whatever their political Sentiments may be," had confidence in Madison's "Virtue & Talent."[91]

Immediately Madison plunged into his work. The State Department not only managed the country's foreign affairs, corresponding with America's five ministers, twenty-five consuls, and seven commissioners; but the secretary of state also handled important domestic functions, such as granting copyrights and patents, supervising the mint, overseeing and publishing laws, corresponding with state and territorial governors, and preparing commissions for all presidential appointments. Furthermore, Madison was President Jefferson's closest and most trusted adviser.

Madison spent most of his time dealing with foreign affairs. A number of crises were awaiting his attention. Tripoli, which along with Algiers had signed a treaty with the United States in 1796, broke away from its subservience to Algiers, revoked the treaty, and in September 1800 captured an American merchantman. The ship was brought to Tripoli and promptly released, but the pasha demanded that America pay Tripoli an annual tribute of $20,000. The newly arrived secretary of state advised the president to send a naval squadron to the Mediterranean without the approval of Congress and at the same time to openly declare America's intent. Opponents in Congress objected to this executive action, which in their opinion was an unconstitutional act of declaring war, a power the Constitution gave exclusively to Congress. Secretary Madison publicly and privately announced the purpose of the naval expedition. It was not to declare war; it was to strengthen the diplomatic leverage of the American consuls in the Barbary States, to preserve the peace as well as to enhance "the dignity and interests of the United States."[92] The ships' commanders were ordered not to fire unless first fired upon. If Tripoli's navy attacked American vessels, that would be a declaration of war to which the American squadron would be forced to respond.

War ensued and went on for four long years. Jefferson and Madison were roundly condemned for their war and for sending insufficient forces to defeat Tripoli quickly. The administration's excessive frugality had prolonged the conflict and endangered American lives.[93] Not until

1805 did the pasha and Algiers and Tunis agree to sign treaties opening their region to American ships without demanding tribute.

A more serious diplomatic problem arose in October 1802 when Spain announced the closing of the port of New Orleans to American trade. It soon became evident that Spain was going to transfer its territory along the Mississippi to France, a dangerous move in the eyes of Jefferson and Madison. Madison instructed Robert R. Livingston, America's new minister to France, to make an offer "on convenient terms" to purchase New Orleans and Florida as the means to end one of America's most "perplexing" problems. The goal was to have "a pacific policy" and "to seek by just means the establishment of the Mississippi, down to its mouth" as America's boundary.[94]

When Napoleon offered to sell America the entire Louisiana territory for $15 million, Jefferson thought about seeking a constitutional amendment to authorize the purchase. Madison, however, advised against such a time-consuming action. In his view the treaty power of the president provided sufficient authority for this grand purchase. If Jefferson felt some constitutional qualms when new states created from this territory were ready to be admitted to the Union, a constitutional amendment could be sought at that time. Satisfied with Madison's advice, Jefferson authorized the purchase, and the Senate ratified the treaty on October 20, 1803.

The Spanish were quite upset with the sale of Louisiana to the United States. The marquis de Casa Yrujo, Spanish minister to the United States, protested that the sale violated the agreement between Spain and France, thus rescinding the Spanish cession to France. Yrujo also vehemently rejected America's assertion that West Florida was included in the sale. Madison strenuously rejected the Spanish arguments, informing Yrujo "that we shall not withhold any means that may be rendered necessary to secure our object." He sent troops, and America took formal possession of Louisiana on December 20. Insisting that the eastern boundary of Louisiana was at the Perdido River (now the western border of the state of Florida), Madison sent James Monroe and Charles Pinckney to Madrid to negotiate a treaty with Spain, but no agreement was reached.

Jefferson's second administration was dominated by European affairs. After a brief truce in 1802, the ten-year-old European war was rekindled. Trying to avoid being drawn into the war, Jefferson and Madison used commerce—including an embargo—to protect American shipping. But as Mathew Carey reported, Jefferson and Madison succeeded only in alienating New England. Increasingly throughout his second term, and especially after 1807 when Jefferson announced that he would not seek reelection, the president deferred to his secretary of state, whom he hoped would succeed him. Many agreed that there was no proper leadership as the president "consulted the other heads of department but little." After Madison was elected president, Jefferson only offered advice while the secretary of state—now the president-elect—made all final decisions. Repeatedly Jefferson expressed confidence in Madison as "eminently qualified as a safe depository by the endowments of integrity, understanding, and experience." According to the outgoing president, his successor possessed "the purest principles of republican patriotism" and "a wisdom and foresight second to no man on earth."[95] But throughout the last year of Jefferson's presidency, the country drifted between war and peace.

President

Because of the restrictive trade policies of the Jefferson administration, Federalists, especially in New England, gained strength both at the state and federal levels in the 1808 elections. In Connecticut the governor and the legislature rejected the Jefferson administration's request for additional legislation to "put an end to the scandalous insubordination" in not enforcing the federal embargo on commerce. Governor Jonathan Trumbull told his legislature that the federal government's Enforcement Act contained "many very extraordinary, not to say unconstitutional provisions for its execution." He called on the legislature "to devise such constitutional measures as in their wisdom may be judged proper to avert the threatening evil." The legislature, in a move reminiscent of Madison's and Jefferson's 1798 Virginia and Kentucky resolutions, agreed that the federal act should not be enforced, stating that it had "a sense of paramount public duty . . . to abstain from any agency in the execution of measures, which are unconstitutional and despotic." Madison's old friend Virginia Federalist Henry "Light Horse Harry" Lee advised the incoming president to separate himself from the diplomatic policies of the previous administration. "I confess I am persuaded the less you connect your administration with the last, the better your chance to do good to your country which I am sure is your sole wish & will be both your best reward and highest glory."[96]

Others, however, expected and wanted Madison to continue Jefferson's policies. The Republican committee of Essex County, New Jersey, anticipated "the same moderate, prudent, & pacific course" as Jefferson's. At the opposite end of the state, the Republican committee of Salem County supported the previous "system of policy characterized by wisdom and economy at home, by justice and impartiality abroad." The committee expected much of Madison. "We trust with the utmost confidence that the powers which the constitution of the general government has allotted you will be employed for the public benefit. We entertain no apprehensions that you who had so distinguished a share in proposing, in forming, and in advocating the adoption of that excellent instrument would suffer it to be injured by the unhallowed hands of its enemies. No, Sir, we remain satisfied that it will be preserved inviolate while you are entrusted with the exercise of the presidential functions." The oppressive policies of Britain and France on the high seas in restraining the rights of neutrals "forced our government to adopt such measures as we believe would have been attended with complete success had all our Citizens been true to their country and its laws." Even with the rampant smuggling that violated the embargo, success was near if the United States stayed the course. But the situation boiled down to a simple choice: "whether Connecticut shall yield to the G[eneral] government, or the G[eneral] Government yield to Connecticut."[97]

In a single paragraph in his inaugural address, Madison outlined the goals of his administration in following the "examples of illustrious services, successfully rendered in the most trying difficulties, by those who have marched before me." Madison promised

To cherish peace and friendly intercourse with all nations having correspondent disposition; to maintain sincere neutrality towards belligerent nations; to prefer in all cases amicable discussion and reasonable accommodation of differences, to a decision of them by an appeal to Arms; to exclude foreign intrigues and foreign partialities, so degrading to all Countries, and so baneful to free ones; to foster a spirit of independence too just to invade the rights of others, too proud to surrender our own, too liberal to indulge unworthy prejudices ourselves, and too elevated not to look down upon them in others; to hold the Union of the States as the basis of their peace and happiness; to support the Constitution, which is the cement of the Union, as well in its limitations as in its authorities, to respect the rights and authorities reserved to the States and to the people, as equally incorporated with, and essential to the success of, the general system.[98]

Despite his strong desire to avoid war, Madison, pushed by "war-hawks" in Congress, stumbled into it. Upset with the continued British harassment on the high seas and the British incitement of Indians in the Northwest Territory, President Madison asked Congress for a declaration of war, which a divided Congress voted to approve on June 18, 1812. From the beginning of the war, American military fortunes fared badly. Old and inept generals, incompetent leadership by the president and his cabinet, poor recruitment and communications, and the continued strong opposition in New England hampered the war effort. Only the navy fared well, especially on the Great Lakes. The low point of the war occurred in 1814 when the British briefly occupied and burned Washington, D.C., destroying many of the public buildings, including the Capitol and the President's Mansion. A similar British assault on Baltimore failed as the city withstood a persistent naval bombardment that inspired Francis Scott Key to write a poem entitled "The Star-Spangled Banner," which after being put to music became the national anthem. General Andrew Jackson's spectacular victory over the British at New Orleans in January 1815, almost two weeks after the signing of the peace treaty at Ghent, ended the war on a high note.[99]

Despite the military problems many Americans viewed the war as successful, and for the remainder of his presidency, Madison rode a wave of patriotic fervor. Federalists, especially New Englanders who had met in a three-week antiwar convention in Hartford from December 15, 1814, to January 5, 1815, were discredited.[100] Americans had a new sense of national pride and unity.

❦ Retirement

Madison started his long retirement on March 4, 1817. For almost twenty years he busied himself reading in a wide variety of subjects and collecting and arranging his papers for a posthumous publication. He rose early, had breakfast between 8:00 and 9:00, and then relaxed on the portico with family and guests, sometimes looking through a telescope at distant plantations and the mountains. For exercise he rode his horse Liberty about the plantation. On rainy days he walked back and forth on the porch, sometimes, it was reported, even racing Dolley. He regularly kept up his correspondence, especially with Jefferson, and served on the Board of Visitors of the University of Virginia from 1819 and then succeeded Jefferson as rector from 1826 to 1834. In June 1824 Samuel Whitcomb, an itinerant bookseller, described the retired president.

> Mr. Madison is not so large or so tall as myself and instead of being a cool reserved austere man, is very sociable, rather jocose, quite sprightly, and active. . . . [He] appears less studied, brilliant and frank but more natural, candid and profound than Mr. Jefferson. Mr. Jefferson has more imagination and passion, quicker and richer conceptions. Mr. Madison has a sound judgment, tranquil temper and logical mind. . . . Mr. Madison has nothing in his looks, gestures, expression or manners to indicate anything extraordinary in his intellect or character, but the more one converses with him, the more his excellences are developed and the better he is liked. And yet he has a quizzical, careless, almost waggish bluntness of looks and expression which is not at all prepossessing.[101]

Two years later, in his last letter to Madison, Jefferson wrote that

> the friendship which has subsisted between us, now half a century, and the harmony of our political principles and pursuits, have been sources of constant happiness to me through that long period. And if I remove beyond the reach of attentions to the University [of Virginia], or beyond the bourne of life itself, as I soon must, it is a comfort to leave that institution under your care,

and an assurance that it will not be wanting. It has also been a great solace to me, to believe that you are engaged in vindicating to posterity the course we have pursued for preserving to them, in all their purity, the blessings of self-government, which we had assisted too in acquiring for them. If ever the earth has beheld a system of administration conducted with a single and steadfast eye to the general interest and happiness of those committed to it, one which, protected by truth, can never know reproach, it is that to which our lives have been devoted. To myself you have been a pillar of support through life. Take care of me when dead, and be assured that I shall leave with you my last affections.

In his will Jefferson, as a symbol of his friendship, gave Madison his silver-hilted walking cane. Madison, in turn, in his will bequeathed this same cane to Thomas Jefferson Randolph, Jefferson's oldest grandson, "in testimony of the esteem I have for him as from the knowledge I have of the place he held in the affection of his grand father."[102]

Visitors besieged Montpelier, and all reported on the conviviality of the last of the founders. According to one visitor, Madison "keeps alive a strong interest in passing events," and he even served in the Virginia state constitutional convention of 1829, in which he played the role of a peacemaker. Jared Sparks, the prolific nineteenth-century historian, lived the dream of any historian in spending

five delightful days at Mr. Madison's. The situation of his residence is charming. The blossoms and verdure of the trees are just springing into perfection, and the scenery, embracing a distant view of the Blue Ridge, is commanding and beautiful. But I have had little time for these objects. . . . The intellect and memory of Mr. Madison appear to retain all their pristine vigor. He is peculiarly interesting in conversation, cheerful, gay, and full of anecdote; never a prosing talker, but sprightly, varied, fertile in his topics, and felicitous in his descriptions and illustrations. He seems busy in arranging his papers. While he was in the old Congress he rarely kept copies of his letters, though he wrote many. He has recently succeeded in procuring nearly all the originals from the descendants of the persons to whom he wrote them.[103]

Throughout his latter years Madison feared for the preservation of the Union. He denied the neo-Antifederalist interpretation of the Constitution as a compact among the states which had the power to nullify federal laws. In a memorandum titled "Advice to My Country" written in 1834, Madison wrote: "The advice nearest to my heart and deepest in my convictions is that the Union of the States be cherished and perpetuated. Let the open enemy to it be regarded as a Pandora with her box opened; and the disguised one, as the Serpent creeping with his deadly wiles into Paradise."[104]

As he got older, Madison's tiny handwriting got even smaller. "In explanation of my microscopic writing, I must remark that the older I grow, the more my stiffening fingers make smaller letters, as my feet take shorter steps; the progress in both cases being, at the same time, more fatiguing as well as more slow."[105] His rheumatism at times became crippling, and Dolley had to attend to him constantly. He suffered from shortness of breath and was obliged to sit or recline for the entire day.

Edward Coles, who had served as Madison's secretary during the presidential years, remembered Madison fondly.

In height he was about five feet six inches, of a small and delicate form, of rather a tawney complexion, bespeaking a sedentary and studious man; his hair was originally of a dark brown colour; his eyes were bluish . . . his form, features, and manner were not commanding, but his conversation exceedingly so, and few men possessed so rich a flow of language, or so great a fund of amusing anecdotes, which were made the more interesting from their being well timed and well told. His ordinary manner was simple, modest, bland, & unostentatious, retiring from the throng and cautiously refraining from doing or saying anything to make conspicuous—This made him appear a little reserved and formal. . . . [He was] the most virtuous, calm, and amiable of men; possessed of one of the purest hearts, and best tempers with which man was ever blessed. Nothing could excite or ruffle him. Under all circumstances he was collected, and ever mindful of what was due from him to others, and cautious not to wound the feelings of any one.[106]

Madison died on June 28, 1836. The entire country mourned. Comparisons were made between Madison and Jefferson. Eulogies abounded. Henry Clay, like other statesmen of the time, praised Madison as second only to Washington as "our greatest statesman and [our] first political writer." The *National Intelligencer* reported that "the last of the great lights of the Revolution . . . has sunk below the horizon . . . [and] left a radiance in the firmament." In writing his last letter the day before his death, Madison reflected on his "public services." He had cooperated sincerely and steadfastly "in promoting such a reconstruction of our political system as would provide for the permanent liberty and happiness of the United States; and that of the many good fruits it has produced which have well rewarded the efforts and anxieties that led to it, no one has been a more rejoicing witness than myself."[107]

Notes

ABBREVIATIONS AND SHORT TITLES

DHRC   Merrill Jensen, John P. Kaminski, and Gaspare J. Saladino, eds., *The Documentary History of the Ratification of the Constitution* (Madison, WI, 1976–)

GW   George Washington

JM   James Madison

PGW, ColS   W. W. Abbot et al., eds., *The Papers of George Washington, Colonial Series* (10 vols., Charlottesville, VA, 1983–95)

PGW, ConfS   W. W. Abbot et al., eds., *The Papers of George Washington, Confederation Series* (6 vols., Charlottesville, VA, 1992–97)

PGW, PresS   W. W. Abbot et al., eds., *The Papers of George Washington, Presidential Series* (Charlottesville, VA, 1987–)

PGW, RetS   W. W. Abbot et al., eds. *The Papers of George Washington, Retirement Series* (4 vols., Charlottesville, VA, 1998–99)

PGW, RevWarS   W. W. Abbot et al., eds., *The Papers of George Washington, Revolutionary War Series* (Charlottesville, VA, 1985–)

PJM   William T. Hutchinson et al., eds., *The Papers of James Madison* (17 vols., Chicago and Charlottesville, VA, 1962–91)

PJM, PresS   Robert A. Rutland et al., eds., *The Papers of James Madison, Presidential Series* (Charlottesville, VA, 1984–)

PJM, SecS   Robert J. Brugger et al., eds., *The Papers of James Madison, Secretary of State Series* (Charlottesville, VA, 1986–)

Plumer's Memorandum   Everett Somerville Brown, ed., *William Plumer's Memorandum of Proceedings in the United States Senate, 1803–1807* (New York, 1923)

PTJ   Julian P. Boyd et al., eds., *The Papers of Thomas Jefferson* (Princeton, NJ, 1950–)

PTJ, RetS   J. Jefferson Looney et al., eds., *The Papers of Thomas Jefferson: Retirement Series* (Princeton, NJ, 2004–)

TJ   Thomas Jefferson

TJ: Writings   Merrill D. Peterson, ed., *Thomas Jefferson: Writings* (New York, 1984)

Writings of GW   John C. Fitzpatrick, ed., *The Writings of George Washington from the Original Manuscript Sources, 1745–1799* (39 vols., Washington, DC, 1931–44)

Writings of TJ   H. A. Washington, ed., *The Writings of Thomas Jefferson* (9 vols., Washington, DC, 1853–54)

PREFACE

1. TJ to William Johnson, March 4, 1823, John P. Kaminski, ed., *The Quotable Jefferson* (Princeton, NJ, 2006), 184.
2. TJ to John Adams, June 27, 1813, Lester J. Cappon, ed., *The Adams-Jefferson Letters* . . . (Chapel Hill, NC, 1959), 336.
3. TJ to William Johnson, March 4, 1823, Kaminski, *Quotable Jefferson*, 185.
4. *Plumer's Memorandum*, March 16, 1806, p. 453.
5. Abigail Adams to John Adams, Oct. 22, 1775, L. H. Butterfield et al., eds., *Adams Family Correspondence* (Cambridge, MA, 1963–), 1:310.

GEORGE WASHINGTON

The subtitle, "The Greatest Man on Earth," is taken from John Marshall to James Monroe, Jan. 3, 1784, Daniel Preston, ed., *The Papers of James Monroe* (Westport, CT, 2006), 2:76.

1. Richard Brookhiser, ed., *Rules of Civility: The 110 Precepts That Guided Our First President in War and Peace* (New York, 1997); GW to George Washington Parke Custis, Nov. 28, 1796, *Writings of GW* 35:295.
2. Sarah S. Hughes, *Surveyors and Statesmen: Land Measuring in Colonial Virginia* (Richmond, 1979), 156.
3. GW to John Augustine Washington, May 31, 1754, *PGW, ColS* 1:118–19.
4. GW to Sarah Cary Fairfax, Sept. 25, 1758, *PGW, ColS* 6:42; officers quoted in James Thomas Flexner, *Washington: The Indispensable Man* (New York, 1969), 17.
5. *PGW, ColS* 6:192–93.
6. Charles Willson Peale, Recollection of Dec. 28, 1773, *Recollections and Private Memoirs of Washington, by His Adopted Son, George Washington Parke Custis* (New York, 1860), 519.
7. Robert Stewart to GW, Sept. 28, 1759, *PGW, ColS* 6:361. For the Indian prophecy, see Frank E. Grizzard Jr., *George Washington: A Biographical Companion* (Santa Barbara, CA, 2002), 157–58.
8. GW to Burwell Bassett, May 23, 1785, to Charles Armand-Tuffin, Aug. 10, 1786, to William Gordon, April 10, 1787, *PGW, ColS* 3:10, 4:203, 5:136; Martha Washington to Fanny Bassett Washington, Feb. 25, 1788, to Lucy Knox, post May 1797, Joseph E. Fields, comp., *"Worthy Partner": The Papers of Martha Washington* (Westport, CT, 1994), 206, 304. For Julian Ursyn Niemcewisz's account of his visit to Mount Vernon, see *Under Their Vine and Fig Tree: Travels through America in 1797–1799, 1805, with Some Further Account of Life in New Jersey*, trans. and ed. Metchie J. E. Budka (Elizabeth, NJ, 1965),

excerpted in Jean Lee's *Experiencing Mount Vernon: Eyewitness Accounts, 1784–1865* (Charlottesville, VA, 2006), 69–88.

9. GW to Arthur Young, Aug. 6, 1786, to Alexander Spotswood, Feb. 13, 1788, *PGW, ConfS* 4:196, 6:111; GW to John Sinclair, July 20, 1794, *Writings of GW* 33:437; Louis B. Wright and Marion Tinling, eds., *Quebec to Carolina in 1785–1786: Being the Travel Diary and Observations of Robert Hunter, Jr., a Young Merchant of London* (San Marino, CA, 1943), 191–98, excerpted in Lee, *Experiencing Mount Vernon*, 31.

10. GW to Clement Biddle, Aug. 22, 1787, *PGW, ConfS* 5:300–301.

11. GW to George Augustine Washington, July 15, 1787, ibid., 260; Paul Leicester Ford, *The True George Washington* (Philadelphia, 1896), 127.

12. GW to Lund Washington, Nov. 26, 1775, *PGW, RevWarS* 2:431–33; GW to Bushrod Washington, Jan. 15, 1783, quoted in Stephen E. Lucas, ed., *The Quotable George Washington: The Wisdom of an American Patriot* (Madison, WI, 1999), 14; GW to George Washington Parke Custis, Nov. 15, 1796, *Writings of GW* 35:283; Ford, *True George Washington*, 161–62.

13. GW to Benjamin Harrison, Oct. 10, 1784, to James Warren, Oct. 7, 1785, *PGW, ConfS* 2:89–90, 3:300. See Stuart Leibiger, *Founding Friendship: George Washington, James Madison, and the Creation of the American Republic* (Charlottesville, VA, 1999), 35–48, for the cooperation between GW and JM in establishing a system of canals.

14. GW to George Mason, April 5, 1769, *PGW, ColS* 8:178.

15. GW to Bryan Fairfax, July 4, 20, Aug. 24, 1774, to Robert McKenzie, Oct. 9, 1774, ibid., 10:109, 129–30, 155, 172.

16. Silas Deane to Elizabeth Deane, Sept. 10, 1774, Paul H. Smith, ed., *Letters of Delegates to Congress, 1774–1789* (26 vols., Washington, DC, 1986–2000), 1:61–62.

17. George W. Corner, ed., *The Autobiography of Benjamin Rush* (Princeton, NJ, 1948), 113.

18. GW to John Augustine Washington, June 20, 1775, *PGW, RevWarS* 1:19.

19. GW to Martha Washington, June 18, 1775, ibid., 3–4.

20. John Adams to Abigail Adams, June 17, 1775, Eliphalet Dyer to Joseph Trumbull, June 17, 1775, John Hancock to Elbridge Gerry, June 18, 1775, Smith, *Letters of Delegates* 1:497, 499–500, 507; Elkanah Watson, Memoirs, 1775, Winslow C. Watson, ed., *Men and Times of the Revolution; or Memoirs of Elkanah Watson* (New York, 1856), 243–44; Abigail Adams to John Adams, July 16, 1775, Butterfield, *Adams Family Correspondence* 1:246; Benjamin Rush to Thomas Ruston, Oct. 29, 1775, L. H. Butterfield, ed., *Letters of Benjamin Rush* (2 vols., Princeton, NJ, 1951), 1:92.

21. GW, Address to the New York Provincial Congress, June 26, 1775, *PGW, RevWarS* 1:41.

22. Richard Henry Lee to GW, Sept. 26, 1775, John Hancock to GW, April 2, 1776, ibid., 2:52, 4:16.

23. GW to John Hancock, Dec. 20, 1776, ibid., 7:382; John Adams to Mercy Otis Warren, Nov. 25, 1775, Jan. 8, 1776, Robert J. Taylor et al., eds. *Papers of John Adams* (Cambridge, MA, 1977–), 3:319, 399; GW to Samuel Washington, Dec. 18, 1776, *PGW, RevWarS* 7:370.

24. Thomas Paine, *American Crisis* I, Dec. 19, 1776, Eric Foner, ed., *Thomas Paine: Collected Writings* (New York, 1995), 91.

25. Corner, *Autobiography of Rush,* 124.

26. Ibid., 125; John Adams to Mercy Otis Warren, Jan. 1777, *Papers of John Adams* 2:151; Paine, *American Crisis* I, Dec. 19, 1776, Foner, *Paine: Writings,* 94; William Hooper to Robert Morris, Feb. 1, 1777, Smith, *Letters of Delegates* 6:191.

27. Benjamin Rush, Notes of Debates in Congress, Feb. 19, April 8, 1777, Charles Carroll of Carrollton to Charles Carroll Sr., Sept. 23, 1777, Smith, *Letters of Delegates* 6:324–25, 558, 8:11.

28. Jonathan Dickinson Sergeant to James Lovell, Nov. 20, 1777, Henry Laurens to the marquis de Lafayette, Jan. 12, 1778, to Isaac Motte, Jan. 26, 1778, ibid., 296, 571, 654.

29. GW to John Hancock, Sept. 8, 1776, *PGW, RevWarS* 6:249.

30. Memorandum of an Interview with Lieutenant Colonel James Paterson, July 20, 1776, ibid., 5:399.

31. GW to General William Howe, Oct. 6, 1777, ibid., 11:409–10.

32. Samuel Shaw to Francis Shaw, Jan. 7, 1777, Josiah Quincy, ed., *The Journals of Major Samuel Shaw* (Boston, 1847), 29–30.

33. Alexander Hamilton to Elias Boudinot, July 5, 1778, Harold C. Syrett, ed., *The Papers of Alexander Hamilton* (27 vols., New York, 1961–87), 1:511.

34. Elias Boudinot to Alexander Hamilton, July 8, 1778, Smith, *Letters of Delegates* 10:238; Lafayette to GW, June 12, 1779, Stanley J. Idzerda, ed., *Lafayette in the Age of the American Revolution: Selected Letters and Papers, 1776–1790* (5 vols., Ithaca, NY, 1977–83), 2:277.

35. Matthias Ogden to GW, April 9, 1778, GW to Matthias Ogden, April 13, 1778, *PGW, RevWarS* 14:440–41, 498–99.

36. JM, Notes of Debates in Congress, Feb. 20, 1783, Smith, *Letters of Delegates* 19:719.

37. GW to Alexander Hamilton, March 4, 1783, Syrett, *Papers of Hamilton* 3:278. GW's address is printed in *Writings of GW* 26:222–27. It also appears as an appendix to Mason Locke Weems, *The Life of Washington,* ed. Peter S. Onuf (Armonk, NY, 1996), 183–87.

38. Quoted in Flexner, *Washington: The Indispensable Man,* 174; Samuel Shaw to the Rev. Eliot, April 1783, *Journals of Shaw,* 104–5; chevalier de La Luzerne to comte de Vergennes, March 29, 1783, George Bancroft, ed., *History of the*

Formation of the Constitution of the United States of America (2 vols., New York, 1882–83), 1:301.

39. GW, Circular Letter to the State Executives, June 1783, *Writings of GW* 26:483–96. The letter is also printed in John P. Kaminski and Jill Adair McCaughan, eds., *A Great and Good Man: George Washington in the Eyes of His Contemporaries* (Madison, WI, 1989), 4–16, and in Don Higginbotham, *George Washington: Uniting a Nation* (Lanham, MD, 2002), 115–27.

40. Ibid.

41. *Writings of GW* 27:222–27. Also printed in Weems, *Life of Washington*, ed. Onuf, 187–91.

42. Stanley Weintraub, *General Washington's Christmas Farewell: A Mount Vernon Homecoming, 1783* (New York, 2003), 85.

43. James Tilton to Gunning Bedford Jr., Dec. 25, 1783, Smith, *Letters of Delegates* 21:232.

44. James McHenry to Margaret Caldwell, Dec. 23, 1783, ibid., 221–22. GW's address surrendering his commission is printed in *Writings of GW* 27:284–85, and Weems, *Life of Washington*, ed. Onuf, 191–92.

45. GW to Charles Thomson, Jan. 22, 1784, *PGW, ConfS* 1:71, 72n-73n.

46. GW to Lafayette, Feb. 1, 1784, ibid., 87–88.

47. GW to Mary Ball Washington, Feb. 15, 1787, to Lee Massey, July 10, 1784, to Samuel Vaughan, Nov. 12, 1787, ibid., 5:35, 1:494, 5:433.

48. GW to George Washington Parke Custis, Jan. 7, 1798, *PGW, RetS* 2:5; Julian Ursyn Niemcewicz, in Lee, *Experiencing Mount Vernon*, 82; GW to James McHenry, May 29, 1797, *PGW, RetS* 1:160.

49. Lafayette to Adrienne de Noailles de Lafayette, Aug. 20, 1784, Idzerda, *Lafayette* 5:237; GW to Lafayette, Dec. 8, 1784, *PGW, ConfS* 2:175.

50. Watson, *Memoirs*, Jan. 23–25, 1785, pp. 243–44.

51. Robert Hunter quoted in Lee, *Experiencing Mount Vernon*, 27; Olney Winsor to Hope Winsor, March 31, 1788, quoted in ibid., 54.

52. Francis Hopkinson to GW, April 19, 1785, GW to Francis Hopkinson, May 16, 1785, *PGW, ConfS* 2:508, 561–62.

53. John P. Kaminski, *George Clinton: Yeoman Politician of the New Republic* (Madison, WI, 1993), 51.

54. GW to Thomas Lewis, Dec. 25, 1787, *PGW, ConfS* 5:506–7.

55. Brookhiser, *Rules of Civility*, 50; GW quoted in John P. Kaminski, ed., *A Necessary Evil? Slavery and the Debate over the Constitution* (Madison, WI, 1995), 277; GW to Alexander Spotswood, Nov. 23, 1794, *Writings of GW* 34:47–48.

56. Ford, *True George Washington*, 139.

57. Ibid., 140.

58. GW to John Francis Mercer, Nov. 6, 1786, *PGW, ConfS* 4:336; GW to Joseph

Whipple, Nov. 28, 1796, *Writings of GW* 35:297; Ford, *True George Washington,* 140–41.

59. GW to James McHenry, Nov. 11, 1786, to William Drayton, Nov. 20, 1786, Edward Moyston to GW, April 4, 1787, *PGW, ConfS* 4:358, 389–90, 5:123.

60. GW to Robert Morris, April 12, 1786, Kaminski, *A Necessary Evil,* 276.

61. Ford, *True George Washington,* 142, 144.

62. GW to John Francis Mercer, Sept. 9, 1786, *PGW, ConfS* 4:243.

63. Ibid., and GW to Mercer, Nov. 6, Dec. 5, 1786, ibid., 336, 442.

64. GW to Mercer, Nov. 24, 1786, ibid., 394.

65. GW to Lafayette, April 5, 1783, Kaminski, *A Necessary Evil,* 24–25.

66. William Gordon to GW, Aug. 30, 1784, *PGW, ConfS* 2:64; Lafayette to GW, July 14, 1785, Feb. 6, 1786, Kaminski, *A Necessary Evil,* 25.

67. See "The Attempt to Abolish Slavery in Virginia," and GW to Lafayette, May 10, 1786, Kaminski, *A Necessary Evil,* 33–36, 26.

68. Kaminski, *A Necessary Evil,* 242.

69. GW to Arthur Young, Dec. 12, 1793, to Tobias Lear, May 6, 1794, *Writings of GW* 33:174–83, 358.

70. GW to the Clergy of Different Denominations, March 3, 1797, ibid., 35:416; GW, first inaugural address, April 30, 1789, *PGW, PresS* 2:175; GW, Farewell Address, Sept. 19, 1796, Higginbotham, *George Washington: Uniting a Nation,* 148.

71. GW, Circular Letter to the State Executives, June 1783, Higginbotham, *George Washington: Uniting a Nation,* 116.

72. GW to Jonathan Trumbull Sr., May 15, 1782, *PGW, ConfS* 1:385.

73. GW, first inaugural address, April 30, 1789, Higginbotham, *George Washington: Uniting a Nation,* 132–33.

74. GW to George Mason, Oct. 3, 1785, *PGW, ConfS* 3:292; GW to Edward Newenham, June 22, 1792, *PGW, PresS* 10:493; GW, Farewell Address, Sept. 19, 1796, Higginbotham, *George Washington: Uniting a Nation,* 141.

75. GW to the United Baptist Churches of Virginia, May 1789, to the Society of New York Quakers, Oct. 1789, to the New Jerusalem Church of Baltimore, Jan. 27, 1793, *PGW, PresS* 2:424, 4:266, 12:53.

76. GW to George Mason, Oct. 3, 1785, *PGW, ConfS* 3:293.

77. TJ to Isaac Story, Dec. 5, 1801, quoted in Kaminski, *Quotable Jefferson,* 366; GW to William Fitzhugh, Nov. 11, 1785, *PGW, ConfS* 3:352; GW to his sister Betty Washington Lewis, Sept. 13, 1789, *PGW, PresS* 4:32; GW to Jonathan Trumbull Jr., Oct. 1, 1785, *PGW, ConfS* 3:289.

78. GW to the marquis de Chastellux, Aug. 18, 1786, *PGW, ConfS* 4:220; Grizzard, *George Washington: A Biographical Companion,* 270; GW to Henry Knox, Feb. 20, 1784, *PGW, ConfS* 1:138.

79. Kaminski and McCaughan, *A Great and Good Man,* 16.

80. GW to Bryan Fairfax, March 1, 1778, *PGW, RevWarS* 14:9.

81. GW to Bryan Fairfax, March 6, 1793, ibid., 12:271; GW to Henry Knox, March 2, 1797, *Writings of GW* 35:409; GW to Betty Washington Lewis, Sept. 13, 1789, *PGW, PresS* 4:32; GW to Lafayette, Feb. 1, 1782, Lucas, *Quotable George Washington*, 21; GW to the marquis de Chastellux, June 2, 1784, *PGW, ConfS* 1:413; GW to Burgess Ball, Sept. 28, 1789, Lucas, *Quotable George Washington*, 21.

82. TJ to Walter Jones, Jan. 2, 1814, *TJ: Writings*, 1319–20.

83. GW to George William Fairfax, Feb. 27, 1785, *PGW, ConfS* 3:390; GW to George Washington Parke Custis, Dec. 19, 1796, *Writings of GW* 35:341.

84. Charles Thomson to GW, April 22, 1785, *PGW, ConfS* 2:517.

85. GW to James Craik, March 25, 1784, ibid., 1:235. See also GW to William Gordon, May 8, 1784, David Humphreys to GW, July 15, 1784, GW to John Witherspoon, March 8, 1785, ibid., 376–77, 527, 3:415.

86. GW to Clement Biddle, May 18, 1786, ibid., 4:54.

87. Lafayette to GW, March 19, 1785, ibid., 2:450.

88. Ebenezer Hazard and Jeremy Belknap quoted in ibid., 2–3, 251.

89. Much of the detail about GW's library is found in Appleton P. C. Griffin's *A Catalogue of the Washington Collection in the Boston Athenæum* (Boston, 1897).

90. GW to Henry Knox, Dec. 26, 1786, *PGW, ConfS* 4:482.

91. GW to JM, March 31, 1787, ibid., 5:115, 116.

92. Edmund Randolph to GW, Dec. 6, 1786, JM to GW, Dec. 7, 24, 1786, John Jay to GW, March 16, 1786, ibid., 4:445, 448, 474–75, 3:601.

93. GW to Henry Knox, March 8, 1787, David Humphreys to GW, Jan. 20, 1787, ibid., 5:75, 4:526, 529.

94. Henry Knox to GW, March 19, 1787, ibid., 5:96.

95. William Pierce's Notes, Max Farrand, ed., *The Records of the Federal Convention of 1787* (rev. ed., 4 vols., New Haven, CT, 1966), 3:86–87.

96. *DHRC* 17:330; Hugh Ledlie to John Lamb, Jan. 15, 1788, ibid., 20:610.

97. Donald Jackson and Dorothy Twohig, eds., *The Diaries of George Washington* (6 vols., Charlottesville, VA, 1976–79), 5:179.

98. *DHRC* 13:211–21.

99. Victor Marie du Pont to Pierre Samuel du Pont, Nov. 28, 1788, Victor du Pont Papers, group 3, box 1, folder 1788, Eleutherian Mills Historical Library, Greenville, DE; Alexander Hamilton to GW, Sept. 1788, Syrett, *Papers of Hamilton*, 5:220–21; Anthony Wayne to Lafayette, July 4, 1776, *DHRC* 18:221; Anthony Wayne to GW, April 6, 1789, *PGW, PresS* 2:37.

100. Gouverneur Morris to GW, Oct. 30, 1787, *DHRC* 13:513–14.

101. GW to Henry Lee, Sept. 22, 1788, *PGW, ConfS* 6:530–31; Martha Washington to John Dandridge, April 20, 1789, Fields, *Worthy Partner*, 213.

102. *PGW, PresS* 2:156–57.

103. Fisher Ames to George Richards Minot, May 3, 1789, Seth Ames, ed., *Works of Fisher Ames* (2 vols., Boston, 1854), 1:34.

104. GW, first inaugural address, April 30, 1789, U.S. Senate to GW, May 16, 1789, GW to the U.S. Senate, May 18, 1789, *PGW, PresS* 2:173–77, 310, 311, 324.

105. William Ellery to Benjamin Huntington, July 21, 1789, Thomas C. Bright Autograph Collection, Jervis Library, Rome, NY.

106. Archibald Stuart to JM, July 31, 1789, *PJM* 12:320; Abigail Adams to Mary Cranch, Jan. 5, 1790, Stewart Mitchell, ed., *New Letters of Abigail Adams, 1788–1801* (Boston, 1847), 35.

107. JM to Edmund Randolph, June 24, 1789, *PJM* 12:258; Abraham Baldwin to Joel Barlow, May 8, 1790, Yale University Library, New Haven, CT; Samuel Osgood to Henry Knox, May 22, 1790, John P. Kaminski, ed., *The Founders on the Founders: Word Portraits from the American Revolutionary Era* (Charlottesville, VA, 2008), 504–5; Abigail Adams to Mary Cranch, May 30, 1790, Mitchell, *New Letters*, 49; John Adams to Thomas Brand Hollis, June 1, 1790, John Disney, ed., *Memoirs of Thomas Brand-Hollis* (London, 1808), 36; Lafayette to GW, Aug. 23, 1790, *PGW, PresS* 6:315–16.

108. Ford, *True George Washington*, 171.

109. Kenneth R. Bowling and Helen E. Veit, eds., *The Diary of William Maclay and Other Notes on Senate Debates*, vol. 9 of *Documentary History of the First Federal Congress of the United States of America* (Baltimore, 1988), 182, 212, 261.

110. Ibid., 253.

111. Ibid., 136–37, 365–66.

112. Ford, *True George Washington*, 173–74.

113. Ibid., 190.

114. Abigail Adams to Mary Cranch, Jan. 5, 1790, Aug. 9, 1789, Mitchell, *New Letters*, 35, 19.

115. Abigail Adams to Mary Cranch, June 23, 1797, ibid., 98.

116. Ford, *True George Washington*, 101. Abigail Adams to Mary Cranch, June 28, July 12, Oct. 11, 1789, Aug. 29, 1790, Mitchell, *New Letters*, 13, 15, 30, 57.

117. This first of two stanzas was printed in the Newburyport, MA, *Essex Journal*, Nov. 4, 1789, and reprinted in the *New York Weekly Museum*, Nov. 14, 1789; *Gazette of the United States*, Nov. 14, 1789; *New York Journal*, Nov. 19, 1789; and *Pennsylvania Packet*, Nov. 19, 1789.

118. Printed in the *Newport Herald*, Sept. 9, 1790, and in Kaminski and McCaughan, *A Great and Good Man*, 179–81.

119. Printed in the *Virginia Herald*, May 26, 1791, and reprinted throughout the country. See Kaminski and McCaughan, *A Great and Good Man*, 191.

120. Richard Venable Diary, June 6–7, 1791, Kaminski and McCaughan, *A Great and Good Man,* 196.

121. *Gazette of the United States,* Sept. 19, 1796, Kaminski and McCaughan, *A Great and Good Man,* 149–51.

122. GW, Farewell Address, Kaminski and McCaughan, *A Great and Good Man,* 216–35.

123. GW to Henry Knox, March 2, 1797, *Writings of GW* 35:409.

124. Lee, *Experiencing Mount Vernon,* 65–66, 67n.

125. Martha Washington to David Humphreys, June 26, 1797, to Lucy Knox, post May 1797, Fields, *Worthy Partner,* 312, 304.

126. Julian Ursyn Niemcewicz in Lee, *Experiencing Mount Vernon,* 81–82.

127. Elizabeth Powel to Martha Washington, Jan. 7, 1798, Martha Washington to Elizabeth Powel, Dec. 18, 1797, From Martha Washington, Sept. 18, 1799, Fields, *Worthy Partner,* 304, 310, 321. For Tobias Lear's account of GW's death, see *PGW, RetS* 4:542–55.

128. Timothy Dwight, *A Discourse, Delivered at New-Haven, Feb. 22, 1800; On the Character of George Washington, Esq. at the Request of the Citizens* (New Haven, CT, 1800), 28, 27.

129. Elizabeth Fleet, ed., "Madison's Detached Memoranda," *William and Mary Quarterly,* 3d ser., 3 (Oct.. 1946): 534–68.

130. TJ to Walter Jones, Jan. 2, 1814, *TJ: Writings,* 1319–20.

THOMAS JEFFERSON

1. Alexander Hamilton to John Steele, Oct. 15, 1792, TJ to James A. Bayard, Jan. 16, 1801, Hamilton to Edward Carrington, May 26, 1792, Syrett, *Papers of Hamilton* 12:569, 25:319, 11:444; *Plumer's Memorandum,* March 16, 1806; John Nicholas to GW, Feb. 22, 1798, *PGW, RetS* 2:101.

2. Margaret Bayard Smith's account of her visit to Monticello, *PTJ, RetS* 1:393.

3. TJ to Edward Rutledge, Dec. 27, 1796, *PTJ* 29:233; TJ to James Monroe, Jan. 13, 1803, *TJ: Writings,* 1112; TJ to James Fishback, Sept. 27, 1809, *PTJ, RetS* 1:565.

4. TJ to Horatio Gates, Feb. 3, 1794, to Ferdinando Fairfax, April 25, 1794, *PTJ* 28:14, 58; TJ to Thomas Law, Jan. 15, 1811, *Writings of TJ* 5:556; TJ to John Cartwright, June 5, 1824, to William Short, Nov. 28, 1814, *TJ: Writings,* 1494, 1356; TJ to George Logan, Oct. 3, 1813, to Louis H. Girardin, March 27, 1815, *Writings of TJ* 6:217, 455.

5. The Kentucky Resolutions, Oct. 1798, *TJ: Writings,* 454, 455.

6. TJ to John Page, Feb. 21, 1770, *PTJ* 1:35.

7. Ibid.; TJ to James Ogilvie, Feb. 20, 1771, ibid., 1:63.

8. Autobiography, 1821, *TJ: Writings,* 10.

9. John Adams Autobiography, 1802, L. H. Butterfield et al., eds., *Diary*

and Autobiography of John Adams (4 vols., Cambridge, MA, 1962), 3:335–37.

10. TJ to Henry Lee, May 8, 1825, *TJ: Writings*, 1501.

11. Adams, *Thoughts on Government . . .*, 1776, *Papers of John Adams* 4:86.

12. TJ, first inaugural address, March 4, 1801, *TJ: Writings*, 492–96.

13. *TJ: Writings*, 510.

14. TJ to George Wythe, Aug. 13, 1786, *TJ: Writings*, 859.

15. Quoted in Norman K. Risjord, *Thomas Jefferson* (Madison, WI, 1994), 42.

16. Quoted in ibid., 47.

17. For more on Jefferson's attitude toward slavery, see Kaminski, *A Necessary Evil.*

18. TJ, *Notes on the State of Virginia*, 1782, *TJ: Writings*, 264–67, 288–89.

19. TJ to Richard Price, Aug. 7, 1785, *PTJ* 8:357.

20. TJ to Edward Coles, Aug. 25, 1814, *TJ: Writings*, 1344, 1346.

21. TJ to Thomas Cooper, Sept. 10, 1814, Kaminski, *A Necessary Evil*, 263; TJ to John Holmes, April 22, 1820, *TJ: Writings*, 1434.

22. TJ to Frances Wright, Aug. 7, 1825, *Writings of TJ* 7:408.

23. TJ to Edmund Randolph, Sept. 16, 1781, *PTJ* 6:118.

24. Marquis de Chastellux, *Travels in North-America, in the Years 1780, 1781, and 1782* (2 vols., London, 1787).

25. Madison to Edmund Randolph, Sept. 30, 1782, *PJM* 5:120.

26. TJ to the marquis de Barbé-Marbois, Dec. 5, 1783, to James Monroe, Nov. 18, 1783, Smith, *Letters of Delegates* 21:182, 156.

27. TJ to George Rogers Clark, Dec. 4, 1783, *TJ: Writings*, 783.

28. TJ to Peter Carr, Dec. 11, 1783, *PTJ* 6:379; TJ to Francis Eppes, Oct. 6, Dec. 13, 1820, Jefferson Papers, Library of Congress.

29. TJ to Martha Jefferson, Nov. 28, 1783, *TJ: Writings*, 782.

30. TJ to Martha Jefferson, Nov. 28, Dec. 11, 1783, ibid., 783, 784.

31. TJ to James Monroe, March 18, 1785, *PTJ* 8:43.

32. Abigail Adams to Mary Cranch, May 8, 1785, to TJ, June 6, 1785, Butterfield, *Adams Family Correspondence* 6:119, 169.

33. TJ to the Rev. William Smith, Feb. 19, 1791, *TJ: Writings*, 975.

34. TJ to JM, Jan. 30, 1787, *PJM* 9:250; Lafayette to James McHenry, Dec. 3, 1785, Idzerda, *Lafayette* 5:355; Lafayette to GW, Feb. 6, Oct. 26, 1786, Jan. 1, 1788, *PGW, ConfS* 3:545, 4:311, 6:6.

35. TJ to Alexandre Giroud, May 22, 1797, *PTJ* 29:387.

36. Autobiography, 1821, *TJ: Writings*, 57; TJ to C. W. F. Dumas, May 6, 1786, *PTJ* 9:463.

37. TJ to John Adams, July 11, 1786, *PTJ* 10:123; TJ, Autobiography, 1821, *TJ: Writings*, 59–61.

38. TJ to Ralph Izard, Nov. 18, 1786, to Abigail Adams, Aug. 9, 1786, to Eliza

House Trist, Dec. 15, 1786, to Thomas Paine, July 3, 1788, *PTJ* 10:541–42, Aug., 203, Dec., 600, 13:307; TJ, Autobiography, 1821, *TJ: Writings*, 98.

39. TJ to Maria Cosway, Oct. 12, 1786, May 21, 1789, John P. Kaminski, ed., *Jefferson in Love: The Love Letters between Thomas Jefferson and Maria Cosway* (Madison, WI, 1999), 44, 121.

40. TJ to Francis Eppes, Aug. 30, 1785, *PTJ* 8:451.

41. TJ to Martha Jefferson, April 7, 1787, ibid., 11:278.

42. TJ to Lafayette, April 11, 1787, *TJ: Writings*, 894; TJ to GW, May 2, 1788, *PGW, ConfS* 6:256.

43. TJ to David Ramsay, Aug. 4, 1787, *PTJ* 11:687.

44. TJ to Ezra Stiles, Dec. 24, 1786, ibid., 10:629; TJ to JM, Jan. 30, 1787, *PJM* 9:248; TJ to Abigail Adams, Feb. 22, 1787, *TJ: Writings*, 889–90; TJ to William Stephens Smith, Nov. 13, 1787, *PTJ* 12:356.

45. TJ to C. W. F. Dumas, Sept. 10, 1787, *PTJ* 12:113; TJ to John Adams, Aug. 30, 1787, *TJ: Writings*, 908–9; TJ to JM, June 20, 1787, *PJM* 10:64.

46. TJ to Francis Hopkinson, March 13, 1789, *TJ: Writings*, 940–41.

47. TJ to Madame d'Enville, April 2, 1790, ibid., 965–66.

48. TJ to GW, May 10, 1789, *PGW, PresS* 2:259.

49. Nathaniel Cutting Journal, *PTJ* 15:498.

50. TJ to William Short, Nov. 21, 1789, ibid., 15:552.

51. GW to TJ, Oct. 13, 1789, *PGW, PresS* 4:174.

52. TJ to GW, Dec. 15, 1789, to GW and to JM, both Feb. 14, 1790, GW to TJ, New York, Jan. 21, 1790, ibid., 412, 5:138, 165n, 29–31.

53. TJ to George Mason, Feb. 4, 1791, *TJ: Writings*, 971–72.

54. TJ, Notes of a Conversation with George Washington on Foreign Affairs, Dec. 27, 1792, *PTJ* 24:793; TJ to Gouverneur Morris, Dec. 30, 1792, TJ, Notes on the Legitimacy of Government, Dec. 30, 1792, *TJ: Writings*, 801, 800, 802.

55. TJ to Lafayette, April 2, 1790, *PTJ* 16:293; TJ to William Short, Jan. 3, 1793, *TJ: Writings*, 1004.

56. TJ to Count de Volney, Dec. 9, 1795, *PTJ* 28:551; TJ to John Adams, June 27, 1813, Cappon, *Adams-Jefferson Letters*, 335; TJ to William Branch Giles, Dec. 31, 1795, *PTJ* 28:566.

57. TJ to William Carmichael, Aug. 2, 1790, to William Carmichael and William Short, June 30, 1793, *PTJ* 17:112, 26:411.

58. TJ to Charles Carroll of Carrollton, April 15, 1791, *TJ: Writings*, 977.

59. TJ to Benjamin Hawkins, Aug. 13, 1786, *PTJ* 10:240; TJ to Benjamin Hawkins, Feb. 18, 1803, *TJ: Writings*, 1115.

60. TJ to JM, June 9, 1793, *TJ: Writings*, 1009–10; TJ to John Adams, April 25, 1794, Cappon, *Adams-Jefferson Letters*, 254; TJ to Henry Knox, Aug. 30, 1795, Knox Papers, Gilder-Lehrman Collection, New-York Historical Society.

61. TJ to Jean Nicolas Démeunier, April 29, 1795, TJ to John Taylor, Dec. 29,

1794, TJ to George Wythe, Jan. 16, 1796, *TJ: Writings*, 1028–29, 1021–22, 1031–32; TJ to Count de Volney, April 10, 1796, *PTJ* 29:61.

62. TJ to JM, Dec. 28, 1794, *TJ: Writings*, 1017.

63. John Adams to Benjamin Rush, Sept. 1807, John A. Schutz and Douglas Adair, eds., *The Spur of Fame: Dialogues of John Adams and Benjamin Rush, 1805–1813* (rept., Indianapolis, n.d.), 101.

64. From Alexander Hamilton, Nov. 8, 1796, Syrett, *Papers of Hamilton* 20:376–77.

65. TJ to JM, Dec. 17, 1796, *PJM* 16:431; TJ to JM, Jan. 1, 1797, *TJ: Writings*, 1039.

66. TJ to Elbridge Gerry, May 13, 1797, TJ to Benjamin Rush, Jan. 22, 1797, *PTJ* 29:362, 275.

67. TJ to John Taylor, June 4, 1798, *TJ: Writings*, 1050.

68. Charles Carroll of Carrollton to Alexander Hamilton, April 18, 1800, Syrett, *Papers of Hamilton* 24:412.

69. Alexander Hamilton to James A. Bayard, Jan. 16, 1801, ibid., 25:320.

70. TJ to Spencer Roane, Sept. 6, 1819, *TJ: Writings*, 1425.

71. TJ, first inaugural address, March 4, 1801, ibid., 492–96.

72. Joseph Story to Samuel P. P. Fay, May 30, 1807, William W. Story, ed., *Life and Letters of Joseph Story* (2 vols., Boston, 1851), 1:151–52.

73. *Plumer's Memorandum*, Dec. 3, 1805, pp. 212–13; Samuel L. Mitchill to Mrs. Mitchill, Jan. 10, 1802, "Dr. Mitchill's Letters from Washington, 1801–1813," *Harper's New Monthly Magazine* 58 (1879): 743.

74. TJ to Aaron Burr, Nov. 18, 1801, Mary-Jo Kline, ed., *Political Correspondence and Public Papers of Aaron Burr* (2 vols., Princeton, NJ, 1983), 2:637; TJ to Larkin Smith, Nov. 26, 1804, Jefferson Papers, Library of Congress; TJ to Governor James Sullivan, March 3, 1808, to Benjamin Rush, Jan. 3, 1808, *Writings of TJ* 5:252, 225.

75. TJ to JM, March 15, 1789, *PTJ* 14:659; *Plumer's Memorandum*, Jan. 7, 1804, p. 102; TJ to Spencer Roane, Sept. 6, 1819, *TJ: Writings*, 1426; TJ to Charles Hammond, Aug. 18, 1821, *Writings of TJ* 7:216.

76. John Marshall to Joseph Story, Sept. 18, July 13, 1821, Herbert A. Johnson et al., eds., *The Papers of John Marshall* (12 vols., Chapel Hill, NC, 1974–2006), 9:183, 179, 184.

77. *Plumer's Memorandum*, Dec. 31, 1804, pp. 234–35.

78. Ibid., Dec. 11, 1806, p. 527.

79. TJ to John Page, June 25, 1804, *Writings of TJ* 4:547.

80. TJ to JM, Aug. 12, 1812, *PJM*, *PresS* 5:149.

81. *Plumer's Memorandum*, March 16, April 8, 1806, pp. 453, 478; TJ to James Monroe, Jan. 28, 1809, *Writings of TJ* 5:420.

82. *Plumer's Memorandum*, March 16, 1806, p. 455.

83. TJ to Pierre Samuel du Pont de Nemours, March 2, 1809, *TJ: Writings*, 1203.

84. TJ to JM, March 17, 1809, *Writings of TJ* 5:437.

85. TJ to Andrew Ellicott, June 24, 1812, to Samuel Brown, April 17, 1813, to Martha Jefferson, July 7, 1793, Jefferson Papers, Library of Congress; Margaret Bayard Smith, Reminiscences, in Gaillard Hunt, ed., *The First Forty Years of Washington Society in the Family Letters of Margaret Bayard Smith* (1906; rept. New York, 1965), 11.

86. TJ to Charles Willson Peale, Aug. 20, 1811, *TJ: Writings,* 1249.

87. For Margaret Bayard Smith's Account of Her Visit to Monticello, July 29–Aug. 1, 1809, see *PTJ, RetS* 1:386–401.

88. Gabriel Duvall to JM, Sept. 5, 1812, *PJM, PresS* 5:272.

89. Richard Rush to JM, Sept. 4, 1812, ibid., 268.

90. John Mason to JM, Sept. 4, 1812, ibid., 265.

91. TJ to William Duane, Oct. 1, 1812, *Writings of TJ* 6:80; TJ to Vine Utley, March 21, 1819, *TJ: Writings,* 1416–17.

92. Benjamin Rush to John Adams, Feb. 17, 1812, Butterfield, *Letters of Rush* 2:1127.

93. TJ to John Adams, Jan. 11, 1817, Cappon, *Adams-Jefferson Letters,* 505; TJ to Vine Utley, March 21, 1819, *TJ: Writings,* 1417.

94. TJ to Samuel H. Smith, Sept. 21, 1814, *TJ: Writings,* 1353–54; TJ to John Adams, June 10, 1815, Cappon, *Adams-Jefferson Letters,* 443.

95. Daniel Webster, Notes of Mr. Jefferson's Conversation, 1824, at Monticello, Jefferson Papers, University of Virginia, Charlottesville. Dated Dec. 1825. A slightly different copy is in the New Hampshire Historical Society and was published in Charles M. Wiltse and Harold D. Moser, eds., *The Papers of Daniel Webster: Correspondence* (4 vols., Hanover, NH, 1974–1980), 1:370–71.

96. TJ to Maria Cosway, Dec. 27, 1820, Jefferson Papers, Massachusetts Historical Society; TJ to John Page, June 25, 1804, *Writings of TJ* 4:547; TJ to John Adams, Aug. 1, 1816, Cappon, *Adams-Jefferson Letters,* 484.

97. TJ to John Adams, Nov. 13, 1818, Cappon, *Adams-Jefferson Letters,* 529.

98. TJ to John Adams, March 14, 1820, ibid., 562–63.

99. JM to Nicholas P. Trist, July 6, 1826, Jack N. Rakove, ed., *James Madison: Writings* (New York, 1999), 812.

JAMES MADISON

1. Fisher Ames to George Richards Minot, May 29, 1789, Charlene Bangs Bickford et al., eds., *Documentary History of the First Federal Congress: Correspondence* (3 vols., Baltimore, 2004), 15:651; Alexander Hamilton, Conversation with George Beckwith, Oct. 1789, Syrett, *Papers of Hamilton* 5:488.

2. Quoted in Ralph Ketcham, *James Madison: A Biography* (New York, 1971), 21.

3. Benjamin Rush to his son James Rush, May 25, 1802, Rush Papers, Library Company of Philadelphia.

4. JM to William Bradford, June 10, 1773, *PJM* 1:89.

5. JM to William Bradford, Nov. 9, 1772, to TJ, April 27, 1785, ibid., 1:75, 8:270.

6. JM to William Bradford, Sept. 25, 1773, Dec. 1, 1771, Sept. 25, 1783, Dec. 1, 1773, July 1, 1774, ibid., 1:97, 100, 96, 101, 114.

7. JM to William Bradford, Jan. 24, April 1, 1774, ibid., 106, 112–13.

8. JM to William Bradford, July 1, 1774, ibid., 115.

9. JM to William Bradford, Aug. 23, Jan. 24, 1774, ibid., 121, 105.

10. JM to William Bradford, Nov. 26, 1774, ibid., 129.

11. Article on Religion Adopted by Convention, [June 12, 1776], ibid., 175.

12. JM to James K. Paulding, Jan. 1832, ibid., 193.

13. JM to Benjamin Harrison, Dec. 16, 1779, ibid., 319.

14. JM to William Bradford, April 28, 1773, Jan. 24, 1774, ibid., 84, 106.

15. JM to William Bradford, Nov. 9, 1772, ibid., 75–76; Thomas Rodney's Character Sketches of Some Members of Congress, post March 1781, Smith, *Letters of Delegates* 17:36; Martha Dangerfield Bland to Mrs. St. George Tucker, March 30, 1781, *PJM* 2:196n; Eliza House Trist to TJ, April 13, 1784, *PTJ* 7:97.

16. Thomas Burke to William Bingham, [Feb. 6?], 1781, Smith, *Letters of Delegates* 16:682.

17. I am indebted to Stuart Leibiger for making this comparison in his *Founding Friendship*, 82, citing GW to his nephew Bushrod Washington, Nov. 9, 1787.

18. For JM's proposed amendment, see *DHRC* 1:141–43.

19. JM, Address to the States, April 25–26, 1783, *PJM* 6:492, 494.

20. "CC" Proctor, ed., "After-Dinner Anecdotes of James Madison: Excerpts from Jared Sparks' Journal for 1829–31," *Virginia Magazine of History and Biography* 60 (1952): 264.

21. William Short to TJ, May 15, 1784, Edmund Randolph to TJ, May 15, 1784, *PTJ* 7:260, 257.

22. Archibald Stuart to John Breckinridge, Dec. 7, 1785, TJ to JM, Dec. 8, 1784, *PJM* 8:446, 178.

23. JM to TJ, Jan. 22, 1786, ibid., 474.

24. Congressional debates, March 6 to April 18, 1783, Kaminski, *A Necessary Evil*, 20–23.

25. JM to James Madison Sr., Sept. 8, 1783, *PJM* 7:268.

26. JM to Edmund Randolph, July 26, 1785, ibid., 8:328; JM to GW, Nov. 11, 1785, Kaminski, *A Necessary Evil*, 36.

27. JM, speech of June 30, 1787, Kaminski, *A Necessary Evil*, 47.

28. JM, speech of Aug. 25, 1787, ibid., 62–63, 64.

29. JM, speech in the U.S. House of Representatives, May 13, 1789, ibid., 207–9.

30. JM, speech in the U.S. House of Representatives, March 23, 1790, ibid., 229.

31. Robert Pleasants to JM, June 6, 1791, ibid., 270.

32. JM to Robert Pleasants, Oct. 30, 1791, ibid., 271–72.

33. See JM, Memorandum on an African Colony for Freed Slaves, c. Oct. 20, 1789, ibid., 269.
34. JM to James Monroe, Jan. 22, 1786, *PJM* 8:483.
35. Ibid.; JM to TJ, March 18, 1786, ibid., 501–2.
36. JM to TJ, Aug. 12, 1786, ibid., 9:96; Stephen Higginson quoted in *DHRC* 1:177.
37. GW to Henry Knox, Dec. 26, 1786, *PGW, ConfS* 4:482.
38. *DHRC* 1:197.
39. JM to GW, Dec. 7, 1786, to TJ, Dec. 4, 1786, *PJM* 9:199, 189.
40. David Stuart to GW, Dec. 25, 1786, *PGW, ConfS* 4:477.
41. JM, Notes of Debates, Feb. 19, 1787, *PJM* 9:278; Worthington C. Ford et al., eds., *Journals of the Continental Congress, 1774–1789* (34 vols., Washington, D.C., 1904–37), 32:177–84.
42. JM to Edmund Randolph, April 8, 1787, to Edmund Pendleton, April 22, 1787, *PJM* 9:371, 395.
43. JM to Edmund Randolph, April 8, 1787, ibid., 369.
44. George Mason to George Mason Jr., May 20, 1787, Farrand, *Records of the Federal Convention* 3:23.
45. Ibid., 94–95; *TJ: Writings*, 37.
46. JM to TJ, July 18, 1787, to TJ, June 6, Sept. 6, 1787, *PJM* 10:105, 29, 163–64.
47. Adrienne Koch, ed., *Notes of Debates in the Federal Convention of 1787 Reported by James Madison* (1966; rept. New York, 1987), 17–18.
48. *Federalist* No. 37, New York *Daily Advertiser*, Jan. 11, 1788, *DHRC* 15:348.
49. Melancton Smith, Notes of the Debate in Congress, *DHRC* 1:335, 337.
50. GW to JM, Oct. 10, 1787, *PJM* 10:189.
51. *DHRC* 13:486; Alexander Hamilton to GW, Oct. 30, 1787, Syrett, *Papers of Hamilton* 4:306.
52. Fleet, "Madison's Detached Memoranda," 565.
53. GW to Alexander Hamilton, Aug. 28, 1788, Syrett, *Papers of Hamilton* 5:207; TJ to JM, Nov. 18, 1788, *PJM* 11:353.
54. TJ to William Carmichael, Dec. 15, 1787, *DHRC* 8:241.
55. JM to Ambrose Madison, Nov. 8, 1787, Edmund Randolph to JM, Jan. 3, 1788, William Moore to JM, Jan. 31, 1788, *PJM* 10:244, 350, 454.
56. JM to Eliza House Trist, March 25, 1788, ibid., 11:5–6; James Duncanson to James Maury, May 8, 1788, *DHRC* 9:604; Cyrus Griffin to JM, April 14, 1788, *PJM* 11:22.
57. James Breckinridge to John Breckinridge, June 13, 1788, *DHRC* 10:1621.
58. JM, speeches on June 6, 16, 1788, ibid., 9:989, 10:1302, 1319.
59. JM, speeches on June 17, 12, 6, 1788, ibid., 1343, 1295, 9:990.
60. JM, speeches on June 14, 6, 1788, ibid., 10:1295, 9:989, 992.
61. JM, speeches on June 7, 6, 24, 1788, ibid., 1031, 990, 10:1507.

62. JM, speech on June 7, 1788, ibid., 9:1028, 1031.

63. JM, speeches on June 16, 17, 6, 24, 11, 19, 1788, ibid., 10:1323, 1340, 9:996, 10:1502, 9:1152, 10:1396.

64. JM, speeches on June 19, 4, 6, 1788, ibid., 10:1409, 9:941, 995.

65. JM, speech on June 7, 1788, ibid., 9:1029, 1034, 1035, 1033.

66. JM, speeches on June 24, 6, 1788, ibid., 10:1499, 9:990–91.

67. JM, speeches on June 6, 24, 25, 1788, ibid., 9:994–95, 10:1501, 1503–4, 1518.

68. JM, speeches on June 14, 20, 1788, ibid., 10:1283, 1417.

69. JM, speeches on June 24, 25, 1788, ibid., 1500, 1518.

70. Bushrod Washington to GW, June 7, 1788, ibid., 1581; "Extract of a letter from Richmond, June 18," *Pennsylvania Mercury,* June 26, 1788, "Extract of a letter from a gentleman of the first information, dated Petersburg, June 9, 1788, received per a vessel in 5 days from Norfolk," *Massachusetts Centinel,* June 25, 1788, Martin Oster to comte de La Luzerne, June 28, 1788, *DHRC* 1688, 1684, 1690.

71. Charles Lee to GW, Oct. 29, 1788, Merrill Jensen et al., eds., *The Documentary History of the First Federal Elections, 1788–1790* (4 vols., Madison, WI, 1976–89), 2:269; Edmund Randolph to JM, Nov. 10, 1788, Henry Lee to JM, Nov. 19, 1788, *PJM* 11:339, 356.

72. "A Marylander," Baltimore *Maryland Gazette,* Dec. 26, 1788, Jan. 2, 1789, Martin Oster to comte de La Luzerne, Feb. 11, 1789, Jensen, *Documentary History of the First Federal Elections* 2:156, 182, 401.

73. Extract of a letter from a Member of the Assembly at Richmond, to his correspondent in this town, dated Nov. 8, 1788, Winchester *Virginia Centinel,* Nov. 19, 1788, ibid., 379.

74. Hardin Burnley to JM, Dec. 16, 1788, ibid., 328.

75. JM to Edmund Randolph, Nov. 23, 1788, Richard Bland Lee to JM, Nov. 25, 1788, Hardin Burnley to JM, Dec. 16, 1788, ibid., 320, 321, 328–29.

76. Edward Carrington to JM, Dec. 2, 1788, ibid., 322. See also Alexander White to JM, Dec. 4, 1788, ibid., 323.

77. An Appeal for the Election of James Monroe, c. Jan. 1789, ibid., 329–30.

78. William C. Rives, *History of the Life and Times of James Madison* (3 vols., Boston, 1866–68), 2:656–57.

79. JM to George Eve, Jan. 2, 1789, Jensen, *Documentary History of the First Federal Elections* 2:330–31.

80. *Fredericksburg Virginia Herald,* Jan. 15, 1789, ibid., 336–37.

81. The Rev. James Madison to JM, March 1, 1789, *PJM* 11:454; Ralph Izard to TJ, April 3, 1789, *PTJ* 15:22.

82. Leibiger, *Founding Friendship,* 1.

83. GW, final version of inaugural address, *PGW, PresS* 2:173–77.

84. U.S. House of Representatives to GW, May 5, 1789, GW to JM, May 5, 1789,

to U.S. House of Representatives, May 8, 1789, to U.S. Senate, May 18, 1789, *PGW, PresS* 2:214–15, 216–17, 232, 324.

85. Fisher Ames to George R. Minot, May 3, 1789, *Works of Ames* 1:35; Henry Wynkoop to Reading Beatty, March 18, 1789, Bickford, *Documentary History of the First Federal Congress, Correspondence* 15:77.

86. Fisher Ames to George R. Minot, May 3, 18, 1789, *Works of Ames* 1:35, 42.

87. JM to Edmund Randolph, March 1, 1789, *PJM* 11:453.

88. Theodore Sedgwick to Benjamin Lincoln, July 19, 1789, Fisher Ames to George R. Minot, July 2, 1789, Robert Morris to Richard Peters, Aug. 24, 1789, Bickford, *Documentary History of the First Federal Congress: Correspondence* 16:1075, 915, 1392.

89. Andrew Craigie to Daniel Parker, May 5, 1790, Theodore Sedgwick to Pamela Sedgwick, March 4, 1790, Benjamin Goodhue to Samuel Phillips, March 14, 1790, Gouverneur Morris to Robert Morris, May 3, 1790, ibid., *Second Session*, vol. 19, forthcoming; John Trumbull to John Adams, June 5, 1790, Adams Family Papers, Massachusetts Historical Society.

90. Jonathan Trumbull Jr. quoted in Ketcham, *James Madison*, 387.

91. William Thornton to JM, March 16, 1801, *PJM, SecS* 1:24.

92. JM to James Leander Cathcart, U.S. Consul at Tripoli, May 21, 1801, ibid., 211.

93. *Plumer's Memorandum*, Dec. 31, 1804, pp. 234–35.

94. JM to Robert R. Livingston, Oct. 15, 1802, Jan. 18, 1803, to Robert R. Livingston and James Monroe, March 2, 1803, *PJM, SecS* 4:25, 259, 364–65.

95. Mathew Carey to JM, Aug. 12, 1812, *PJM, PresS* 5:149; *Plumer's Memorandum*, April 8, 11, 1806, p. 478; TJ to James Monroe, Jan. 28, 1809, to Henry Guest, Jan. 4, 1809, to Tadeusz Kosciusko, Feb. 26, 1810, *Writings of TJ* 5:420, 408, 508.

96. *PJM, PresS* 1:13; Henry Lee to JM, March 5, 1809, ibid., 20.

97. Republican Committee of Essex County, NJ, to JM, March 4, 1809, Republican Committee of Salem County, NJ, to JM, March 3, 1809, Epaphras W. Bull to JM, March 7, 1809, ibid., 18, 11–12, 27.

98. JM, first inaugural address, March 4, 1809, ibid., 15–18. For a general overview of JM's presidency, see Robert A. Rutland, *The Presidency of James Madison* (Lawrence, KS, 1990).

99. For JM and the War of 1812, see J. C. A. Stagg, *Mr. Madison's War: Politics, Diplomacy, and Warfare in the Early Republic, 1783–1830* (Princeton, NJ, 1983), and Donald R. Hickey, *The War of 1812: A Forgotten Conflict* (Urbana, IL, 1989).

100. For the Hartford Convention, see James M. Banner, *To the Hartford Convention: The Federalists and the Origins of Party Politics in Massachusetts, 1789–1815* (New York, 1970).

101. Samuel Whitcomb quoted in Ketcham, *James Madison*, 630.

102. TJ to JM, Feb. 17, 1826, *TJ: Writings*, 1515; Robert A. Rutland, ed., *James Madison and the American Nation, 1751–1836: An Encyclopedia* (New York, 1994), 285.

103. Daniel Webster to Jeremiah Mason, Dec. 29, 1824, Wiltse and Moser, *Papers of Webster: Correspondence* 1:379; Jared Sparks, Journal, April 23, 1830, *Virginia Magazine of History and Biography* 60 (1952): 264.

104. Rutland, *James Madison and the American Nation*, 284.

105. JM to James Monroe, April 21, 1831, William C. Rives and Philip R. Fendall, eds., *Letters and Other Writings of James Madison* (4 vols., Philadelphia, 1867), 4:179.

106. Edward Coles to Hugh Blair Grigsby, Dec. 23, 1854, Grigsby Papers, Virginia Historical Society.

107. Henry Clay quoted in Ketcham, *James Madison*, 670–71; JM to George Tucker, June 27, 1836, Rives and Fendall, *Letters and Other Writings of James Madison* 4:436.

For Further Reading

GEORGE WASHINGTON

Abbot, W. W., et al., eds. *The Papers of George Washington, Colonial Series.* 10 vols., Charlottesville, VA, 1983–95.

———. *The Papers of George Washington, Confederation Series.* 6 vols., Charlottesville, VA, 1992–97.

———. *The Papers of George Washington, Presidential Series.* Charlottesville, VA, 1987–.

———. *The Papers of George Washington, Retirement Series.* 4 vols., Charlottesville, VA, 1998–99.

———. *The Papers of George Washington, Revolutionary War Series.* Charlottesville, VA, 1985–.

Brookhiser, Richard. *Founding Father: Rediscovering George Washington.* New York, 1996.

———. *Rules of Civility: The 110 Precepts That Guided Our First President in War and Peace.* New York, 1997.

Cunliffe, Marcus. *George Washington: Man and Monument.* Boston, 1958.

Ellis, Joseph. *His Excellency: George Washington.* New York, 2004.

Ferling, John E. *The First of Men: A Life of George Washington.* Knoxville, TN, 1988.

Fischer, David Hackett. *Washington's Crossing.* Oxford, 2004.

Flexner, James Thomas. *Washington: The Indispensable Man.* Boston, 1969.

Ford, Paul Leicester. *The True George Washington.* Philadelphia, 1896.

Freeman, Douglas Southall. *George Washington: A Biography.* 7 vols. New York, 1948–57.

———. *George Washington.* New York, 1968. An abridgment by Richard Harwell of the 7-vol. *George Washington.*

Grizzard, Frank E., Jr. *George Washington: A Biographical Companion.* Santa Barbara, CA, 2002.

Higginbotham, Don. *George Washington: Uniting a Nation.* Lanham, MD, 2002.

Hirschfeld, Fritz. *George Washington and Slavery: A Documentary Portrayal.* Columbia, MO, 1997.

Hofstra, Warren R. *George Washington and the Virginia Backcountry.* Madison, WI, 1998.

Kaminski, John P., and Jill Adair McCaughan, eds. *A Great and Good Man: George Washington in the Eyes of His Contemporaries.* Madison, WI, 1989.

Lee, Jean B., ed. *Experiencing Mount Vernon: Eyewitness Accounts, 1784–1865.* Charlottesville, VA, 2006.

Leibiger, Stuart. *Founding Friendship: George Washington, James Madison, and the Creation of the American Republic.* Charlottesville, VA, 1999.

Longmore, Paul K. *The Invention of George Washington.* Berkeley, CA, 1988.

Lucas, Stephen E. *The Quotable George Washington: The Wisdom of an American Patriot.* Madison, WI, 1999.

Smith, Richard Norton. *Patriarch: George Washington and the New American Nation.* Boston, 1993.

Weems, Mason Locke. *The Life of Washington: A New Edition with Primary Documents and Introduction.* Ed. Peter S. Onuf. Armonk, NY, 1996.

Wiencek, Henry. *An Imperfect God: George Washington, His Slaves, and the Creation of America.* New York, 2003.

Wills, Garry. *Cincinnatus: George Washington and the Enlightenment.* Garden City, NY, 1984.

THOMAS JEFFERSON

Boyd, Julian P., et al., eds. *The Papers of Thomas Jefferson.* Princeton, NJ, 1950–.

Burstein, Andrew. *The Inner Jefferson: Portrait of a Grieving Optimist.* Charlottesville, VA, 1995.

———. *Jefferson's Secrets: Death and Desire at Monticello.* New York, 2005.

Cunningham, Noble, Jr. *In Pursuit of Reason: The Life of Thomas Jefferson.* Baton Rouge, LA, 1987.

Ellis, Richard E. *The Jeffersonian Crisis: Courts and Politics in the Young Republic.* New York, 1971.

Gordon-Reed, Annette. *Thomas Jefferson and Sally Hemings: An American Controversy.* Charlottesville, VA, 1997.

Kaminski, John P. *The Quotable Jefferson.* Princeton, NJ, 2006.

Looney, J. Jefferson, et al., eds. *The Papers of Thomas Jefferson: Retirement Series.* Princeton, NJ, 2004–.

Malone, Dumas. *Jefferson and His Time.* 6 vols. Boston, 1948–81.

Mayer, David N. *The Constitutional Thought of Thomas Jefferson.* Charlottesville, VA, 1994.

Risjord, Norman K. *Thomas Jefferson.* Madison, WI, 1994.

JAMES MADISON

Banning, Lance. *Jefferson and Madison: Three Conversations from the Founding.* Madison, WI, 1995.

———. *The Sacred Fire of Liberty: James Madison and the Founding of the Federal Republic.* Ithaca, NY, 1995.

Brant, Irving. *James Madison.* 6 vols. Indianapolis, 1941–61.

Brugger, Robert J., et al., eds., *The Papers of James Madison, Secretary of State Series*. Charlottesville, VA, 1986–.

Hutchinson, William T., et al., eds. *The Papers of James Madison*. 17 vols. Chicago and Charlottesville, VA, 1962–91.

Ketcham, Ralph. *James Madison: A Biography*. 1971; rept. Charlottesville, VA, 1990.

Koch, Adrienne. *Jefferson and Madison: The Great Collaboration*. New York, 1950.

Leibiger, Stuart. *Founding Friendship: George Washington, James Madison, and the Creation of the American Republic*. Charlottesville VA, 1999.

Madison, James. *Notes of Debates in the Federal Convention of 1787*. Ed. with introduction by Adrienne Koch. 1966: rept. New York, 1987.

McCoy, Drew R. *The Last of the Fathers: James Madison and the Republican Legacy*. Cambridge, 1989.

Matthews, Richard K. *If Men Were Angels: James Madison and the Heartless Empire of Reason*. Lawrence, KS, 1995.

Rakove, Jack N. *James Madison and the Creation of the American Republic*. New York, 2002.

Rutland, Robert A. *James Madison: The Founding Father*. New York, 1987.

———, ed. *James Madison and the American Nation, 1751–1836: An Encyclopedia*. New York, 1994.

Rutland, Robert A., et al., eds., *The Papers of James Madison, Presidential Series*. Charlottesville, VA, 1984–.

Index